The Canadian Regime

2nd edition

The Canadian Regime

An Introduction to Parliamentary

Government in Canada

2nd edition

Patrick Malcolmson & **Richard Myers**

broadview press

National Library of Canada Cataloguing in Publication Data
Malcolmson, Patrick N., 1953–
    The Canadian regime: an introduction to parliamentary government in Canada

2nd ed.
Includes bibliographical references and index.
ISBN 1-55111-465-8

1. Canada--Politics and government. I. Myers, Richard M. (Richard Morley), 1957–
II. Title.

JL75.M34 2001   320.971   C2001-903158-0
Broadview Press Ltd. is an independent, international publishing house, incorporated in 1985.

North America:
P.O. Box 1243, Peterborough, Ontario, Canada K9J 7H5
3576 California Road, Orchard Park, NY 14127
TEL: (705) 743-8990; FAX: (705) 743-8353;
E-MAIL: customerservice@broadviewpress.com

United Kingdom:
Thomas Lyster Ltd
Unit 9, Ormskirk Industrial Park
Old Boundary Way, Burscough Road
Ormskirk, Lancashire L39 2YW
TEL: (01695) 575112; FAX: (01695) 570120; E-mail: books@tlyster.co.uk

Australia:
St. Clair Press, P.O. Box 287, Rozelle, NSW 2039
TEL: (02) 818-1942; FAX: (02) 418-1923

www.broadviewpress.com

Broadview Press gratefully acknowledges the financial support of the Book Publishing Industry Development Program, Ministry of Canadian Heritage, Government of Canada.

Book design and composition by George Kirkpatrick

PRINTED IN CANADA

Contents

Preface   9

Preface to the Second Edition   11

A Note to Political Scientists   13

PART I: INTRODUCTION

Chapter 1: Canada's Regime Principles   19
   1.1 Political Regimes   19
   1.2 Equality   21
   1.3 Liberty   24
   1.4 The Canadian Regime   27

Chapter 2: The Constitution   29
   2.1 Constitutions and Their Functions   29
   2.2 Constitutional Forms   31
   2.3 The Canadian Constitution   37
   2.4 Amending the Constitution   43
   2.5 Judicial Review of the Constitution   46
   2.6 Contemporary Constitutional Politics   47

PART II: BASIC PRINCIPLES OF THE CANADIAN CONSTITUTION

Chapter 3: Responsible Government   53
   3.1 The Emergence of Responsible Government   53
   3.2 The Conventions of Responsible Government   56
   3.3 Responsible Government as "Cabinet Government"   58
   3.4 Forming a Government   59
   3.5 Majority and Minority Government   62
   3.6 Institutional Implications of Responsible Government   64
   3.7 Responsible Government and Separation of Powers Compared   69

Chapter 4: Federalism   73
   4.1 What is Federalism?   73
   4.2 Why a Federal Union?   75
   4.3 The Original Design of the Federal Union   77

4.4 The Historical Development of Federalism in Canada   78

4.5 Fiscal Federalism   81

4.6 The Challenge of Canadian Federalism   84

4.7 Current Controversies: The Pressure to Decentralize   88

Chapter 5: The Canadian Charter of Rights and Freedoms   91

5.1 What is a Charter of Rights?   91

5.2 The Adoption of the Charter   94

5.3 Opposition to the Charter   97

5.4 The Notwithstanding Clause   99

5.5 Section 1   101

5.6 The Political Impact of the Charter   103

PART III: INSTITUTIONS

Chapter 6: The Crown and Its Servants   109

6.1 The Crown   109

6.2 The Governor General   111

6.3 The Functions of the Governor General   112

6.4 The Cabinet   116

6.5 The Cabinet Committee System   118

6.6 The Prime Minister   119

6.7 Prime Ministerial Government?   122

6.8 The Civil Service   123

Chapter 7: Parliament   127

7.1 The Role of Parliament   128

7.2 The Parliamentary Calendar   129

7.3 The House of Commons: Membership and Officers   130

7.4 The Business of the House of Commons   132

7.5 The Rules of Procedure of the House of Commons   134

7.6 The Backbencher   135

7.7 House of Commons Reform   137

7.8 The Senate   139

7.9 Senate Reform   141

Chapter 8: The Judiciary   145

8.1 The Role of the Judiciary   145

8.2 The Fundamental Principles of the Canadian Judiciary   150

8.3 Canada's Courts   156

8.4 The Supreme Court of Canada   161

8.5 The Politicization of the Judiciary   162

PART IV: PARTICIPATION

Chapter 9: Elections   169
 9.1 Elections and Representation   169
 9.2 Canada's Electoral System   172
 9.3 The Effects of SMP   174
 9.4 Proportional Representation   177
 9.5 Voting in Canada   179

Chapter 10: Political Parties   183
 10.1 Political Parties in the Canadian Regime   183
 10.2 The Functions of Political Parties   185
 10.3 Parties and Ideology   186
 10.4 The Organization of Political Parties   189
 10.5 The Canadian Party System   191
 10.6 Canada's Federal Parties   194
 10.7 Party Government and Party Politics   197

Chapter 11: Interest Groups, Public Opinion, and Democratic Citizenship   201
 11.1 Forms of Political Participation   201
 11.2 Interest Groups   202
 11.3 Women in Politics   206
 11.4 Public Opinion   208
 11.5 The Media   210
 11.6 The Question of Public Opinion Polls   212
 11.7 Civic Education and Democratic Citizenship   214

Appendix: The Constitution Acts 1867 to 1982   217

Questions for Discussion   265

Index   269

Preface

Of all regimes, a democratic regime is most in need of a politically educated populace. The democratic principle requires the rule of the people. Such rule demands that the people have an education in politics that makes "government by the people" both possible and prudent. If the great body of voting citizens lacks such an education, two consequences follow. First, people become passive and unwitting followers of the opinion leaders of the day. Demagoguery becomes indistinguishable from principled political rhetoric, and the tyranny of the majority — the Achilles' heel of democracy — grows more probable. Second, people come to have entirely unrealistic expectations of politics. Lacking any clear understanding of what is possible, they let their hopes, desires, and dreams govern their political demands.

There is ample evidence to suggest that both of these characteristics are easily observable in Canadian politics today. We believe that this is due, in large part, to the poor condition of civic education in contemporary Canada. This book has been written in the hope of strengthening that Canadian civic education.

Our book is an attempt to explain and describe the most important political institutions of Canada's national government. Its premise is that Canadians — citizens, university students, and even many of our politicians — need a straightforward, explanatory introduction to these institutions. Our aim is to educate Canadians to a more sober and realistic set of expectations about politics by explaining the institutional limitations that structure all political action. Our objective is to present the reader with a short and clear account of Canadian government. We have tried to focus on the logic of how our institutions work and how they fit together. For that reason, this book, unlike similar texts, concentrates more on explaining basic principles and less on describing the arcane details of our institutions. We have tried to ensure that our account is written in straightforward language and that all technical terms are clearly explained. Finally, we have tried to write the book so that it presupposes little prior knowledge of the subject matter.

Every Canadian adult should know the material in this book as a matter of civic duty. We hope that our book makes the performance of that duty a pleasure.

Preface
to the Second Edition

This second edition is the result of the need to update the book and to respond to a number of thoughtful criticisms and suggestions from colleagues. We would like to thank Peter Aucoin, Craig Cameron, Sheldon Cardinal, Heather Lunergan, Rob Sheppard, Heidi Studer, and our editor at Broadview Press, Betsy Struthers. A special thanks goes to our new colleague, Gerry Baier. We would also like to thank the Canadian Centre for Management Development for adopting the book for use in its courses and for supporting the publication of a French version, *Le regime politique canadien*.

While we have made a number of corrections, added a new section on the media, and updated the book where necessary, our fundamental argument remains the same. We believe that there is an underlying logic to the conventions, laws, principles, and institutions that make up the Canadian regime. A clear understanding of the logic of the regime is essential if citizens are to play their role in it.

Patrick Malcolmson
Richard Myers

A Note to
Political Scientists

One might characterize our approach to Canadian government as an "institutional approach." We happily agree with this description, but we think it is important to explain at the outset why we have proceeded in this way. Instead of focusing on the constitutional design of government and the institutions of parliament and federalism, political scientists in the last three decades have shifted their attention to political "systems" and "cultures." The classic texts of Canadian politics, Dawson's *The Government of Canada* and Mallory's *The Structure of Canadian Government*, gave way to books with titles like *The Canadian Political System* and *Politics in Canada*. Political science moved away from the study of government and political institutions in an attempt to explain political phenomena in terms of economics, sociology, psychology, and anthropology. In other words, political science seems to have lost confidence in itself as a discipline, succumbing to the tendency to reduce political to sub-political phenomena. Having once prided itself as the "master-art," political science seems to have taken on the meek and submissive posture of a grateful baggage handler to the rest of the social sciences.

What is noteworthy about the changed nature of political science is that it has given rise to textbooks that few who are not required to read for political science courses would ever open. These books do not start by explaining politics from the common-sense perspective of a citizen or politician, but usually begin with mystifying sketches of abstract theories about the nature of "political systems." As political scientists, we are both well aware that there is far more to understanding Canadian politics than can possibly be conveyed in an introductory analysis of Canada's political institutions. Studying the country's political economy and its underlying social structure is crucial for a full understanding of the Canadian regime. Even more important is understanding the historical development of the political culture and the dominant schools of political thought that have given rise to the ideas that have structured Canadian political life through the twentieth century. Still, we argue that the starting point for a sound understanding of Canadian politics is to focus on the basic institutions of government. Such a starting point supplies one with the ideas and concepts that allow for a more in-depth and comprehensive understanding of the regime itself.

We have taken an approach that begins from the common-sense perspective of the citizen and active political participant. There are a number of good reasons for proceeding in this way. One is that it is difficult, if not impossible, to discuss political issues of the day intelligently without a solid understanding of the political institutions that provide the conceptual framework for such discussions. How can one intelligently discuss problems concerning the tax structure without some understanding of federalism? Or censorship without some understanding of the *Charter of Rights* and the Supreme Court? Or the role of an MP without understanding the nature of parliamentary or responsible government? Yet all too often one finds that people want to discuss current political problems without giving any consideration to how these issues are tied to the structures and institutions of government. The local MP is thus criticized for always voting the party line, with little consideration as to how the Canadian form of parliamentary democracy makes it exceedingly difficult for MPs to vote against their party on any crucial political issue. One might liken such discussions to criticizing a chess game without understanding the rules.

A second reason why we have focused on the institutions of government is that such a focus supplies us with a vocabulary and perspective that is close to those used in political life. We can thus intelligently discuss politics in an everyday and practical context as opposed to the abstract, and practically irrelevant, context of contemporary social science. The concepts and jargon of functionalism, neo-institutionalism, rational choice theory, and so on, are not the stuff of contemporary political debate. For the purposes of providing a starting point for understanding contemporary politics, they obscure and distort more than they illuminate.

Finally, it is important to consider how politics has traditionally been understood and written about by Canadian political scientists — scholars like Stephen Leacock, Eugene Forsey, James Mallory, and

R. M. Dawson. In its English-speaking variety, Canadian political science has been an interesting combination of American and British influences. It typically defined itself, over and against its American counterpart, by a more traditional and institutional approach to the study of government in Canada. Such is no longer the case, and textbooks in Canadian political science bear the heavy imprint of American influence. Our view is that the traditional Canadian approach is superior. It is better not simply because it is ours, but because the traditional institutional approach begins from the common-sense perspective of the educated citizen and thus provides both a theoretical and practical education. It is this unity of theory and practice that is the greatest strength of the Canadian tradition. Canadians have always been more sober and pragmatic in comparison with our American counterparts. When it comes to both political knowledge and action, pragmatism and prudence are the signs of a superior political education.

One does not have to be a specialist in methodological theory to see the influence of American political science on the way Canadian government is taught today. The problem is evident at the very surface. Note, for example, how many of our textbooks discuss our institutions in terms of the legislative and executive branches of government. Such a framework makes perfect sense for a book on the government of the United States because the American constitution is built around the theory of "separation of powers." But the Canadian constitution is not. Our constitution provides for a "fusion of powers" rather than a "separation of powers." The work done by cabinet ministers is of both a legislative and executive nature. It is therefore misleading and confusing to frame one's discussion of Canadian government in terms of chapters on the legislative and executive "branches." We have no such thing, and pretending we do leads to significant deficiencies in the way Canadian government is described. For instance, because they operate on the basis of "separation of powers" assumptions, most texts are grossly inadequate in their accounts of the principles of responsible government, the principles which create our "fusion of powers." In this book, by contrast, we attempt to describe the institutions of Canadian government on their own terms. Instead of fitting Canadian institutions into some foreign framework, we try to present them in terms of responsible government, the framework that is natural to them.

The failure of Canadian political science to articulate and defend the coherence of our institutions has to some extent contributed to the increasing Americanization of our regime. In 1982 our constitution was expanded to include an American-style Charter of Rights. Now the call is for an American-style Senate, an American-style procedure for screening Supreme Court nominees, American-style primaries for leadership selection, and American-style representation (where MPs vote according to the wishes of their constituents instead of following the "party line"). Such innovations strike many Canadians as being more democratic or more "advanced" than what we have here now, but it is doubtful whether many appreciate the difficulties involved in grafting features from one regime onto a very different one.

Years ago, Canadians adopted the American practice of choosing their party leaders at leadership conventions. It was thought that this innovation would further democratize our regime by taking leadership selection out of the hands of a small minority (the caucus) and sharing it with a wider body of Canadians. In practice, however, the introduction of leadership conventions has probably made our institutions *less* democratic. When the leader was chosen by the caucus, the caucus maintained a certain influence over the leader. Because today's party leaders are chosen by several thousand party delegates, they have a "mandate" that allows them to dominate their caucus to an unprecedented degree. It is in this innovation as much as in anything else that we find the roots of "prime ministerial government." Thus an American-inspired innovation which was designed to democratize our party leadership has in the long run made it even more elitist.

One of the objectives of this book is to describe and explain Canada's political institutions in such a way as to minimize the appeal of seductive but facile calls for further Americanization of our regime. By approaching Canadian institutions on their own terms, we hope to articulate the inner logic and coherence of the regime as a whole. This should make the reader more aware of the problems inherent in borrowing practices from other regimes. More importantly, it should give the reader a deeper appreciation of, and respect for, our own.

Patrick Malcolmson
Richard Myers
St. Thomas University
Fredericton

Part one: Introduction

Canada's Regime Principles

1.1   Political Regimes

1.2   Equality

1.3   Liberty

1.4   The Canadian Regime

1.1   Political Regimes

To the casual observer, it may seem that Canada's political institutions are an arbitrary, perhaps even whimsical, hodge-podge of archaic ideas and quaintly-named offices. To the political scientist, however, the political institutions of this, or any other country, have an inner logic that ties them all together into a coherent whole. The term traditionally used by political scientists to describe that whole is **regime**.

The English word regime is derived from the Latin word *regere*, which means to rule. From this Latin root come related words like "regent" (the person who rules on behalf of a monarch who is not yet of age) and "regulate." In common speech, the word regime is sometimes used to refer to a particular group of rulers (we might talk, for example, of "the Castro regime" in Cuba). Strictly speaking, however, it has a more precise meaning. For political scientists, the term regime refers to two interconnected things: a country's institutions of government and the principles that inform those institutions.

The classic discussion of regime types is to be found in Aristotle's *Politics*. Aristotle's account is not comprehensive enough to provide a complete analysis of contemporary regimes, but it provides an excellent starting point for understanding the differences between them. According to Aristotle, the first question one must ask about any particular political order is how those who rule understand the purpose of political rule. This is the question that each of us would likely ask first if we were being ruled: are the rulers just or unjust? Do they rule in their own interest, or do they look to the common good of the political community? The second question that Aristotle asks is who rules: one person, the few, or the many?

Applying these two considerations, Aristotle generated a typology that included six regimes, three of them just and three of them unjust:

FIG. I.I

To What Purpose Do The Rulers Rule?

Who Rules?	Common Good	Own Interest
one	Kingship	Tyranny
few	Aristocracy	Oligarchy
many	Polity	Democracy

When we look back on history, we commonly and quite correctly distinguish between good and bad monarchs. Some kings and queens ruled with the interests of their country and subjects uppermost in mind. Others were concerned primarily with their own benefit. Aristotle calls a monarchy of the first type **kingship** and one of the second type **tyranny**.

The distinction between the common good and self-interest forms the basis of the other regime types. Aristotle calls an elite few ruling for the sake of the common good an **aristocracy**. However, political history does not provide many examples of small elites ruling in the common good. In most cases where political power is in the hands of the few, they use it for their private economic advantage. Aristotle calls this unjust regime **oligarchy**. Today we find oligarchies in many developing countries where rich elites use political power to maintain and increase their wealth.

Aristotle's analysis of rule by the many will come as something of a surprise to the reader. He says that a regime in which the many rule for the sake of the common good could be called **polity**, but he argues that such a regime is non-existent. The reason for this is that in his time, political communities were divided into two classes: the many poor—the *demos*—and the few rich. Aristotle had never seen a community in which rule by the demos was anything but an attempt by the poor majority to use its superior force to despoil the rich minority. In other words, Greek democracies had a tendency to degenerate into mob rule. This explains why Aristotle puts **democracy**—rule by the demos— on his list of bad or selfish regimes.

Aristotle's unflattering portrait of majority rule may offend our democratic ears, but his point should be considered very seriously. It is undeniable that majority rule can, and too often does, involve unjust treatment of those in the minority. For instance, a majority of voters could elect a government that would forbid members of a non-white minority to own property. Such legislation would be democratic in that it expresses the will of the majority, but it would also be unjust. The fact that something is democratic does not necessarily mean that it is right. In contemporary terms, we would distinguish between a decent democratic regime and **tyranny of the majority**. For us, democracy has come to mean rule by the majority that respects the rights of all individuals, including those who may be in the minority. We use constitutions to provide protection against unrestrained majoritarianism.

It is important to appreciate the danger posed by tyranny of the majority if one is to understand the foundations of the Canadian regime. Canada's regime, as we all know, is a democratic regime. But it has been carefully crafted so as to minimize the dangers of tyranny of the majority. This will become apparent as we examine our most fundamental principles. We call these "regime principles," and there are two of them: **equality** and **liberty**.

1.2 Equality

The fundamental principle of democracy is the principle of equality. In its pure form, democracy grants political power to all citizens equally (excluding children) because democrats believe that no one has any special title to rule. In a democratic regime, there is no special privilege granted to those who come from particular families or to people who own particular lands or businesses. It should be noted that the democratic principle of equality is a political principle, not a social or economic one. Strictly speaking, democracy means that people share equally in political rule; it does not mean that they share equally (or even equitably) in wealth or social status. Still, there may be some respects in which political equality is interconnected with questions of social and economic equality. Genuine political equality may be undermined by massive social or economic inequalities. For instance, if those with great wealth are able to use their money to influence the political process in a significant way, that gives them unequal political power. This is why democracies usually enact legislation to regulate donations to political campaigns.

The basic democratic principle of political equality can take different forms. In the democracies observed by Aristotle, the principle was given its fullest expression. The democrats of ancient Greece understood equality to mean that all citizens were equally capable of exercising political power. These were **direct democracies**—regimes in which all of the citizens were directly involved in political decision-making. Moreover, to the extent that special officers were needed, they were to be chosen by lottery on the assumption that all citizens are equally capable of exercising political power. The Fathers of Confederation were democrats, but they did not support such a fully egalitarian form of democracy. Their preference was for **parliamentary democracy**, a regime they thought superior to direct democracy precisely because it was a more limited form of democracy.

Parliamentary democracy must be understood in the first instance as a variety of **representative democracy**. The direct form of democracy practised by the ancient Greeks has been replaced by an indirect form. Instead of managing political matters themselves, the equal citizens of modern democracies delegate the responsibility for public matters to a small group of elected representatives. There are two chief reasons for the emergence of representative democracy. The most obvious is that modern democracies are simply too large to be governed by the people directly: while the direct democracies of ancient Greece may have had only a few thousand citizens, the democracies of the modern world typically have millions. The second justification for representative democracy, though somewhat less obvious, is no less important. We are used to thinking of elections as a democratic exercise, and in one sense they obviously are: all voters get an equal say in the choice of the winner. But elections are also an aristocratic exercise: to attain office, the candidate has to convince the voters that he or she is the *best* person for the job. The founders of modern democracies believed that the introduction of representation would minimize the tendency to mob rule observed in the direct democracies of ancient Greece. The fact that the representatives would be accountable to the people through elections would keep the regime democratic. But at the same time, the exercise of power would be given to a small elite of the best people, an elite that would be less likely than the people as a whole to behave like a mob.

Parliamentary democracy is a regime in which political decisions are made by a representative body called parliament. It is therefore, like all representative democracies, an indirect and, hence, limited form of democracy. Indeed, it is important to understand that the Fathers of Confederation valued the institutions of parliamentary democracy precisely because it was a more limited form of representative democracy than the alternative.

As we shall see in subsequent chapters, when the Fathers of Confederation created our regime, they borrowed heavily from the United States in some respects. When it came to representative government, however, they emphatically rejected the American congressional/presidential model in favour of the British model of parliamentary government. Their concern was that American-style democracy, though indirect, was nonetheless still too directly linked to the people and thus subject to the dangers of mob rule. One of the problems they noted was that the chief officers of the American regime—the president, the governors, and some of the judges—were chosen directly by the people. The Fathers of Confederation preferred the model of parliamentary government where (as we shall see in Chapter 3) the chief officers of the government are chosen only indirectly: the voters do not directly elect either the prime minister or the ministers of the cabinet; through a complex process called "responsible government," those officers are selected by our elected representatives. Parliamentary democracy is thus in some sense the most indirect of indirect democracies.[1]

The other feature of parliamentary democracy that was important to the Fathers of Confederation was the fact that it gave the Crown a role (albeit, a weak one) as last-chance safety valve. The constitution of the United States established a **republican** regime, that is, a regime in which full and final authority is placed in the hands of the people's elected representatives and officers. The Fathers of Confederation believed that it would be important to have the monarchy present as a stabilizing influence, one that would prevent democratic politicians from rash action. Today, of course, it would be unthinkable for the Crown to interfere in the normal political process. Still, the anti-republican attitudes of the Fathers of Confederation are worth noting, for it was precisely their desire to avoid the "evils of republicanism" that led them to reject annexation to the United States and to work so hard to create an independent Canada.

While there has been some evolution in our political ideas since the time of the Fathers of Confederation, it is still important to appreciate

---

1   Contemporary thinking on this point has changed somewhat. Canadians now believe that our indirect democracy should provide clear and direct lines of accountability to the electorate. See Chapter 9.1, below.

that the Canadian regime is a relatively limited form of democracy. We do not believe that people are so equal that all of us should share equally in the making of political decisions. Nor do we believe that all citizens ought to share equally in the election of all political officers. What makes our regime a fundamentally democratic one is the notion that *the regime belongs to us all equally*: Canadian political equality is an equality of citizenship. This implies two things. The first is that we all have an equal right to run for public office. Second, (and more important), whoever is elected or appointed to political office must in some way be accountable (that is, answerable) to the people as a whole for their actions and decisions.

1.3 Liberty

While Canadians view democracy as a key political principle, we do not see it as the only fundamental principle of our regime. Indeed, Canadians believe that democracy can go wrong if it is not tempered by another fundamental principle — the principle of liberty. This explains why our regime is commonly referred to as a liberal democracy.

Liberty is the idea that there is a sphere of human thought and action that is private, and that, within that **private sphere**, all individuals have the right to make choices for themselves. According to the political theory of **liberalism**, then, we are free to do whatever we wish provided there is no law prohibiting us from doing so. We have rights, which means that we are free to decide for ourselves whether we will or will not do something. This freedom to decide for ourselves about such matters as which ideas we shall believe and what religion we shall practise is an essential element of the liberal understanding of politics. And from these initial freedoms flow a number of others, notably freedom of expression and freedom of the press.

But what provides the philosophical foundation for the principle of liberty? In contemporary liberal democracies, there are two schools of thought that predominate: **natural rights** and **utilitarianism**. The natural rights school argues that every individual possesses certain rights — for example, the rights to life, liberty, property, or privacy — simply because they are human beings. These rights, now often called human rights, are rights that all human beings possess everywhere and always, whether they are recognized or not. They are "inalienable" rights in that they cannot be given up or taken away. According to the natural rights school, these inalienable or natural rights establish both the purpose and the limits of political power. The purpose of government is to secure these universal and permanent rights; and no government is ever allowed to act in a manner that violates them.

The utilitarian justification for liberty is fundamentally different. For utilitarians, the importance of liberty derives from its usefulness ("utility") as a means of promoting human happiness. Utilitarians do not believe that there are universal and permanently valid "natural" rights. They believe, rather, that rights are created within each regime in response to circumstances. If it is conducive to the general well-being of the citizens to establish a right to separate schools for Roman Catholics, then such a right could be proclaimed. But utilitarians would deny that such a right exists by nature; they deny, in other words, that the establishment of separate schools is a universal moral imperative binding all governments in all times and places.

It is important to appreciate, however, that utilitarians believe the articulation of rights to be guided by certain ground-rules. The most important of these rules would be the famous **harm principle** elaborated by John Stuart Mill. According to the harm principle, governments cannot interfere with the actions of individuals so long as those individuals are not harming others. Mill argued that happiness was most likely to be arrived at if all individuals were allowed to develop their own individuality as fully as possible. The full development of our individuality requires that we each be left as free as possible to explore our own ideas and to act on the basis of those ideas. Provided we do not harm others, even harming ourselves is, according to Mill, within the province of liberty.

The harm principle means two things for politics. The first point is that the onus of proof is always on the government to show why any law that limits our individual liberty is necessary. The second point is that such a law will be valid only if it is necessary to prevent some direct harm to other human beings. We cannot, for example, pass laws forbidding people to smoke or drink when they are acting in ways that harm only themselves. But when their actions harm others, such as driving while drunk, we are allowed to invade their liberty for the protection of others' rights.

The best examples of liberal democratic regimes that take their bearings from the natural rights school of liberalism are the United States and France. The leading example of the utilitarian approach to liberty is Britain. Here in Canada, our liberalism was historically of the utilitarian type. The doctrine of natural rights was for many years seen as an abstraction foreign to our traditions. In recent years, however, especially since the adoption of the Charter of Rights and Freedoms, Canadian thinking about rights has shifted dramatically. While our traditional utilitarian approach to rights remains, it is now common for Canadians to think of many of their rights as human rights, just as our American neighbours do. Given that the utilitarian and the natural rights schools are incompatible in important respects, it seems likely that our thinking about rights will be in flux for some time to come.

The list of specific rights enjoyed by citizens of liberal democracies is a long one. It is also a list that varies from one liberal democracy to another. Still, it is possible to summarize the essence of those rights in three general principles:

A) *Protection of the private sphere*

Liberals draw a deep (though not necessarily sharp) distinction between the private sphere and the public sphere. The public sphere includes those areas of human activity where governmental regulation of our conduct is necessary to protect the rights of everyone. The private sphere includes everything else, and liberals insist that governments may not interfere in these areas of our lives. For a liberal, then, government may legitimately tell us how fast we may drive a car or what kind of guns we may own, but it has no right to tell us what religion to believe in or whether we should refrain from engaging in extra-marital sex. Former prime minister Pierre Trudeau once articulated this principle of liberalism in his famous remark that "the government has no place in the bedrooms of the nation."

B) *Respect for minority rights*

A liberal regime will proscribe all discrimination on the basis of race, religion, and other politically irrelevant characteristics. This injunction against discrimination is part of a wider principle, the principle that those in power must assure equal treatment for those in the minority. According to liberals, the fact that 51% of the population can win any vote does not entitle that majority to anything it pleases. For instance, would it not be unjust for a majority of the population to compel an ethnic, religious, or regional minority to pay all of the taxes?

c) *The rule of law*

Liberals believe that the effective protection of the various rights of citizens depends on the principle of the **rule of law**. At a minimum, this principle states that citizens must be able to count on what we often call "law and order," for without the protection of an effective legal order, the rights of everyone would be in jeopardy. But the principle of the rule of law goes far beyond simple law and order. It dictates, first of all, that the government is not itself above the law. Second, it stipulates that the law must be applied equally and impartially. Finally, every action taken by the government must be grounded in some legal authority. The reason for this principle is simple: if those in control of public power were able to treat citizens arbitrarily, that is, however they saw fit, we would all be at the mercy of the powerful.

Insisting that government act on the basis of established legal authority is a crucial mechanism for guaranteeing our rights. One especially important aspect of the rule of law is the idea of **constitutionalism**, the idea that the regime itself must be ordered in accordance with agreed-upon rules which will be supreme. A dictatorship may be defined as a regime in which those in power rule by force and recognize no limitations on their capacity to act; in a liberal regime, however, we insist on fixing clear limitations to the power of those who rule, and these limitations are to be found in a set of fundamental rules called the constitution.

1.4 The Canadian Regime

Equality and liberty constitute the regime principles of all of the world's liberal democracies. Sweden, Australia, Japan, Israel—all of these countries share the regime principles sketched above. It is important to note, however, that every liberal democracy will apply those principles in its own way.

In Part II of this book (Chapters 3-5), "The Basic Principles of the Canadian Constitution," we will explain the way in which the Canadian constitution adapts and applies the regime principles of liberal democracy to create a uniquely Canadian regime. Chapter 3 discusses the principle of responsible government. We will see in that chapter that the rules of responsible government are the mechanism we use in Canada to apply the principles of democracy in general and parliamentary democracy in particular. In Chapter 4 we examine federalism, the division of political authority between a national government in Ottawa and 10 provincial governments. As we will see, Canadians adopted a federal regime as the best means of ensuring respect for the rights of regional and linguistic minorities. In Chapter 5, we turn to the Charter of Rights and Freedoms, the constitutional document which serves to protect our liberal rights and freedoms from violation by the governments.

Before turning to Part II, however, we must first complete our introduction to the Canadian regime by describing and explaining Canada's constitution. We have seen in Section 1.3 above that liberal democracies are based on constitutionalism, the idea that the rules of the regime must be set down in a constitution. The constitution is thus the skeleton or framework of the regime, and any study of the regime will therefore entail frequent reference to it. For this reason, it is important to begin by familiarizing the reader with Canada's constitution.

Key Terms

regime
kingship
tyranny
aristocracy
oligarchy
polity
democracy
tyranny of the majority
equality
liberty
direct democracies

parliamentary democracy
representative democracy
republican
private sphere
liberalism
natural rights
utilitarianism
harm principle
rule of law
constitutionalism

The Constitution

2.1   Constitutions and Their Functions

2.2   Constitutional Forms

2.3   The Canadian Constitution

2.4   Amending the Constitution

2.5   Judicial Review of the Constitution

2.6   Contemporary Constitutional Politics

2.1   Constitutions and Their Functions

A constitution may be defined as *a set of rules that authoritatively establishes both the structure and the fundamental principles of the political regime.* We call this set of rules a "constitution" because it is these rules that "constitute" (that is, create or establish) the regime. A constitution will normally do so by performing up to three major functions.

The *first major function of a constitution* is to establish what person or persons will exercise the various forms of political authority. In modern times, political power is understood to consist of three distinct types. **Legislative power** is the power to make law or policy. For instance, a political community might use its legislative power to pass a law stipulating that no one may drive an automobile when their blood has an alcohol content above .08 per cent. **Executive power** is the power to "execute" or administer that law or policy. This would include the power to establish and maintain a police force to catch drunk drivers. **Judicial power** is the power to settle questions about specific violations of law (is there appropriate evidence to prove the driver's blood-alcohol level exceeded .08 per cent?) and to choose a suitable punishment from among those permitted in the relevant legislation for those found guilty.

Every constitution will, at some point, assign legislative, executive, and judicial powers to some specific persons or bodies of persons. The constitution of a student council, for example, might stipulate that legislative power, the power to set policy, will be exercised by a council consisting of some fixed number of persons who represent specific constituencies of the student population: the senior class, the off-campus students, and so on. It will probably also establish certain fundamental rules to govern the manner in which the council will proceed in its work (for instance, how many members must be present to make a meeting official). The student council's constitution will also specify who is to exercise the executive power. It may, for example, confer this power on a group called "the executive" and stipulate that this executive will have a number of specific members (president, secretary, treasurer), each of whom will have certain specific responsibilities.

The constitution of a national political regime will set down similar rules. It will stipulate that legislative power is to be exercised by a "parliament," by a "congress," by an "assembly," or by some other body. It will then dictate the composition of that body (one chamber or two, how many members, how they are to be selected) and probably establish some basic ground-rules for its functioning. The constitution will also determine whether executive power will be in the hands of a president, a prime minister, a cabinet, or perhaps even a queen. Finally, it must establish the broad outlines of a judicial system by stipulating what kind of courts the country will have and by setting down rules for the selection of their judges.

The second major function of a constitution is to provide an authoritative division of powers between national and regional governments in federal countries. Countries like Britain or France are said to have "unitary" regimes in the sense that they have only one government for the entire country. Yet in very large countries (for example, the United States) or countries divided into distinct ethnic or cultural regions (Russia or Germany), it is common to establish two independent levels of government. In these "federal" regimes, a "national" or "federal" government will handle those matters on which it is thought there should be common policy across the country (national defence, for instance). At the same time, however, "state" or "provincial" governments take responsibility for matters on which different parts of the country want distinct policies—education, for example—or which might be more

effectively managed by local authorities (the construction and maintenance of roads).

A workable federal system requires a clear division of powers
between the two levels of government. If it were left up to each level to
decide for itself what its powers were, the result would be chaos. Citizens might find themselves torn between a federal law requiring them
to drive on the right hand side of the road and a state or provincial law
requiring them to drive on the left! This is why the constitution in federal countries establishes the powers and responsibilities of each level of
government. In theory, this can be done by drawing up two lists, each of
which spells out the specific jurisdictions of each level of government.
The practical problem, however, is that it is difficult, if not impossible, to
make the two lists sufficiently comprehensive. Governments legislate in
a wide variety of areas, and new areas emerge on a regular basis (regulating the use of the Internet, for example). It is therefore typical for a
constitution in a federal regime to furnish a list of specific jurisdictions
reserved for the exclusive attention of one level of government and then
to stipulate that everything else (the "**residual power**") is reserved for the
other.

The *third major function of a constitution* is to delineate the limits of
governmental power. The very existence of a constitution is in some
sense a limitation on the power of government. The idea of constitutionalism implies that the constitution is supreme and that government
is subordinate to it. Beyond this general limitation, it is not uncommon
for constitutions to establish a list of fundamental rights and liberties in
some sort of charter or "bill" of rights. Such a charter might specify, for
example, that the citizens of a country have a right to freedom of religion. What this means is that no government, national or provincial, has
the power to take measures that would violate its citizens' right to religious freedom. Thus, even though a provincial government might
under the division of powers have jurisdiction over education, it could
not use that jurisdiction to pass legislation requiring schools to indoctri-
nate their students in some specific religious tradition.

2.2 Constitutional Forms

The fundamental rules that make up a country's constitution are of two
basic types: conventions and laws. Conventions are political rules; laws
are rules enforced by the courts. Constitutional laws may in turn be
divided into two types: organic statutes and entrenched constitutional

laws. A country may choose to embody its constitutional rules in any one (or any combination) of these three distinct forms.

A) *Constitutional convention*

A **constitutional convention** is not a big meeting where people get together to talk about the constitution. In constitutional terms, the word "convention" refers to a constitutional rule based on implicit political agreement and enforced in the political arena rather than by the courts. Think, for example, of the custom of shaking hands when you meet someone. There is no law that says people must shake right hands, but everyone accepts that it is the right hand one offers to another person (except, perhaps, in extraordinary circumstances). Constitutional rules can be made to operate in much the same way. For instance, in the British constitution, there is a rule stipulating that the prime minister may not wait more than five years to call a general election. This rule takes the form of an unwritten agreement, accepted as binding by everyone, and sanctioned by the force of tradition.

But it is not mere tradition that makes a particular practice a convention. The essential point in any convention is its rationale. Today we shake right hands because that just happens to be the custom. Originally, however, people greeted others by extending their right hand for a specific reason: that was the hand in which one would normally hold one's weapon. Extending an empty right hand was thus a way of demonstrating that one's intentions were not hostile. The British convention requiring elections every five years is also based on an obvious rationale: if there were no limitation on the timing of elections, unpopular prime ministers could stay in office forever by postponing elections indefinitely. The fact that this convention has existed for centuries will certainly strengthen its hold on British politicians and voters, but its legitimacy rests on the British people's perception that there are good reasons for such a rule, not on the length of time it has been followed.

The question, of course, is what happens if someone violates a convention? If politicians break a law, they can be brought before a court, tried, and punished if found guilty. But precisely because the court is a "court of law" and not a court of "conventions" its judges cannot, and will not, enforce constitutional conventions. So who does enforce them?

The answer is the voters. In a constitutional system based on conventions, it is assumed that the voters will know what those conventions are and will guard them jealously. Therefore, politicians will respect these conventions out of fear of invoking the wrath of the voters. In Britain, for example, unpopular prime ministers would never consider trying to improve their electoral chances by postponing parliamentary elections beyond the five-year limit, for they would know that when elections were finally held, the voters, outraged at this violation of constitutional convention, would severely punish the government party.

But this is not to say that constitutional conventions are always respected. The great advantage of having constitutional rules in the form of conventions rather than laws is that they can be applied with a certain amount of flexibility. We normally greet other people by shaking their right hand, but if one's right hand is in a cast, it is acceptable to offer the left. This same flexibility is evident in the realm of constitutional convention. The British electorate would never permit a prime minister to violate the convention on the timing of elections for partisan advantage. Yet prime ministers always have the option of ignoring the convention if they think they can persuade the public that there are good reasons for doing so. For instance, Winston Churchill postponed the parliamentary elections that were due in 1944 until early 1945. This was a violation of constitutional convention, but Churchill knew he could persuade the public that there was a good reason for making an exception to the rule: Britain needed to focus its attention on the war, not an election campaign. Now had this rule been in the form of a law, it would have been virtually impossible to act with such flexibility, for any single citizen would have been able to take the government to court, and the courts would have had no choice but to order the prime minister to follow the letter of the law.

B) *Organic statutes*

The second form in which a country may embody its constitutional rules is what we call **organic statutes**. The term "statute" refers to an act of the authoritative legislative body. Statutes establishing constitutional rules are called "organic" to distinguish them from statutes dealing with non-constitutional matters — statutes regulating health care, automobile traffic, or unemployment insurance.

The classic example of this form of constitutional rules is, once again, Great Britain. Because of that country's extensive use of constitutional convention, textbooks will often describe the British constitution as an "unwritten" one. This is a somewhat misleading description. A good deal of the British constitution is actually written out in the form of organic statutes, laws passed by the British Parliament to spell out certain constitutional rules in black and white. The *Bill of Rights* of 1689, which placed important new restrictions on the powers of the Crown, is a classic example of such a statute. So too are the *Reform Act* of 1832 and the *Parliament Act* of 1911, both of which dramatically altered the nature and functioning of Britain's legislative institutions.

There are two basic reasons for adopting some constitutional rules as organic statutes rather than conventions. The first is that some rules, especially those which establish and describe institutions, are probably too complex and too detailed to be left to the realm of unwritten agreement. The second is that organic statutes provide a more effective means of introducing substantial innovation to the existing constitutional order. Each of the three statutes cited as examples in the previous paragraph represented a dramatic change in the nature of the British regime. Putting those measures in statute form improved their chances of taking hold because statutes, as opposed to conventions, can be enforced by the courts. For instance, if in 1690 the king had tried to impose new taxes without Parliament's consent (an act prohibited by the *Bill of Rights* of 1689), his subjects could have used the courts to resist the new taxes on the grounds that they were in violation of British law.

c) *Constitutional laws*

The third form in which a country may embody its constitutional rules is what experts refer to as **constitutional laws**. This is a somewhat confusing term since organic statutes are, in effect, laws of a constitutional nature. But a "constitutional law" differs from an "organic statute" in two important respects. The first difference is that constitutional laws tend to be more comprehensive than organic statutes: while organic statutes usually deal with one particular institution or situation, constitutional laws tend to be comprehensive codifications of all (or most) of a country's constitutional rules. The second, and more important, difference is one of status or authority. The authority of an organic statute derives from the fact that it represents the will of the body that exercises legislative power. This means its authority is always somewhat precarious since any body that has a right to adopt a statute must of necessity have the right to repeal or amend it. The British Parliament that adopted the *Reform Bill* of 1832 could have repealed that same bill the day after they adopted it. The authority of a constitutional law is more absolute because constitutional laws are not as easily changed as statutes. In the United States, for example, the constitution itself proclaimed that changes (or "amendments") could be made only if they were supported by two-thirds of the members of each chamber of congress, by the president, and by three-quarters of the state legislatures.

The logic of this concept is best explained in the writings of the great English political philosopher, John Locke. Locke's theory of government begins with the argument that since no one has any natural title to rule over anyone else, government can be legitimate only if it is based on the consent of all those who are governed. In saying this Locke does not mean that all political decisions have to be made democratically. He means only that the regime has to meet with the approval of its citizens. Locke suggests that this approval comes in a two-stage process, which he called the "social contract." In the first stage of the contract, human beings who are naturally free and equal decide to come together in "civil society" and establish a political regime to govern themselves. In the second stage, they establish the ground-rules of the regime by majority vote. They can vote to set up a democratic regime, but they also have the right to institute an aristocracy or even a monarchy. It is not the institutions that have to be democratic for government to be legitimate, but the underlying contract that establishes them.

According to Locke, once the people have put the social contract in place, they turn the process of governing over to those who fill the offices established by the contract. But this government is not free to act in any way it pleases. It is always limited by any conditions stipulated in the social contract, because it is on that contract that the legitimacy of the government's very existence depends. If the social contract says that the government may not tax citizens without obtaining the consent of their representatives, then a new tax which has not been approved by the representatives of the people would be in violation of the social contract and hence illegitimate.

In conceptual terms, what we mean by a "constitutional law" is very close to what Locke meant by a "social contract." A constitutional law is a kind of fundamental pact emanating from the will of the people, which provides the foundation for the entire regime. It is therefore of higher status than ordinary laws — statutes adopted by legislative bodies — because those bodies owe their very existence to it. A constitutional law is thus a kind of "super-law," the supreme law of the regime, and this means that any action or statute inconsistent with it can have no validity.

The special authority or status of a constitutional law is the key to understanding a crucial constitutional concept known as **entrenchment**. There are many political principles so fundamental that citizens will want to ensure that their government will never be able legally to violate them. Freedom of religion might be an example of such a principle, or the right to use either French or English in the courts. The best way to ensure the inviolability of such principles is to "entrench" them by writing them into the text of a constitutional law. The foundational status of that law will then serve to put those principles safely out of the reach of any institution of government that might seek to violate them.

The classic example of a constitutional law is the Constitution of the United States. Prior to declaring their independence, the American colonists were, of course, British subjects. As such, their constitutional traditions might have led them to opt for a constitution similar in form to the British one, a constitution based on conventions and organic statutes. But for a number of reasons, the Americans opted instead to embody their constitutional rules in a constitutional law. One reason was the fact that the leading figures in colonial America—people like Jefferson, Franklin, and Madison—were enthusiastic devotees of the works of John Locke. The so-called "Founding Fathers" insisted that the constitution of the United States take the form of a fundamental law emanating from the will of the people rather than a set of conventions and organic statutes devised by those politicians who held the legislative power, because this was the approach most consistent with Lockean theory.

But the Americans also had two practical reasons for using a constitutional law instead of conventions and organic statutes. One was the fact that they had decided to establish a federal regime in which responsibilities were to be divided between a "federal" government and a number of "state" governments. It would have been impractical to establish a federal division of powers in the form of a constitutional convention, because a federal division of powers has to be formulated in more precise, detailed, and rigid terms than can be managed in unwritten agreements. It would have been equally impractical to try to embody the division of powers in an organic statute, because that statute would have to be adopted by some particular legislative body. But which one? The state governments would never agree to concede the task to the legislative body of the federal government, for then that body, by virtue of its right to amend its own statutes, would be able at any time to rewrite the division of powers so as to transfer jurisdictions from the state governments to itself. By the same token, leaving the adoption of a division of powers to the state legislatures would put the federal government at the mercy of the state governments. The federal division of powers had to be put in a constitutional form that would be beyond the unilateral reach of either the state or federal governments. This meant it had to take the form of a constitutional law.

The other reason for preferring constitutional law to convention or organic statute was the belief that constitutional law provides the most effective means of guaranteeing citizens' rights and liberties. It should not be forgotten that the 13 colonies broke away from Great Britain precisely because they believed that the British government was not respecting the American colonists' constitutional rights (for example, the right to "no taxation without representation"). These rights had been guaranteed to all British subjects, including the American colonists, by various conventions and organic statutes. But guarantees offered by conventions and statutes are not iron-clad. A government can ignore conventions or repeal statutes if a majority of voters is willing to support it. And in the 1770s the American colonists believed that their constitutional rights were being systematically violated by a government more concerned with the interests of the British majority than the rights of the American minority.

Here, then, was another reason to place the constitutional rules of the new American regime in a constitutional law. Constitutional laws are the preferred constitutional form for rights and liberties because constitutional laws have a higher status than any particular political institution. In a constitutional system based on convention and statute, politicians can adopt the most oppressive of measures as long as they have the support of a majority of voters. But no matter how much public support they have, politicians cannot legally adopt measures that violate a constitutional law.

2.3 The Canadian Constitution

In subsequent chapters, we will see that the Canadian regime is to a large extent a mixture of the British and American forms of government. This is evident in the form of the Canadian constitution. Like the Americans, we have entrenched many, if not most, of our constitutional rules in two constitutional laws: the *Constitution Act, 1867 (CA 1867) and the Constitution Act, 1982 (CA 1982)*. Like the British, however, we rely on constitutional conventions and organic statutes for a substantial number of our constitutional rules. Our entire system of responsible government, for example, is embedded in constitutional convention rather than constitutional law. Specific examples of Canadian constitutional conventions and organic statutes will be discussed later in the book. In this section, we will focus our attention on Canada's two constitutional laws.

It is essential that students of the Canadian regime learn to work with Canada's constitutional documents. In this book, we shall refer to the constitution on a regular basis, and for that reason we have included a copy of *CA 1867* and *CA 1982* in Appendix A. It will be useful to examine these acts briefly in order to familiarize the reader with their structure and contents.

FIG. 2.1 **Main Elements of Canada's Constitutional Laws**

CA 1867	CA 1982
Executive powers	Charter of Rights
Legislative powers	Aboriginal Rights
Provincial constitutions	Equalization and Regional Disparities
Federal division of powers	Amending Formulas
Judicial power	Definition of the Canadian Constitution

A) *CA 1867*

Canada's first constitutional law was originally called the *British North America Act* (*BNA Act*). Its name was changed to *Constitution Act, 1867* in 1982.

CA 1867 served to create a union of three British colonies into a new political entity called the "Dominion of Canada." The term "dominion" was a new one, invented to describe a regime that was too self-governing to be considered a colony, but not entirely independent of the mother country either: under the terms of "confederation," Canadians were to remain subjects of the British Crown; their foreign policy was to be directed by the British government; the Judicial Committee of the Privy Council, Britain's highest court, would be the final court of appeal for Canadian legal disputes; and Britain would maintain control of Canada's constitution.

It is this last point that is of particular interest to us here. Constitutional laws normally derive their supreme status from the fact that they emanate from the will of the people, usually as expressed in some kind of popular referendum. Because those creating the new confederation were already subjects of the British Crown, however, their new constitution was not adopted as some kind of Lockean social contract; instead, it was legislated for them, at the request of their colonial legislatures, by the British Parliament. Thus, the status of *CA 1867* as Canada's supreme law depended on the fact that it was an act of our colonial mother-country and on the fact that we Canadians, being less than fully independent of her, had no right to disobey her laws.

CA 1867 consists of a **preamble** (an introduction stating the reasons for the act that follows) and 11 "parts." The most noteworthy feature in the preamble is the suggestion that Canada is to have "a Constitution similar in Principle to that of the United Kingdom." This clause is of the greatest importance for understanding the Canadian constitution. As we have seen, the constitution of the United Kingdom is to a large extent based on conventions. In declaring that Canada's constitution is to be "similar in Principle to that of the United Kingdom," the preamble serves notice that many of those conventions are to be incorporated into it. This would certainly include those conventions governing the operation of "responsible government," a subject we shall discuss in detail in Chapter 3.

Part I of *CA 1867* deals with relatively unimportant preliminary matters. Part II establishes some basic points about the union of the provinces. Parts III and IV are much more important, for it is here that the *CA 1867* sketches the fundamental outlines of executive and legislative power in the federal government. We shall examine the particular "sections" of Parts III and IV in some detail in Chapter 7 (Parliament) and Chapter 6 (The Crown and Its Servants). Part V deals with "provincial constitutions" and describes some of their distinctive features. For the most part, the constitutions of the provinces are governed by the same principles as that of the federal government.

In Part VI, we find the division of powers between the two levels of government. Of particular importance are the description of the legislative authority of the federal government in Section 91 and the list of provincial jurisdictions in Section 92. Part VII lays down some of the fundamental rules governing judicial power in Canada. Note, however, that nothing is said about the Supreme Court of Canada. Section 101 gives the federal parliament the right to establish a "General Court of Appeal for Canada," and in 1875, Ottawa used this power to create a supreme court in *The Supreme Court of Canada Act*. Because the Supreme Court of Canada is this country's highest institution of judicial power, the act that establishes it must certainly be considered a constitutional act, even though it is not a constitutional law. Here, then, is a good example of a Canadian "organic statute." Part VIII establishes various provisions governing the financial details of Confederation. Part IX lays down a number of miscellaneous provisions, including Section 133 on the use of the French and English languages.

Part X, which committed the federal government to the immediate construction of the Intercolonial Railway between Quebec and Halifax, became obsolete upon the termination of that project and was repealed in 1893. It is a good example of the way in which a constitutional law is sometimes used in Canada to entrench guarantees that have nothing to do with constitutional matters. Part XI establishes two procedures for the admission of new provinces. Existing colonies, such as British Columbia or Prince Edward Island, may be admitted to Canada by an act of the British Parliament if it receives a request to that effect by both the colony and the federal government of Canada. The federal government may pass acts of its own to create new provinces out of "Rupert's Land" and did so when it founded the provinces of Manitoba, Saskatchewan, and Alberta. In either case, the act creating a new province is a constitutional measure and may thus be classified as an "organic statute." This is why in 1994 it was necessary to seek a constitutional amendment in order to clear the way for the construction of a bridge to take the place of ferry service between New Brunswick and Prince Edward Island. The British Parliament's *Prince Edward Island Terms of Union Act, 1871*, passed pursuant to Section 146 of *CA 1867*, had specifically guaranteed that the federal government would provide ferry service to the Island, and Ottawa therefore could not unilaterally cease providing that service.

B)   *CA 1982*

For well over 100 years, *CA 1867* and its attendant statutes and conventions formed the core of Canada's constitutional order. Through much of that period, however, there was a sense that this constitutional order was significantly incomplete. From the 1920s right up to the beginning of the 1980s, Canadian politicians struggled to add another element to our constitution: a constitutional amending formula.

Constitutions need to be amended from time to time when certain of their provisions either become outdated (for example, the section of *CA 1867* dealing with the Intercolonial Railway) or are found to be problematic. Constitutional laws will therefore always (or almost always) contain an amending formula, a rule explaining how the law can be changed. The constitution of the United States, for example, specifies that it may be amended if the text of a proposed amendment is support-ed by a two-thirds vote in each of the two houses of Congress and then a majority vote in three-quarters of the state legislatures.

CA 1867 is perhaps the only constitutional law in the history of the world that contained no comprehensive amending formula. Until 1982, Section 92.1 gave each province the right to amend its own internal constitution. And from 1949 to 1982, Section 91.1 gave the federal par-liament the right to make changes to most aspects of its own internal structure. But nowhere in the *Act* is there a formula for the amendment of such crucial matters as the federal-provincial division of powers, the judiciary, or language rights. This, of course, did not mean that the con-stitutional provisions governing such matters could not be amended. Because *CA 1867* was a statute of the British Parliament, that body retained the right to amend any section of the *Act*. Until 1982, then, Canada could make changes to those parts of *CA 1867* not governed by 91.1 or 92.1 by sending a formal request for amendment to the British Parliament at Westminster. The request took the form of a resolution of the federal parliament, but a practice emerged according to which Ottawa would not request any amendments that would alter the powers of the provincial governments without first obtaining their consent.

Over time, this arrangement came to be seen as unsatisfactory. As a result of our nation's substantial contributions and sacrifices during World War I, it was agreed by Britain and Canada that the time had come for the Canadian regime to become fully independent. This meant, among other things, that it was time for Canada to take full con-trol of its own constitution. As early as the 1920s, Britain had invited Canada to **patriate** (literally, to "bring to the fatherland") its constitu-tion, but Canada was unable to do so. The problem was that before the British government could hand *CA 1867* over to us, it had to put a comprehensive amending formula into the act. Unfortunately, Canadian politicians were unable to agree what that formula should be. Numer-ous constitutional conferences were held over the years, but agreement remained elusive.

The problem in these negotiations was not patriation itself: everyone agreed that patriation was a good idea. The catch was that various par-ties insisted on using the patriation negotiations to pursue other agen-das. From the early 1960s on, the government of Quebec took the posi-tion that it would agree to patriation only if it were accompanied by the transfer of specific legislative jurisdictions from Ottawa to Quebec City. In the 1970s, many other provincial governments made similar demands. On the other side of the table, Pierre Trudeau, then prime minister, opposed any such transfer, and sought to link patriation of the constitution to a project of his own: the adoption of an entrenched bill of rights which would, among other things, provide constitutional protection for the bilingual regime of language rights he favoured. His proposal was fiercely resisted by the government of Quebec.

In the early 1980s, Trudeau brought the matter to a head by announcing that if Ottawa and the provinces did not soon come to an agreement on patriating the constitution, his government was ready to proceed with a patriation request unilaterally. Two provincial governments supported Trudeau, but the other eight (the "Gang of Eight") opposed him and went to court to challenge the constitutionality of a unilateral initiative.[1] The case was eventually heard by the Supreme Court of Canada, which handed down a complicated split decision: in terms of constitutional law, there was nothing to prevent the federal government from making a unilateral request for patriation, but the court also declared that Trudeau's proposed amendment would diminish the powers of the provincial governments and that it was now a convention that amendments having an impact on the powers of the provinces required the support of a substantial number of the provinces. The effect of this decision was to compel both sides to go back to the negotiating table and show more flexibility. The "Gang of Eight" could not be intransigent knowing that Ottawa had the legal right to proceed unilaterally if no agreement was reached, and Ottawa had a powerful incentive to compromise because it wanted to avoid the stigma that comes from violating constitutional convention.

These negotiations resulted in a compromise agreement that obtained the support of every provincial government except Quebec. On the basis of that agreement, the British Parliament passed *The Canada Act, 1982*, which created a second major constitutional law for Canada, *The Constitution Act, 1982*.

CA 1982 is divided into seven parts. Part I is the Canadian Charter of Rights and Freedoms, a document we shall examine in Chapter 5. Part II is a constitutional declaration of the rights of Canada's aboriginal peoples. Part III entrenches the federal government's practice of making equalization payments to provinces whose revenues are below the national average. This practice will be explained in Chapter 4. The

---

1 Ontario and New Brunswick sided with the federal government, and the remaining 8 provinces were opposed.

fourth part committed the governments of Canada, the provinces, and the territories to hold a conference on aboriginal people's constitutional concerns. The conference was held soon after the adoption of *CA 1982* and resulted in certain amendments to Section 35 of *CA 1982*. Part V outlines the new procedure for amending the constitution of Canada, and we shall examine its contents in detail in the next section of this chapter. Part VI makes an amendment to Section 92 of *CA 1867* strengthening the powers of provincial governments in the area of energy, forestry, and non-renewable resources. This was one of the demands of the "Gang of Eight." Part VII of the *Act* contains a number of miscellaneous provisions. For our purposes, the most noteworthy is Section 52, which gives a legal definition of the Constitution of Canada and proclaims in no uncertain terms its status as Canada's "supreme law."

It should not be forgotten, however, that Section 52 is a clause in an act that is itself a creation of Britain's *Canada Act, 1982*. The supremacy of Canada's constitutional laws is thus still grounded in the fact that they are statutes of our mother-parliament in Westminster. In order to give our constitutional order a more independent foundation, it was proposed that the federal parliament and the 10 provincial legislatures should each pass a resolution adopting *CA 1982*. This, it was suggested, would make our constitution more like a Lockean social contract. The problem with this strategy, however, is that the government of Quebec, which has always opposed the agreement now embodied in *CA 1982*, refuses to pass such a resolution. Nevertheless, the *Act* is valid in Quebec, as well as in the rest of Canada, because the British Parliament has declared it so.

2.4   Amending the Constitution

Part V of *CA 1982* establishes an amending formula for the constitution, or, to speak more precisely, five distinct formulas for five distinct situations. A brief summary is sketched in Figure 2.2.

Section 44 stipulates that amendments to constitutional provisions regarding the executive or legislative offices of the federal government may be made by Parliament[1] on its own. This is essentially the same provision that formerly existed as Section 91.1 of *CA 1867*. In like fashion, Section 45 reproduces the former Section 92.1 of *CA 1867*, stipulat-

---

1   In constitutional language, the term "Parliament" refers to the Parliament of Canada. Provincial governments do not have parliaments; the provincial equivalent of parliament is a "legislature."

ing that amendments to the constitution of a province may be made by the legislature of that province. Section 43 contains a third amending formula. This section stipulates that amendments which concern some, but not all provinces (for example, the alteration of a provincial boundary) or that deal with constitutionally entrenched language rights in a particular province may be made only with the consent of the federal government and the provinces concerned. The reason for including the second category of amendments is to ensure that a temporary majority in a single province cannot unilaterally diminish or abolish the constitutional language rights of a minority.

The other two formulas are somewhat more complex. Section 41 provides that for five specific matters — the Crown, the right of provinces to a number of members of Parliament not less than the number of its senators, the use of French and English, the composition of the Supreme Court, and the amending procedures themselves — a constitutional amendment must have the support of the federal parliament and the legislatures of every province. This is an extremely rigid amending formula, but it is argued that the matters in question are so fundamental that they should not be altered without the unanimous consent of Canada's federal and provincial governments.

Any provision of the constitution not covered by one of these four formulas is to be amended with the "general" formula established in Section 38, which requires the consent of the federal parliament and the legislatures of two-thirds of the provinces which, taken together, contain at least half of Canada's population. This formula ensures that no single province can **veto** (that is, block) a proposed amendment, but at the same time it ensures that no amendment can be adopted without widespread support, including the support of one of the two largest provinces, Ontario and Quebec. Section 38 also establishes that a province may choose to exempt itself from an amendment made under this formula. If, for example, nine provinces were willing to transfer to Ottawa their jurisdiction over prisons (a provincial responsibility under *CA 1867*, 92.6) but Quebec was not, the amendment could be made, so that prisons would thereafter be a federal responsibility in the other nine provinces but a provincial responsibility in Quebec. Section 40 adds an interesting twist to this arrangement. This section stipulates that if an amendment involves a transfer of some part of provincial jurisdiction over education or culture, the federal government, which will now take up those responsibilities in all the other provinces, must offer financial compensation to the province that is retaining them. This is

FIG. 2.2   **The Five Amending Formulas**

Sections of CA 1982	Subject of Amendment	Amending Formula
General Procedure (secs. 38 –40; 42)	• all sections of the constitution not covered by secs. 41, 43, 44, 45. • prov. representation in the Senate • Supreme Court reform • principle of proportionate rep. in the House of Commons • the establishment of new provinces • extension of provincial boundaries into the territories	Parliament + 7 provinces with 50% of the population
Unanimous Agreement (sec. 41)	• changes to the executive offices (Queen, Gov. Gen., Lt. Gov.) • right of province to have no fewer MPs than Senators • use of French and English language • composition of the Supreme Court • amendments to sec. 41	Parliament + all provinces
Some Provinces (sec. 43)	• alteration of boundaries between provinces • provisions relating to the use of French and English languages within the province(s)	Parliament + relevant provinces
Parliament (sec. 44)	• laws amending the executive of the Parliament alone • Govt. of Canada or the Senate or the House of Commons (not falling under secs. 41-2)	
One Province (sec. 45)	• amendments to the constitution of a Provincial govt. alone (not falling under sec. 41)	province

because it would be unfair for the taxpayers of a particular province to have to pay a share of the cost of those responsibilities in the other nine provinces through their federal taxes as well as the total cost of those responsibilities in their own province.

2.5 Judicial Review of the Constitution

Our overview of the constitution would be incomplete if we did not say a word about judicial review.

By their very nature, constitutions have to regulate every single aspect and activity of a political regime. This means that constitutional rules must be applicable to an almost infinite number of possible situations. But the number of constitutional rules cannot itself be infinite. For this reason, constitutional laws are of necessity written in language that is highly general and seemingly vague. A constitutional division of powers cannot list every possible object of legislative activity: the regulation of automobile engine emissions, the regulation of industrial effluents, the regulation of garbage disposal, and so on. It will therefore collect all of these matters under a general heading such as "protection of the environment." By the same token, the Charter of Rights cannot specify all the types of police searches that are acceptable and all those that are not. It therefore defines our rights in general terms: the right to be secure against "unreasonable" searches.

The problem, however, is that it is often difficult to know how to apply general rules in specific cases. Let us take as a hypothetical example a constitution which stipulates that "protection of the environment" is a jurisdiction of the federal government and that "management of natural resources" is a provincial jurisdiction. Which level of government has the authority to regulate the clear-cutting of forests? The answer is not self-evident, and it is likely that each of them would insist that it had exclusive jurisdiction over the matter. Obviously, then, someone has to be in a position to offer an authoritative interpretation of what the constitution means in these circumstances.

This is a task that normally falls to the judiciary. "Judicial review" of the constitution refers to the judiciary's task of defining and applying its terms. The courts will decide, for example, whether the constitution says that a particular legislative matter is of federal or provincial jurisdiction or whether a particular statute is in violation of some right entrenched in the Charter. To do so, they will determine the concrete meaning of abstract phrases such as "the Peace, Order, and good Government of Canada," "subject only to such reasonable limits prescribed by law as can be demonstrably justified in a free and democratic society," or "the right to be secure against unreasonable search or seizure." It is therefore essential that students of Canadian politics pay close attention to judicial review, for to understand our regime, one has to understand the constitution, and to understand the constitution, one must understand how the courts have interpreted and applied it.

2.6 Contemporary Constitutional Politics

Canada's constitutional struggles did not end with the adoption of *CA 1982*. The government of the province of Quebec was resolutely opposed to the agreement made by Ottawa and the other nine provinces in 1982. This led Prime Minister Mulroney to initiate negotiations between Ottawa and the 10 provincial premiers aimed at producing a new package of constitutional amendments designed to meet Quebec's concerns. The result of those negotiations was the so-called Meech Lake Accord. Among other things, this accord would have declared Quebec to be a "distinct society" and would have given Quebec and all the other provinces a veto over constitutional amendments affecting the matters listed in Section 42, matters which in *CA 1982* are governed by the two-thirds/50 per cent formula in Section 38.

Because the accord proposed a change to the amending formula—one of the subjects mentioned in Section 41 of *CA 1982*—its adoption required the consent of all of the provincial legislatures. This requirement proved to be a problem. Although all the premiers who participated in the Meech Lake negotiations personally endorsed the final package, a number of them were defeated in provincial elections before they were able to get the necessary resolution of approval passed in their legislatures. In the face of mounting public opposition to the accord, the new governments that replaced them were reluctant to proceed. A series of complex federal-provincial negotiations ensued in a last-ditch effort to save it. Finally, in 1990, with the three-year window for approval fast closing, Elijah Harper, an aboriginal member of the Manitoba Legislature, effectively killed the accord by opposing a crucial procedural motion that required unanimous consent.

Two years later, Prime Minister Mulroney initiated a new round of negotiations. One of the reasons for the defeat of the Meech Lake Accord was that it focused almost exclusively on the constitutional concerns of the government of Quebec. Aboriginal Canadians, women's groups, and Western Canadians, among others, were unwilling to endorse a constitutional package that did not address their constitutional concerns. The 1992 negotiations produced a new proposal, the Charlottetown Accord, which was designed to address the concerns of not only Quebec, but other constituencies as well. The Charlottetown Accord retained the essential elements of Meech Lake—a distinct society clause, the Meech Lake amending formula, and limitations on new federal spending in provincial jurisdictions. It added to that formula a constitutional commitment to aboriginal self-government; a new Senate, designed to meet the demands of Westerners (as well, perhaps, of women) for better representation in Ottawa; and a "Canada Clause" that was meant to encapsulate the fundamental political principles of the regime.

Once the Charlottetown Accord was drafted, the federal government announced that it would not be willing to support a parliamentary resolution adopting the accord unless a majority of voters in each province gave it their approval in a national referendum, because there had been many complaints that the process that produced the Meech Lake Accord had been "undemocratic." Although *CA 1982* places the responsibility for amending the constitution in the hands of Parliament and the 10 legislatures, many Canadians thought they should have been directly consulted on the matter. Confident that the "something-for-everyone" approach of Charlottetown would prove popular, Prime Minister Mulroney gave in to those who advocated putting the accord to a referendum. To the surprise of many, however, a majority of voters in six provinces voted against it. The "something-for-everybody" approach turned out also to be a "something-to-offend-everybody" approach.

Ottawa's recourse to a referendum leaves us with an interesting constitutional question: do proposed amendments to the constitution now have to be submitted to the people for a popular vote of approval? If we look at the relevant constitutional law, Part V of *CA 1982*, in which there is no mention of the term "referendum," the answer appears to be no. Nevertheless, it is difficult to believe that Canadian voters would not insist on the right to have a direct voice in future decisions about the constitution now that they have had that opportunity in the Charlottetown process. If this is so, then perhaps we are witnessing the emergence of a new constitutional convention.

The most significant constitutional development since the rejection of the Charlottetown Accord was the Supreme Court of Canada's decision in the *1998 Reference re Secession of Quebec*. After separatist forces had come within a whisker of winning a referendum on Quebec sovereignty in 1995, the Chrétien government asked the Supreme Court of Canada to clarify whether unilateral secession was permitted under the Canadian constitution. The court held unanimously that the constitution does not permit unilateral declarations of independence, but went on to say that if a "clear majority" of Quebecers voted in favour of a clear proposal for secession, that would confer on the rest of Canada an obligation to enter into negotiations for separation. The court also stipulated that it would be up to political leaders to determine what constitutes "a clear majority on a clear question." Acting upon the judges' invitation, Parliament adopted in 2000 the **Clarity Act**, under which the right to determine whether a "question" and a "majority" are "clear" is reserved to Parliament itself.

Key Terms

legislative power

executive power

judicial power

residual power

constitutional convention

organic statute

constitutional laws

entrenchment

preamble

patriate

veto

Clarity Act

Part two: Basic Principles of the Canadian Constitution

Responsible Government

3.1   The Emergence of Responsible Government

3.2   The Conventions of Responsible Government

3.3   Responsible Government as "Cabinet Government"

3.4   Forming a Government

3.5   Majority and Minority Government

3.6   Institutional Implications of Responsible Government

3.7   Responsible Government and Separation of Powers Compared

We have seen that one of the chief functions of a constitution is to determine who will exercise legislative, executive, and judicial power. It is therefore not surprising that this should be one of the very first topics addressed in *CA 1867*. In the preamble to that act, it is stipulated that Canada is to have "a Constitution similar in Principle to that of the United Kingdom." Above all else, this phrase means that legislative and executive power are to be organized in accordance with a set of principles that may be summarized by the term **responsible government**. The purpose of this chapter is to explain the meaning, the application, and the rationale of those principles.

3.1   The Emergence of Responsible Government

The British regime is one that has evolved through a number of different forms. In its earliest stage, which may roughly be described as absolute monarchy, the Crown wielded both legislative and executive power. In other words, the king or queen both made the laws and administered them. But the possession of so much power by unelected (and hence, unaccountable) monarchs inevitably led to abuses of that power. In reaction to such abuses, the English nobles and commoners were gradually able to compel the Crown to turn legislative power over to their assembly, which they called Parliament.

By the mid-eighteenth century, the political philosopher Montesquieu could cite the British regime as an example of the principle of **the separation of powers**. Following an argument first made by John Locke, Montesquieu claimed that the best way to protect freedom and to prevent the abuse of political power is to ensure that legislative and executive powers are assigned to separate people or bodies. Since any tyrannical act would ultimately require the application of both legislative and executive power, placing those powers in different hands would minimize the chances that such acts could be taken. Because it assigned executive power to the Crown and legislative power to Parliament, the British constitution of his day was held by Montesquieu to be the very model of a free political order.

The principle of the separation of powers also became one of the cornerstones of the American regime. The American Founding Fathers were well versed in the ideas of Montesquieu and Locke, and their experience with British "tyranny" made them keenly concerned with the control of political power. They therefore opted for a constitution which placed legislative power in the hands of an assembly known as Congress and executive power in the hands of a president. Indeed, the Americans extended Montesquieu's principle. Not only did they place legislative and executive power in separate hands; because both the president and the Congress were elected democratically, each would to some extent be in competition with the other for public favour. It was thought that this competition or rivalry would reduce further still the chances of tyrannical collusion between the two branches of government.

In the early years of British rule, the colonies of what would later become Canada were ruled by imperial governors appointed by the British Crown. As early as 1748, the subjects of Nova Scotia gained the right to elect legislative assemblies with authority to legislate on most internal matters. The subjects of Upper Canada (Ontario) and Lower Canada (Quebec) received the same right late in the eighteenth century. Yet, since executive power remained in the hands of the governors and their advisors, our colonial constitutions were based on a kind of separation of powers, such as that set out in the American constitution. The difference, of course, was that we had a separation of powers for imperial reasons (i.e., to ensure British control) rather than for the liberal reasons advanced by Montesquieu and Locke. These colonial constitutions were unworkable precisely because of the separation between legislative and executive power. When those powers are placed in different hands, friction between the two branches of government is inevitable. Such friction is tolerable when each of the branches is elected, as is the case in the United States. But when only the legislative branch is elected, as was the case in our colonial constitutions, conflict between the two branches comes to be seen in terms of democratic rights.

The experience of Upper Canada provides a good illustration of the problem. In the early nineteenth century, political life in Upper Canada centred on the attempts of "reformers" to break the power of the so-called "family compact," a small clique of wealthy citizens who controlled much of the colony's political and economic life. Even when the reformers won control of the Legislative Assembly, they found the governors unwilling to cooperate in the implementation of the reform program, because they had appointed as their advisors an executive council composed almost exclusively of members of the family compact. For Upper Canada's reformers, the separation of legislative and executive powers amounted to a constitutional subversion of democratic self-rule. Discontent with this constitutional order led to armed rebellions in both Upper and Lower Canada in 1837. These were easily crushed by British troops, but they showed the British government that some kind of reform was necessary. The government therefore dispatched to the Canadas one of the leading political figures of the day, Lord Durham, asking him to investigate the situation and to recommend appropriate measures. The central recommendation of Durham's famous *Report* was that the colonial constitutions be amended so as to replace the principle of separation of powers by the principle of responsible government. The fundamental feature of responsible government is that it makes the executive responsible for its actions to a democratically elected legislative body. Instead of choosing as his advisors anyone he liked, the governor would have to choose them from among those who had been democratically elected to the Legislative Assembly. This principle had recently been incorporated into the ever-evolving British regime, and the Canadian rebels of 1837 had demanded that the same step be taken in the colonies. The British government hesitated at first, but agreed after a few years to introduce responsible government first in Nova Scotia and then in the other colonies. By the time of Confederation, then, responsible government was well established as a fundamental principle of Canadian political life.

In the British and Canadian regime, responsible government makes the executive accountable to the House of Commons. This accountability implies firstly that the executive is required to defend its actions in the House. But accountability is meaningless if the House before which the executive defends its actions is unable to do anything about executive actions it finds unacceptable. The principle of responsible government therefore demands of those exercising executive power that they obtain the approval of the House for their use of that power. In this way, responsible government allows for meaningful democratic control of executive power.

The achievement of responsible government requires the adoption of a number of rules, which take the form of constitutional conventions. There are five such conventions which are of particular importance. The *first convention* is that the Crown, which still has formal title to executive power, will act only "on the advice of" its ministers. In other words, it is the ministers themselves who exercise executive power; their "advice" to the Crown is really a command, and the Crown is thus a mere figurehead when it comes to the use of executive power. The *second convention* is that the Crown normally appoint as ministers or advisors only persons who are members of Parliament (MPs). This rule is intended to facilitate executive accountability: putting the Crown's ministers in the House itself makes them more accessible to MPs who wish to question or criticize them. A certain amount of flexibility is always shown in the application of this rule. It is generally acceptable to appoint one or two senators as ministers. It is also possible to appoint people who are neither senators nor MPs, as happened in 1996 when Université de Montréal political scientist Stephane Dion was named Minister of Intergovernmental Affairs. In such cases, however, the persons appointed must take the first possible opportunity to run for a seat in the House of Commons; if they lose that election, they must immediately resign their position as minister. The *third convention* is that the ministers will act together as a team or "ministry," led by a prime minister (or "first" minister), with each minister sharing in the responsibility for all policy decisions made by any member of the ministry. This third rule is known as the convention of **collective responsibility**. The *fourth convention* is that the Crown will appoint and maintain as ministers only people who "have the **confidence** of" (that is, the support of) a majority of members of the House of Commons. Without this rule, responsible government would not necessarily be democratic, for the Crown could appoint a ministry consisting only of MPs from some minor party whose views were representative of only a small minority of the electorate.

If the House of Commons expresses a lack of confidence in a ministry (either by adopting an explicit motion of non-confidence or by voting down a proposal that the ministry deems a matter of confidence), responsible government has in a sense broken down, because the executive is no longer acting in a manner that reflects the wishes of a majority of the people's representatives. In order to keep responsible government going, then, either the ministry or the House must be replaced. Therefore the *fifth convention* of responsible government is that when the ministry loses the confidence of the House, the prime minister must either resign (which entails the resignation of the entire ministry) or request new elections. The first of these options clears the way for the formation of a new ministry, one in which the House will have confidence. The second option (elections) will resolve the problem by producing one of two possible results. One is that the voters will take the side of the ministry and return a new contingent of MPs who will be more favourably disposed towards it. (This is what happened in the 1974 elections. The Trudeau ministry had lost a vote of confidence in the House, but in the subsequent elections, the voters elected a large majority of MPs who supported that ministry. Trudeau therefore remained in office.) The other possibility is that the voters will take the side of the House and elect a majority of MPs who do not support the existing ministry. (This is what happened in the elections of 1980, when voters elected a House with a strong majority of Liberal members who would not support the Progressive Conservative ministry headed by Prime Minister Joe Clark. Clark, seeing that he would not have the confidence of the House, promptly resigned.)

Taken together, these five conventions create a political order which makes those who exercise executive power fully accountable to the elected representatives of the people, and thus, indirectly accountable to the people themselves. (This relationship is expressed schematically in Figure 3.1). By law, executive power is invested in the Crown. But the conventions described above modify the law of the constitution dramatically. Under the principle of responsible government, the Crown must in effect delegate its executive power to a ministry composed of members of Parliament. This ministry (or "cabinet" as it is usually called) must have the confidence (i.e., the support of a majority of the members) of the House of Commons and must resign or face elections if it loses that confidence. In sum, these arrangements provide the kind of democratic accountability sought by the reformers of 1837.

FIG. 3.1 **Responsible Government**

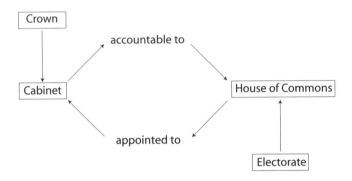

3.3 Responsible Government as "Cabinet Government"

From the description of the principle of responsible government given above, one would likely conclude that the introduction of that principle substantially weakened the cabinet by subordinating it to the control of the House of Commons. This is why responsible government is often referred to as **parliamentary government**. In theory, responsible government makes the House of Commons (the dominant chamber of Parliament) the ultimate authority for both legislative and executive action. In reality, however, the introduction of responsible government actually strengthened the power of the cabinet. It is therefore more accurate to think of responsible government as **cabinet government**.

To understand why, it is essential to grasp that the introduction of responsible government entails a transfer of effective legislative power from the House to the cabinet. We have noted that the cabinet must be composed of MPs who have the confidence of a majority of the members of the House. The cabinet and its supporters in the House are thus by definition in a position to control the legislative activity of that body.

This control becomes especially tight if the members of the House have formed themselves into highly disciplined parties—as has been the case in Canada since the late nineteenth century. For reasons we shall discuss below, modern Canadian parties are able to ensure that almost every member elected to the House will vote as his or her party wishes. In such a situation, the cabinet can count on virtually automatic support from a majority in the House for any measure it proposes. It is thus a natural result of the introduction of responsible government that the cabinet comes to dominate the legislative agenda of the House that supervises it.

In a regime based on responsible government, then, the cabinet becomes the dominant political institution. Under the law of the constitution, it possesses no power of its own, but constitutional convention gives it control of both executive and legislative power. Although constitutional law places legislative and executive powers in separate hands, then, responsible government leads in practice to a **fusion of powers** in the hands of the cabinet. Indeed, one may say that responsible government is best defined as *a regime in which legislative and executive power are fused together in a cabinet which is accountable to an assembly of the people's elected representatives.*

3.4 Forming a Government

To say that Canada is governed by a cabinet is to imply something very surprising about our regime: we do not elect our government—at least, not directly. Canadians often talk about having "elected" the "Chrétien government" or the "Mulroney government," but in this they are mistaken. In a regime based on the principle of responsible government, the people's role in the selection of their government is an indirect one.

This is no accident. The principle of responsible government is inconsistent with the notion of a directly elected executive. We have seen that at the core of responsible government is the idea that the government must be accountable to the House of Commons. Having the people elect the government directly would necessarily make the government accountable to the people as well. As the old proverb teaches, however, no one can serve two masters because the two masters may demand contradictory things. What if the voters were to elect a Conservative government pledged to free trade and a House of Commons dominated by Liberal and NDP members who were opposed to it? The government would either have to drop its free trade policy (thereby repudiating its accountability to the voters) or it would have to introduce free trade by executive decree (thereby repudiating responsible government).

In responsible government, then, we do not directly elect our government. It is more accurate to speak of the "formation" of a government. This is a complex process in which the Crown, the prime minister, and the House of Commons work together to provide Canadians with a government that has the confidence of the elected representatives of the people.

One may summarize this process in four basic rules. The *first rule* is that the ultimate responsibility for choosing the government must rest with the Crown. In practice, this means that the Crown will select a prime minister, who will in turn nominate the other members of the government. There are good reasons for this rule. To begin, the Crown is uniquely suited for choosing the government. For obvious reasons, the government cannot choose itself: in that case, every member of Parliament might proclaim himself or herself the head of a new government. It would be workable (though perhaps cumbersome) to leave the choice of government in the hands of the House of Commons, but this would be inconsistent with certain aspects of our regime. It will be recalled that, formally speaking, the ministers who compose the government are merely advising the Crown on the use of the Crown's powers. The Crown must, therefore, have a formal role in the appointment of its own advisors.

The *second rule* for forming a government is that in appointing a prime minister, the Crown must choose the person who is most likely to have the confidence of the House of Commons. This rule is obviously necessary for the functioning of responsible government, the regime in which the executive is accountable to the legislature. It also brings a democratic element into the process by ensuring that the person who heads the government and chooses its other members has the support of a majority of the elected representatives of the people. The *third rule* for forming a government is that the government remains in power until the prime minister resigns on its behalf. The *fourth rule* is that the prime minister must resign if his or her government has lost the confidence of the House of Commons and has no prospect of winning the confidence of a newly-elected House.

These rules may seem complicated, but working through a couple of historical examples will make them easier to understand.

At the beginning of 1993, Brian Mulroney was Canada's prime minister. He was the leader of the Progressive Conservative party, which held a substantial majority of the seats in the House of Commons. Mulroney decided to retire from politics. The Conservative party called a leadership convention, at which Kim Campbell was chosen to succeed him as party leader. The governor general, Ramon Hnatyshyn, then had no difficulty deciding whom to appoint as the new prime minister. The Conservative party still controlled a majority of the seats in the House of Commons. Campbell was its leader, and therefore Campbell would obviously be able to form a government that would command the confidence of the House. In October of 1993, parliamentary elections were held. In those elections, Campbell was defeated in her own constituency, and her party lost all its seats but two. Her party's main rival, the Liberals, now had a majority of seats. Technically, Campbell was still the prime minister because governments remain in office until the prime minister resigns. Yet, it was obvious to Campbell that when the new House convened, it would not have confidence in her government. It was equally obvious that Liberal leader Jean Chrétien would be able to command the confidence of the House of Commons. Consequently, within a few days of the election, Campbell resigned.

It is important to appreciate that this was a resignation, not a firing. As the elections of 1972 and 1957 illustrate, it is the prime minister, and not the voters, who decides the future of his or her government. From 1968 to 1972, Pierre Trudeau's Liberal Party held well over half of the seats in the House of Commons. In the elections of 1972, Trudeau and his party won fewer than half the seats, only two more than their main rivals, the Progressive Conservatives. Trudeau suspected that the not insignificant block of members elected for the New Democratic Party would prefer his government to the Conservative alternative, and he knew that this would give him enough votes to command the confidence of the House. He therefore chose not to resign. In 1957, on the other hand, a Liberal prime minister who found himself in virtually the same situation opted to resign rather than to continue. As a result of that year's elections, Louis St. Laurent's Liberals no longer had a majority of seats in the House of Commons, but they did have more seats than any other party. St. Laurent interpreted the results of the election to mean that the voters were not happy with his government. Suspecting that he would not have the confidence of the House, he resigned. The governor general then invited John Diefenbaker, the leader of the Progressive Conservatives, to form a new government.

What these examples demonstrate is that the process of forming a government is more complex than it appears. Canadians like to think that they elected a Chrétien government or a Trudeau government; in fact, however, Canadians elect members of the House of Commons. Because no ministry may govern without the confidence of the House, the choices made by the voters have an important, and usually decisive, influence on the formation of government. Yet that influence is not always decisive. After the 1993 elections, it was obvious that Kim Campbell would have to step down, and it was equally obvious that the new prime minister would have to be Jean Chrétien. As the elections of 1957 and 1972 demonstrate, however, when the voters give no party a clear-cut majority in the House, the prime minister may have the decisive role in determining who will form the government. Alternatively, if several opposition parties with a majority of seats between them publicly agree to a coalition — a formal partnership — the governor general would have to appoint as prime minister the person they had designated as the leader of the coalition. In this case — which is essentially what happened in the Ontario elections of 1985[1] — the decisive role was played by the opposition parties, not by the prime minister. Finally, should Canadians ever elect a House in which three or four parties have roughly equal strength, the choice of the new prime minister (should the incumbent resign) might well require the exercise of some discretion by the governor general. Such a situation has not yet occurred, but it now seems a somewhat more likely possibility given the recent emergence of strong regional parties like the Canadian Alliance and the Bloc Québécois.

3.5   Majority and Minority Government

In a political order based on the principle of responsible government, the ministry which takes office is said to have either a **majority government** or a **minority government**. The term "majority government" refers to a situation in which the party that forms the government possesses over half of the seats in the House of Commons. Because party organizations are able to exercise a high degree of control over the way their members vote in the House of Commons, a cabinet backed by a parliamentary majority is almost guaranteed the automatic confidence of the House. This does not mean that such a ministry can do whatever it likes: the cabinet will back away from any measure that is resolutely opposed by its parliamentary "caucus" (the group of MPs who are members of that party) whose votes are essential for sustaining the House's confidence in the government. But a majority government that

---

1   In that election, the ruling Conservative party won the most seats, but not a majority. The NDP formally supported the Liberal party, and the Liberals subsequently formed the new government

has the support of its caucus can govern as it wishes.

The term "minority government" refers to a situation in which no single party possesses a majority of the seats in the House of Commons. In such a situation, the government must be formed by some party which controls less than half the seats. In the 1963 elections, for example, 265 members were elected: 129 of these were members of the Liberal party, 95 were Progressive Conservatives, 17 were members of the New Democratic Party, and 24 were members of the Social Credit Party. Obviously, no party had a majority of seats. The Conservative prime minister, John Diefenbaker, did not expect that his government would maintain the confidence of the House, and he therefore resigned. The governor general called on the leader of the Liberals, Lester Pearson, to form a government. Pearson's party did not have enough seats to control the House of Commons. Under the rules of responsible government, however, it is sufficient if a government is able to command the confidence of the House. Pearson knew that he would be able to win and maintain that confidence as long as he adopted policies that would either find favour with, or not be opposed by, the members of one of the two smaller parties. In this, he was quite successful: his Liberal government remained in office for five years, despite the fact that it never had a majority of seats in the House.

In Canada, it is much more common to have majority rather than minority governments, but minority governments are not rare: since 1867, there have been seven of them, not all as stable as Pearson's. Arthur Meighen's minority government lasted a mere three months in 1921 before the House declared a lack of confidence in it. In 1979, Joe Clark formed a minority government for the Progressive Conservative party, yet announced that he would govern as if he had a majority. By this he meant that, unlike Pearson, he would not attempt to tailor his policies to maintain the confidence of the House. This rather bold stance cost Clark dearly: his government lost the confidence of the House after eight months in office, and new elections were held. In those elections the Liberals won a majority of seats in the House, and Clark was therefore compelled to resign.

There is a general (though not universal) opinion in Canada that majority government is better than minority government. The superiority of majority government is said to rest on its greater stability, longevity, and vigour. But this opinion is open to debate. As the examples cited above suggest, minority government is not necessarily unstable and short-lived. In the right circumstances, and with appropriate leadership, minority governments can last as long as majority governments. Concerning the relative vigour of minority and majority governments, one should consider the arguments made by the distinguished constitutional specialist Eugene Forsey. Forsey notes that sometimes a government backed by an absolute majority of seats may vigorously ride off in the wrong direction. Conversely, minority governments are often compelled by their need for support from outside their own party to govern in a more moderate and less arrogant fashion.[1] In sum, it is probably wrongheaded to ask which regime is superior, minority or majority. It is more sensible to recognize that each has potential advantages and disadvantages, and that circumstances and personalities will do much to determine which form is more desirable in a given situation.

3.6   **Institutional Implications of Responsible Government**

As was mentioned in the first chapter of this book, we have chosen the term "regime" to emphasize the extent to which political rules and institutions form a complex web with an internal logic of its own. Nowhere is this more evident than when one considers the principle of responsible government. For the most part, our arrangements with respect to legislative and executive power are highly complex—certainly much more complex than the relatively straightforward arrangements to be found in the Constitution of the United States. Canadians often wonder why we don't jettison some of our quaint practices and institutions and adopt American alternatives instead. The difficulty, of course, is that the logic of responsible government will not permit it.

It is essential to appreciate that responsible government and separation of powers each has its own internal logic, a logic that will determine many of the regime's institutional features. The decision to adopt responsible government as a fundamental principle will, by the internal logic of the principle, necessitate certain institutional arrangements and rule out others. The same would be true if one opted for the principle of the separation of powers. To demonstrate this point, let us explore a few of the key institutional differences between Canada's regime and that of the United States: elections, cabinet appointments, head of state, and party discipline.

---

1   Eugene Forsey, "The Problem of 'Minority' Government in Canada," in *The Canadian Journal of Economics and Political Science* 30, No. 1 (February 1964):, 1-11.

A) *The timing of elections*

In the United States, the principle of separation of powers implies that each "branch" of government is elected separately. Congress is chosen by the people in one set of elections. The president is chosen by the people in a separate election. Each branch thus has its own mandate and neither depends on the confidence of the other for its legitimacy; even if the Congress believes the president is doing a terrible job, the president will remain in office for four full years because the presidential election gives him a four-year mandate. Because the term of office is fixed by the constitution (two years for the House of Representatives, four years for the presidency, and six years for the Senate), elections in the United States are held at fixed, predictable intervals. George W. Bush was elected on the Tuesday after the first Monday of November in 2000. We know that the next US presidential elections will be held on the Tuesday after the first Monday of November in 2004, 2008, 2012, and so on.

In a regime based on the principle of responsible government, the fundamental logic of the regime makes such an orderly, predictable schedule impossible. In Canada, the timing of parliamentary elections is normally decided by the prime minister. Strictly speaking, it is the Crown (i.e., the governor general) that dissolves Parliament and calls elections, but the decision to do so is made on the basis of "advice" tendered by the prime minister, advice which is almost always followed. There is one fixed rule governing the prime minister's choice of election date. Section 4(1) of *CA 1982* specifies that the interval between elections may not exceed five years. In the Canadian tradition of responsible government, the prime minister traditionally looks to call new elections after four years.

Of course, leaving the timing of the elections to the prime minister gives him or her a significant partisan advantage over the opposition. The prime minister will typically call elections when the polls are most favourable for his or her own party, or perhaps when the main opposition party is in disarray. Jean Chrétien twice called elections (1997 and 2000) after less than three and a half years in office, primarily because opinion polls indicated that early elections would work to his advantage. Each time, Chrétien's decision led to (somewhat predictable) calls to change Canada's electoral practice in this respect and to adopt the American practice of holding elections at fixed intervals. There is little doubt that moving to fixed election dates would be more equitable.

The problem, however, is that the practice of fixed election dates is simply incompatible with the principle of responsible government. Under responsible government, the prime minister and cabinet are not directly elected by the people (as is the US president) and therefore have no direct mandate of their own. Their democratic legitimacy thus depends entirely on their capacity to maintain the confidence of the House of Commons. Because a ministry can, in principle, lose that confidence at any time (especially if no party commands a majority in the House), it is essential to be able to hold elections at any time; for as we have seen, holding new elections is sometimes the only way to resolve the impasse that results when the House and the ministry are in disagreement. The existence of a floating or non-fixed election date is thus an inescapable consequence of the logic of responsible government. While it might be nice for Canadians to have a fixed, predictable schedule of elections from now until eternity, as do our neighbours in the United States, it is simply not possible to graft such a practice onto our regime.

B) *Cabinet membership*

A second important institutional difference between Canada and the United States is the selection of cabinet ministers (or cabinet secretaries, as they are called in the United States). Here the practice in one country is almost the exact opposite of what is done across the border. An American president may choose for his cabinet virtually any citizen of the United States; the only restriction is that if he selects a member of Congress, that person must resign his or her congressional seat. This flexibility allows presidents to seek out the most talented people in the nation to run the government. John F. Kennedy, for instance, plucked Robert McNamara from the presidency of the Ford Motor Company to be his Secretary of Defence. Richard Nixon reached out to Harvard University to bring to Washington the famous international relations expert, Dr. Henry Kissinger, as his Secretary of State. More recently, Bill Clinton selected Harvard economist Robert Reich to be his Secretary of Labour, and George Bush chose retired General Colin Powell to be his Secretary of State. In Canada, on the other hand, a prime minister looking for cabinet material is essentially restricted to the membership of the House of Commons; other Canadians might be appointed to cabinet temporarily, but may not stay unless they are able to get themselves elected quickly to a vacant seat in the House. A Canadian prime minister's choice of cabinet ministers is thus restricted to a very small group of people, few of whom have meaningful technical expertise in the area for which they will be responsible.

Here, too, the difference between the two regimes is a direct consequence of the difference between the principles of separation of powers and responsible government. The constitution of the United States bars members of Congress from holding cabinet posts precisely because its underlying objective is to have the two branches of government "check and balance" each other as a means of protecting liberty. In Canada, on the other hand, it is the logic of responsible government that requires us to restrict a prime minister's choice of cabinet ministers to members of the House of Commons. Because the prime minister and cabinet are not directly elected to their positions by the people, their democratic legitimacy depends on their capacity to maintain the confidence of the House of Commons. If the prime minister and cabinet were not themselves members of the House, it is hard to imagine how the House would be in a position to hold them accountable for their actions and determine whether they deserve its continued confidence.

C) *Head of government and head of state*

Another noteworthy difference between the two regimes is that the Canadian regime draws a distinction between the "head of government" (the prime minister) and the "formal head of state" (the governor general). No such distinction exists in the United States, where the president fulfills both roles. Why this difference? Once again, the crucial point is the difference between the logic of responsible government and the logic of separation of powers. In a regime based on the principle of responsible government, democratic legitimacy depends on our capacity to maintain agreement between the House and the government, to ensure that we always have a government that commands the confidence of the House of Commons. Yet such agreement does not arise on its own; someone must actively intervene to ensure that a ministry that has lost the confidence of the House steps down and that a new ministry more likely to have the confidence of the House will take its place. In the Canadian version of responsible government, that official is the governor general. As the official whose job it is to keep the system of responsible government running, the governor general is, in effect, responsible for the regime; that is why, logically, the governor general, rather than the prime minister, serves as Canada's formal head of state. In the United States, on the other hand, there is no office corresponding to our governor general because, in a regime based on separation of powers, democratic legitimacy is maintained automatically by the system itself. Each branch of government is elected by the people for a fixed period of time and thus has its own democratic mandate. No one is required to oversee the system or to intervene to ensure that one branch has confidence in the other.

D) *Party discipline*

One final illustration of our general point is the matter of party discipline. Party discipline in Canada is quite strong—so strong that it is common for Canadians to complain that their MPs, who almost always vote the party line in the House of Commons, are little better than trained seals. In the United States, by contrast, members of both the Senate and the House of Representatives are freer to vote as they wish and it is not unusual for them to vote against the position favoured by their own party. This is a practice many Canadians would like to see adopted in this country.

The difficulty, however, is that here, too, the different approach of the two countries is to a large extent determined by the basic difference in their fundamental principles. The United States can afford to have weaker party discipline because under separation of powers, the president's mandate does not depend on the support of Congress. The president has a direct mandate from the people and can legitimately remain in office even if Congress consistently votes against his program. There is thus no pressing reason for members of Congress to follow their party line. In Canada, on the other hand, the internal logic of responsible government makes necessary a relatively strict form of party discipline. Because the prime minister and cabinet are not directly elected by the people, their democratic legitimacy depends entirely on the continued confidence of the House of Commons. If members of the party in power do not stick together in support of the ministry, the ministry will not have the confidence of the House, thereby losing its only title to rule. Unless Canadians are willing to see their governments change on a semi-annual basis, they have to accept that responsible government will of necessity require a high level of party discipline.

As these examples illustrate, when contemplating reforms to our political institutions and practices, it is essential to consider very carefully whether specific proposals for change are consistent with the internal logic of responsible government. The fact that certain practices work well in the United States does not mean that they will work here. A political regime is somewhat like an eco-system. Species from one eco-system may not be able to adapt to another. Or they may be able to adapt, provided certain adjustments are made. Of course, the introduction of a new plant or animal species to a particular eco-system may have unintended (and undesirable) side-effects, as well. Our point, then, is not that change is impossible; rather, it is that advocates of reform need to reflect very carefully on whether—and to what extent—practices imported from other regimes are consistent with the internal logic of responsible government.

3.7 Responsible Government and Separation of Powers Compared

The principle of responsible government is of British origin, but it now forms the cornerstone of many, if not most, liberal democratic regimes. In one way or another, all the nations of Western Europe, as well as most of the members of the British Commonwealth, subscribe to the principle that the executive must be responsible for its actions to a legislative body consisting of the elected representatives of the people. In almost all of the world's other liberal democratic regimes, the most influential constitutional model has been the United States rather than Britain. (This is especially true in Latin America.) One may thus think of responsible government and separation of powers as the two great alternative principles for the formation of a liberal democratic regime.

As we have noted, the political objective which inspires the principle of separation of powers is liberty. Montesquieu and Locke argued for a separation of powers on the grounds that placing legislative and executive power in different hands would minimize the chances of the government becoming tyrannical. What they argued for in theory seems to be validated by the experience of the United States. In that country, even when the legislative and executive branches of government are held by members of the same political party, the relationship between them is one of rivalry rather than collusion. It is thus very difficult to imagine the two branches cooperating for anti-democratic purposes. Indeed, the rivalry between the two is so strong that it often becomes a problem. In 1993, for example, the US government came to a standstill when the president and the Congress (both in the hands of the Democratic party) could not agree on a budget. One may thus say that the price of liberty in regimes based on the separation of powers is a substantial inefficiency in government.

In contrast, regimes based on the principle of responsible government are remarkable for their efficiency. Because of the fusion of powers, the same small group exercises both legislative and executive power. In such regimes, standstills of the sort seen in the United States simply do not take place. Once a cabinet backed by a parliamentary majority decides what it wants to do, there is almost nothing to stand in its way. When the Pearson cabinet decided to introduce universal medical insurance in Canada, the adoption and implementation of the policy followed quickly and smoothly. This is in striking contrast to the United States. Though most Americans agree that action is needed to extend coverage of medical insurance, former President Clinton's initiatives on that issue were stalled and then blocked by Congress, which favoured different policies. As a result, no action was taken, and the issue has dropped off the political agenda.

Yet some people would argue that the efficiency of responsible government is purchased at the price of a certain loss of political liberty. Because it is very difficult to stop a cabinet that has a solid majority supporting it in the House of Commons, it is sometimes said that responsible government amounts to a four-year elected dictatorship. Critics of our regime will point to the introduction of the highly unpopular Goods and Services Tax (GST) as an example of the way in which Canadian governments can introduce and impose policies that have little public support. It is probably safe to speculate that the separation of powers in the constitution of the United States would make it far more difficult for politicians to introduce a similar tax in that country.

Nevertheless, it would be an exaggeration to suggest that responsible government equals an elected dictatorship. In the first place, it should not be forgotten that all governments seek re-election. Since no government will be re-elected if it consistently or conspicuously ignores public opinion, those in power will have great incentives to behave democratically. Secondly, one must keep in mind that the activity of the government is subject to the authority of the constitution, especially the Charter of Rights. Finally, in responsible government, there is an important political check on the power of the cabinet: the presence of an institutionalized parliamentary opposition. As we shall see in Chapter 7, the House of Commons, to which the cabinet is responsible, affords those who oppose government policy a wide range of opportunities to question and attack the government, opportunities that do not exist in a regime like that of the United States. One can thus plausibly argue that the cabinet's accountability to the House of Commons makes responsible government as favourable to liberty as does a regime based on the separation of powers.

There is, of course, a more general issue of accountability to be considered, and that is accountability to the voters. In certain respects, democratic accountability appears to be stronger under separation of powers. The leading executive and legislative officers are directly elected by the people under separation of powers, while only the legislative officers are directly elected in responsible government. Moreover, under separation of powers, legislative officers can respond more directly to the wishes of their constituents since they are not restricted by party discipline. In responsible government, when members of Parliament have to choose between voting in support of their party and voting in response to the wishes of their constituents, they will almost always take the side of their party.

On the other hand, responsible government offers substantially greater accountability in that it is much easier for the voters to judge the performance of their elected servants. Under separation of powers, it is often difficult to know who is responsible for the state of the nation's affairs. When the economy is doing well, for example, both the president and the Congress will take credit for it. On the other hand, when the economy is doing poorly (or when there is a crisis over the budget, medicare, or some other issue), the president and the Congress will each insist that everything is the fault of the other branch. The voter has a difficult time evaluating office-holders because it is frequently difficult to know who was responsible for what. In responsible government, on the other hand, one always knows exactly who deserves praise or blame for the state of things. Because responsible government fuses legislative and executive power in the hands of the prime minister and cabinet, there is no debate over who to praise or blame for specific situations. US President Harry Truman was famous for having a sign on his desk that said "The Buck Stops Here." Such a sign would be infinitely more appropriate on the desk of a prime minister, since a president has relatively little control over the nation's legislative activity while a prime minister controls it almost completely. Accountability to the voters is in this sense much greater in regimes based on responsible government than in regimes based on separation of powers.

In a simple, abstract comparison, then, a strong case can be made that responsible government is a superior choice to separation of powers. This case is especially compelling in the twenty-first century, when people are generally less inclined to worry about government tyranny than were the American Founding Fathers and more inclined to expect government to intervene effectively in economic and social life. This probably explains why one regularly sees influential figures in the US advocating reforms that would move the American regime in the direction of responsible government.

Yet politics does not take place in a vacuum, and abstractions that do not take proper account of context can be very dangerous. The attractions of responsible government may not be equally compelling in all situations. One variable that has a considerable impact on the debate over the relative merits of responsible government and separation of powers is federalism. As we shall see in the next chapter, responsible government is substantially inferior to separation of powers with respect to the capacity to manage the tensions that arise in countries that decided to embrace the principle of federalism.

Key Terms

responsible government	cabinet government
separation of powers	fusion of powers
five conventions of government	majority government
collective responsibility	minority government
parliamentary government	confidence

Federalism

4.1   What is Federalism?

4.2   Why a Federal Union?

4.3   The Original Design of the Federal Union

4.4   The Historical Development of Federalism in Canada

4.5   Fiscal Federalism

4.6   The Challenge of Canadian Federalism

4.7   Current Controversies: The Pressure to Decentralize

The preamble to *CA 1867* indicates that the Dominion of Canada is to have "a Constitution similar in Principle to that of the United Kingdom." We have seen, in Chapter 3, that this phrase is primarily a reference to Canada's adoption of the British tradition of responsible government. Yet the constitution of the United Kingdom was not the only model for the Fathers of Confederation. Their new dominion was to be a *federal* union, although the principle of federalism was utterly foreign to the constitution of the United Kingdom. In developing the federal aspect of the Canadian regime, then, the Fathers of Confederation had to look south of the border to see what could be learned from the constitution of the United States of America, the blueprint of the first great modern federal regime. It is thus through federalism that American constitutional practice first enters the Canadian regime.

4.1   What is Federalism?

In order to understand what federalism is, we must first understand the distinction between **unitary** and **federal** systems of government. As the name suggests, a unitary system of government is a system in which all sovereign authority of that nation-state resides in one governing body — the national government. That national government may delegate some of its authority to lower levels of government, such as the governments of counties, towns, cities, or administrative districts. But the national government decides how much power it will delegate; it gives the power, and it can always take that power away. In a unitary system, there may be other governments besides the national government, but they will always be simply the servants of the national government. The country has one sovereign government.

Modern federalism is a relatively recent phenomenon, invented by the American founders in 1787 when they designed the constitution of the United States. Canada, Australia, India, Switzerland, and Germany are examples of countries that have used some version of the federal principle to organize their governments. They stand in contrast to countries such as Great Britain, France, Ireland, Sweden, and Japan—all of which have unitary systems of government.

In a federal system of government, sovereign authority is constitutionally divided between two levels of government. This means that neither level of government can be understood to have sovereign authority. Each receives its authority from the constitution and is thus subordinate to it. The constitution gives legal jurisdiction over matters of national concern to the national government and legal jurisdiction over matters of local or regional concern to the provincial or state governments. In some instances, the two levels of government may share jurisdiction. The point of fundamental importance is that in a federal system, the provincial or state governments are not beholden to the national government in the way that local governments are beholden in a unitary system. In a unitary system, authority flows from the centre out; in a federal system, authority is constitutionally divided.

In Canada, we commonly speak of three levels of government: national, provincial, and local. The national government is also referred to as the federal government because it is the government of the whole federal union. Each level of government has jurisdiction over legally specified matters and hence carries on the business of government concerning different, albeit often related, matters. It is important to understand that the relationship between the federal and provincial governments is not the same as that between the provincial and local governments. Local governments fall within the jurisdiction of the provincial governments, which can alter or abolish them. But the provincial governments are not subordinates of the federal government any more than the federal government is subordinate to the provinces. Both are equally subordinate to the constitution.

This equal subordination is made clear in the constitution itself. *CA 1982* contains a complex amending formula, which works on the basic principle that the provinces and the federal government must agree on changes to the federal division of powers. In this respect, federalism can be understood as a contract between two levels of government. Neither party can change the terms of the contract on its own.

4.2 Why a Federal Union?

In order to understand why the Fathers of Confederation opted for a federal union, we must consider the political situation that confronted the founders of the country in the 1860s. British North America consisted of six colonies — British Columbia, New Brunswick, Nova Scotia, Prince Edward Island, Newfoundland, and the Province of Canada (now Ontario and Quebec). It also included a vast expanse of territory under the charter of the Hudson's Bay Company. Each of the six colonies had its own colonial government. The government of the Province of Canada was a massive failure, as the divisions that existed between the French and English colonists made it unworkable. Politicians from the Province of Canada were thus eager, if not desperate, to reform the system of government.

The scheme that seemed most logical was to unite the British colonies within North America under one government. This would have numerous advantages. First, the new government would break the deadlock that existed between the French and English in Canada by tilting the balance of power in favour of the English-speaking colonists. Second, the new Dominion government could provide for a coordinated plan of economic development of railways, canals, and roads. Third, it could provide greater security for the small colonies, who were concerned about American imperial designs on the unsettled parts of North America. Fourth, it would help to relieve the burden on Great Britain of providing troops and personnel to administer the colonies; the British believed that the time had come for Canada to begin to stand on its own. Finally, it would make expansion into the western part of North America easier. The intention to include British Columbia in Confederation was there from the start. Linking the western colony with the rest of Canada would ensure that the United States would not be able to expand northward.

Those seeking union faced immense political obstacles. The English-speaking colonists in central Canada were enthusiastically in favour of a "legislative union" (a unitary system) rather than a federal union. But a legislative union of government was not a realistic political option. The French-speaking colonists in Lower Canada would never have agreed to a unitary system in which they would be a minority. They had to have their own provincial government, which would have jurisdiction over those matters relating to their preservation as a people. And the Maritime colonies were similarly ill-disposed toward a legislative union. They were among the oldest British colonies, and their governments were long established. They were not inclined to see their interests submerged as they became a small minority in a large Dominion dominated by central Canada. Thus from the very beginning, Canada was confronted with two serious political divisions: the split between French and English and a division between the centre and the periphery.

The obvious solution to the objections of the French Canadians and the Maritimers was the creation of a federal union. Yet Canadians were reluctant to organize the government on the federal principle for a number of good reasons. First, federalism was perceived to have been a great failure in the United States. That country had just emerged from one of the worst civil wars in human history, a war fought in order to preserve the United States as one country without slavery. The Southern states had argued that every state had the right to decide for itself whether it should be a slave state or a free state. Federalism and the doctrine of states' rights were thus associated with war and slavery. Moreover, it was often argued that federalism had created a divided system of government, and the weakness of the national government in Washington was one of the main causes of the war. Thus, it is easy to see why Canadians would have been less than enthusiastic about federalism, given the obvious problems that plagued our federal neighbour to the south.

The second objection to federalism was that it would create two levels of government and hence be more costly than unitary government. The colonies in British North America could not easily afford one level of government, let alone two. Moreover, it was suggested that federalism would be a weaker regime. Who would speak for Canadians? Under a unitary system, the people of the country could speak with one voice. But federalism would mean that each Canadian would be the citizen of both a country and a province, and it was easy to foresee that this would create divided loyalties. The challenge for the Fathers of Confederation, then, was to find a form of federalism that would minimize the perceived defects of federal unions and yet meet the objections of those colonists who opposed a unitary system.

The Fathers of Confederation believed that the federal arrangements agreed to at the Quebec Conference of 1864 constituted a workable solution to their problem. The key was the creation of a federal system in which the federal government would have a clear preponderance of power. A brief examination of some of the essential sections of *CA 1867* will make that preponderance obvious.

The first point to notice is those sections of the constitution which outline the division of powers between the two levels of government. Sir John A. Macdonald argued that the Fathers of Confederation had given "all the great subjects of legislation" to the federal parliament. A comparison of **Sections 91 and 92**— which establish the exclusive legislative jurisdictions of Ottawa and the provinces, respectively — shows that Macdonald was indeed correct.

Section 91.2 grants to the federal parliament exclusive jurisdiction over the essential matter of trade and commerce. Unlike the constitution of the United States, which restricted Washington to the regulation of international and inter-state commerce (as well as commerce with the "Indians"), Section 91.2 grants to the federal parliament exclusive jurisdiction over trade and commerce. This was intended to provide a constitutional basis for putting the general management of the economy in Ottawa's hands. Section 91.27 gives the federal government exclusive control over the important matter of criminal law, a jurisdiction that had been reserved for the individual states in the American constitution. Section 91.3 makes Ottawa the financial powerhouse of Confederation, granting it the right to any form of taxation. Finally, Section 91 appears to place the residual power in the hands of the federal government; anything not specifically reserved for the provinces is to be part of a general federal power to legislate for the "peace, order, and good government of Canada."

In comparison, the powers of the provincial governments appear paltry. The legislatures of the provinces are to have jurisdiction over "all matters of a strictly local or private nature in the province" (92.16). This includes such mundane items as hospitals and charities (92.7), local works (92.10), property and civil rights (92.13), and municipal institutions (92.8). Significantly, the provinces' powers to raise revenue are limited to two modest sources: "direct taxation" (92.3), which was relatively unimportant in 1867, and "shop, saloon, tavern, auctioneer and other licenses" (92.9).

The preeminence of the federal government was evident in a number of other provisions of *CA 1867*. Section 58 provides that the representative of the Crown for each of the provincial governments—the lieutenant-governor—is to be appointed by Ottawa. The lieutenant-governors are given the right to **reserve** provincial legislation, that is, to withhold royal assent, so as to give the federal government a chance to examine it. Under Section 56, Ottawa is granted the power of **disallowance**, by which means the federal government can annul provincial legislation of which it disapproves. These powers of reservation and disallowance actually make the provincial governments subordinate to the federal government in a certain sense. Since true federalism rests on the principle that the two levels of government are equally sovereign in their own jurisdictions, it has been said that *CA 1867* establishes not a federal system, but a **quasi-federal system**, in which the federal government is the dominant partner.

4.4 The Historical Development of Federalism in Canada

Although the Fathers of Confederation intended to create a highly **centralized** federal union—one in which the federal government would dominate—Canada now has one of the most **decentralized** federal unions in the world. This may sound confusing, but one must remember that federal systems, like the constitutions that describe them, are not rigid; they evolve over time in response to a number of factors.

We saw in Chapter 2 that the meaning of a constitution will depend on judicial review—how the courts interpret it. Constitutional provisions that appear to establish a highly centralized form of federalism may be given a decentralized interpretation, thus changing the nature of the federal system. Moreover, it may turn out that jurisdictions that were unimportant in the nineteenth century become extremely important in the twentieth. Because medical science was relatively crude in 1867, it seemed to the Fathers of Confederation that jurisdiction over hospitals (and by extension, health) was not a major item. Today, however, health care is one of the largest areas of public expenditure. The fact that it is a provincial jurisdiction makes provincial governments more important than they were in 1867. The same is true of provincial taxing powers. *CA 1867* restricts provincial governments to "direct taxation." Before the invention of personal and corporate income taxes, direct taxation was not very lucrative. The introduction of such taxes by provincial governments has given those governments revenue sources that would have made the premiers of 1867 green with envy.

Perhaps the most influential factor shaping the relative strength of the two levels of government is public favour. There are a number of decentralizing forces that sometimes lead the public to favour a greater role for provincial governments, including the regional pattern of economic development in Canada, the lack of a strong Canadian identity and the corresponding strength of local attachments, and the demands of Québécois nationalists for a strong *état du Québec*. On the other hand, a number of forces can push the public to favour a strong central government, including the desire for national standards in both social services and human rights and the desire to protect our economy and our culture from American domination. The balance between these forces at a given point in time will determine whether the public favours greater centralization, greater decentralization, or the status quo.

Over the years, the interplay of these various factors has left us with remarkably different federal systems at different points in our history. Without undue simplification, one can divide the historical development of Canadian federalism into four basic periods.

A) *Quasi-federalism (1867-1896)*

The era of Macdonald's long tenure as prime minister and ascendancy of the Conservative Party was one in which the national government proved much stronger than the provincial. For most of this era, the relationship between the national and provincial governments was analogous to the colonial relationship between the United Kingdom and Canada. Provincial legislation was frequently reserved or disallowed, and most of the great initiatives were undertaken by Ottawa, not the provinces.

B) *Classical federalism (1896-1914)*

Beginning with the election of Laurier and the rise of the Liberal Party to national pre-eminence, the balance of power clearly shifted to a more equal relationship between the provinces and Ottawa. The Liberal Party had championed provincial rights in Ontario, and a French-Canadian prime minister was naturally more sensitive to such rights for Quebec. During this period, the courts handed down a series of important constitutional decisions, each of which contributed to a steady erosion of important federal powers (notably the "peace, order, and good government" clause, and Section 91.2, trade and commerce) while at the same time expanding the scope of provincial jurisdictions such as 92.13, property and civil rights. Of particular note was the *Maritime Bank* case of 1892, in which our highest court explicitly repudiated the notion that provincial governments are subordinates of the federal government. The court declared that the constitution would henceforth be interpreted in light of the principles of classical federalism, according to which each level of government is sovereign in the jurisdictions assigned to it.

c) *Emergency federalism (1914-1960)*

In this era, the balance of power swung back toward the federal government. The two world wars required strong and decisive leadership that could be given only by a national government. Moreover, the period between the wars was marked by the economic collapse of the Western democracies and the massive depression that ensued. The Great Depression fostered increased centralization because it led to the idea that the purpose of government should be expanded to include ensuring the welfare of the people; since the Depression had virtually bankrupted most of the provincial governments, it was evident that only Ottawa would be able to afford the costs involved in this new responsibility.

d) *"Cooperative" federalism (1960-present)*

In the post-war era, the economies of the Western democracies have steadily grown. Canada's provincial governments now have a much greater ability to raise revenues and exercise power over their respective jurisdictions. Moreover, as the public level of expectations continued to rise and people demanded ever more services from the government, the jurisdictions of the provincial government continued to grow in importance. With both levels of government often supplying services in each other's jurisdictions, federalism has become a system of federal-provincial "cooperation," meaning that the two levels of government must constantly bargain and coordinate their actions.

Increasingly over the past three decades, this process of federal-provincial negotiations has involved regular meetings of first ministers and of cabinet ministers with common responsibilities. It is not unusual, for example, for there to be yearly meetings of the eleven ministers of health to discuss Canada's health system. Because of the proliferation of such meetings between federal and provincial executive officers, this era is sometimes referred to as the age of **executive federalism**.

Classical federalism was an era in the development of federalism where the two levels of government could, for the most part, operate independently of each other. Thus, one might imagine classical federalism as a layer cake, each level of government being a separate layer. Cooperative federalism, however, involves the inter-penetration of each level of government into the jurisdiction of the other. The layers of the federal cake are thus no longer separate.

4.5 Fiscal Federalism

One of the major problems associated with federalism is the need to balance a government's responsibilities with its ability to finance its role. A federal system will not work well if this balance is not attained, for it does little good to give a level of government the responsibility for providing a service if it cannot afford to provide it. The jurisdictional rights and responsibilities of government are mere legal niceties if the government lacks the will or the means to act.

This problem of balancing revenues with jurisdiction has plagued the Canadian federal system from the outset. In one sense, our federal system was designed to create an imbalance so that the provinces would always be subordinated to the federal government. But as the provinces grew more powerful, their inability to finance themselves also grew, which in turn has put enormous stress on the federal system. In response to that stress, federal and provincial politicians have developed an elaborate web of financial relations that usually goes by the name of **fiscal federalism**. This fiscal federalism may be divided into three distinct branches: taxation, the federal spending power, and equalization.

A) *Taxation*

If we go back and examine *CA 1867*, we find that the federal government was given both a much greater ability to raise revenues and the ability to spend money within provincial jurisdiction. It was clear from the outset that the provincial governments were to be the poor cousins of the federal government and that the federal government would be able to play a major role in areas of provincial jurisdiction because they would have the superior financial resources.

In the area of jurisdiction over taxation, the federal government can raise money "by any mode or system of taxation" (Sec. 91), whereas the provincial government has only the more specific jurisdiction over "direct taxation within the province" (Sec. 92). At the time the constitution was written, government financing was done largely through systems of indirect, as opposed to direct, taxation. A **direct tax** is one in which the taxpayer is taxed directly by the government. A good example is the income tax. An **indirect tax** is one in which the tax is not collected directly from the taxpayer. Examples of such taxes are custom duties and excise taxes. The merchant pays the tax, but then passes it on in the price paid by the individual buyer. The buyer ultimately pays the tax indirectly, through the merchant.

Jurisdiction over taxation was thus divided between the federal and provincial governments so as to favour the former. And up until the early part of the twentieth century, the provincial governments were heavily dependent on federal subsidies. As the field of government responsibilities expanded, governments sought new areas of finance. In the early part of this century, both the federal and the provincial governments introduced income taxes. Both levels of government have resorted to sales taxes.[1] What is important to note is that the federal government has historically been ahead of the provincial government in occupying and thus dominating these fields. It is politically difficult for the provincial government to raise provincial income tax when the federal tax is already widely perceived as burdensome enough. Taxation is thus one of the major areas of conflict between federal and provincial governments. Joint occupancy of what are now the major fields of taxation requires constant negotiation between the two levels of government over "tax room" or "tax points."

B) *Federal spending power*

The federal division of powers divides the areas of jurisdiction in a fairly precise fashion. Nonetheless, today we find the federal government involved in many important areas of provincial jurisdiction. One reason is that the federal government has the financial resources, which it uses to aid the provinces in areas such as education and health care.

---

1   It was thought, in 1867, that a sales tax was a form of indirect tax, and hence, not within the jurisdiction of the provinces. In the 1943 case of *Atlantic Smoke Shops vs. Conlon*, however, the courts declared that a sales tax could be seen as a direct tax, if one considered the merchant as a government tax collector. This decision opened the door to provincial sales taxes.

Although health care is a matter of provincial jurisdiction, that need not prevent the federal government from establishing and financing programs in that area. The **federal spending power** (Ottawa's power to spend its money as it pleases) has been a major factor in determining how the federal system operates.

The most important aspect of this spending power is the way it has allowed the federal government to wield massive political power in areas that legally belong to the provinces. The federal government will supply monies for programs in health care, education, or transportation, for example, but will also attach conditions as to how that money can be spent. Thus, while the federal government is not exercising direct legal control over an area of provincial jurisdiction, it can nonetheless establish substantial political influence. Perhaps the best-known example is in the area of health care. The federal government transfers billions of dollars to the provinces so that they may run their provincial health care programs. In exchange for this money, however, the federal government demands that provinces respect certain principles (such as the prohibition of user fees). While it is constitutionally within a province's power to allow for medical user fees, it is difficult for a province to do so if that means losing millions of dollars in federal monies.

This type of federal spending was traditionally known as a **conditional grant**. In response to political pressure from the provinces, particularly Quebec, the federal government has in recent decades moved more in the direction of **unconditional grants.** These involve a transfer of a large block of funds to each province, which allows for greater provincial discretion in how the monies are spent. Programs must still meet some broad national standards set by the federal government. Most federal funding to the provinces is used to finance health care, post-secondary education, welfare, and social services. This funding is now accomplished through the Canada Health and Social Transfer (CHST), a combination of cash payments and tax transfers. In 2000-2001, the total transfer to the provinces and territories via the CHST was roughly $31.4 billion.

C) *Equalization payments*

The federal government is also responsible for providing monies to provinces that fall below the national average economically. The precedent for such responsibility was established by *CA 1867*. It required the federal government to provide subsidies to the provinces for the expenses of their governments. This responsibility has developed into a responsibility to ensure that social and economic conditions across the country remain roughly equal and that regional disparities not become too great.

Attempts by the federal government to ameliorate regional dispari-ties were once made mainly by means of shared cost programs and fed-eral grants. But today, the more well-known means for doing this are the unconditional **equalization payments**. This type of financing was established in the 1950s and was entrenched in the Constitution in Sec-tion 36 of *CA 1982*. Equalization payments are an attempt to redistrib-ute money from the richer to the poorer regions in order to ensure that Canadian citizens have roughly the same level of government services and taxation. In 2000-2001, transfers to the provinces via equalization payments amounted to roughly $10.8 billion.[1]

4.6   **The Challenge of Canadian Federalism**

The Fathers of Confederation imported the federal element of the Canadian regime from the constitutional practice of the United States. To be sure, significant modifications were made to the US model of federalism. For instance, our constitution lays out (at least on paper) a more centralized division of powers than is to be found south of the border. Still, the basic principle of federalism is the same in the Canadi-an and the American regimes — two levels of government, each supreme in its own areas of jurisdiction, and both subordinate to a writ-ten constitution law.

Given this fundamental similarity, it is at first somewhat surprising to see how strikingly different our experience with federalism has been from the experience of our southern neighbours. To put the matter simply, federalism is not a central issue in American political life. The constitution of the United States established a relatively decentralized form of federalism. Over time, the American regime has evolved into a much more centralized federation in which Washington plays the dom-inant political role, and the governments of the states are clearly less important. The current pre-eminence of the federal government is rel-atively uncontroversial, and there is no interest in undertaking signifi-cant reform of the status quo.

In Canada, on the other hand, just the opposite is true. Almost from the beginning, Canadian political life has been dominated by quarrels

---

1   Figures above are taken from the Department of Finance Website: http://www.fin.gc.ca/

over the nature of our federal arrangements. The point should be obvious if one considers for a minute only a few of the semi-permanent issues that plague our political agenda, all of which are problems of federalism: Quebec separatism, Western alienation, responsibility for funding health care and other services, regional economic development, and constitutional reform. Canada is probably the only country in the world where issues of federalism are the national political obsession.[1]

Certainly part of the explanation for the difference between Canada and the US on this point is the fact that the US does not have a "Quebec question." The "Quebec question" has always been, at bottom, a dispute over the division of jurisdiction between the government of Quebec and the federal government. Rightly or wrongly, a majority of Quebecers believes that the current division of powers does not give the "state of Quebec" (as Quebecers like to call their government) sufficient control over those matters which are essential to the protection and development of the Quebec "people." Over the past 30 years, this dispute has been at the centre of six major constitutional conferences, as well as the 1980 referendum on sovereignty-association, *CA 1982*, the Meech Lake Accord, the Charlottetown Accord referendum, and a referendum on Quebec sovereignty in 1995. The underlying issue throughout this process has been whether Quebec can acquire the powers it believes are necessary to govern itself within the bounds of some federal form of political union, or whether that objective can be achieved only by becoming a sovereign state. Sovereignty or "renewed federalism"—for most Quebecers, these are the only serious options; the status quo is generally considered to be simply unacceptable.

There can be little doubt that Quebec's presence in Confederation is a large part of the reason why federalism has been so much more of a

---

1   The validity of this observation is confirmed by the oft-repeated joke about the elephant, which runs something like this. A Frenchman, a German, and a Canadian were asked to give a speech on the subject "the elephant." The German began with a learned discourse on how the elephant's strength could be used in industry. The Frenchman followed with a talk about the love-life of the elephant. When the Canadian was called upon to speak, he announced that his theme would be "The Elephant: federal or provincial responsibility?" Another illustration of the point may be found in comparing Canadian and American television panels. In Canada, it seems almost mandatory that every political panel on television must have members from the four main regions of the country (or at least three of them). In the United States, it would be incomprehensible to suggest that a panel must include "representation" from the Northeast, the South, the Mid-West, and the West. Americans are much more likely to see gender, race, or political ideology as the politically-relevant categories.

problem or question in Canada than it has in the United States. Yet the role of Quebec does not explain everything. Even if Quebec had never been a part of Canada (or alternatively, if Quebec were to someday secede from Canada), federalism would still be far more controversial here than it is in the United States.[1] The reason for this is that, in one key respect, federalism does not work as well with responsible government as it does with separation of powers. The issue here is representation within the national government.

The citizens of a federal regime will by definition have dual loyalties, feeling themselves to be both citizens of a province or state and citizens of the country as a whole. By extension, they will also, of necessity, have a dual view of the union itself: on the one hand, it will be seen as a union of individual Americans, Canadians, or Australians; on the other, it will be seen as a union of states or provinces. To the extent that we are democrats and respect the principle of equality, this duality leads to a dilemma: should political representation within the national government be based on the principle of the equality of all individual citizens or on the principle of the equality of all the states or provinces?

The Founding Fathers of the United States resolved this dilemma by adopting **bicameralism**. In a bicameral legislative body, power is shared by two separate chambers so that neither can act without the agreement of the other. The Founding Fathers created a legislature (Congress) in which representation in one chamber was based on the principle of the equality of all individual citizens (the House of Representatives), and representation in the other was based on the principle of the equality of the states (the Senate). In the House of Representatives, states with larger populations have more seats, and states with smaller populations have fewer seats. In the Senate, however, all states have the same number of seats—two—regardless of population. The United States Congress thus gives equal voice to the two visions of union—the US as a union of individual Americans (in which all Americans are equal) and the US as a union of states (in which all states are equal). This bicameral solution was essential to the adoption of the US constitution. If legislative power had been assigned only to a chamber based on equality of the states, the small states would have dominated the national government—something the large states would never have accepted. If

---

1   In his separatist manifesto, *An Option For Quebec*, René Lévesque claimed that separatism would be good for English Canada because once Quebec had left, the rest of the country would no longer have any disputes about federalism. On this point, at least, Mr. Lévesque certainly misunderstood political life in English Canada.

legislative power had been assigned only to a chamber based on equality of individual citizens, the large states would have dominated the national government—something the small states would never have agreed to. Bicameralism allowed the Founding Fathers to give fair weight to both claims, so that neither the small states nor the large states would dominate.

The Fathers of Confederation learned from the experience of the United States that bicameralism would be essential to Confederation. This is the main reason why Canada's Parliament includes both a House of Commons and a Senate. Representation in the House of Commons is based on the principle of the equality of all Canadians, so that provinces with larger populations have a larger number of seats. Representation in the Senate, on the other hand, is based on the principle of the equality of the regions, with each of the four main regions of the country receiving about the same number of seats. The problem in the Canadian case, however, is that responsible government makes it difficult, if not impossible, for the two chambers to be equal in power. The House of Commons is not merely a legislative body; under the rules of responsible government, it is also the chamber from which the executive is drawn and to which the executive must be responsible. To the extent that this role cannot be shared with the Senate, the House will of necessity dominate Parliament, and the Senate will always have a peripheral role. This means, however, that the principle of representation embedded in the Senate—the equality of the regions—is not really given meaningful expression within our national government. The chamber with real power is one where the two largest provinces possess 70 per cent of the seats. Not surprisingly, this leads citizens in the other eight provinces to believe they have little control over their national government. (This feeling is dangerously prevalent in the four Western provinces.) Accordingly, the eight smaller provinces must look to their provincial governments to champion their causes, and these provincial governments typically court public favour by "running against Ottawa," by blaming the federal government for all their province's woes. Instead of being dealt with *within* the federal government, regional concerns are thus funnelled through the federal-provincial division of powers, which has the effect of making federalism our country's main battleground. This divisive political dynamic does not prevail in the United States, for the Senate ensures that the interests of the small states are well-protected *within* Washington. In some respects, then, it is our system of responsible government that, by making full bicameralism impossible, promotes and institutionalizes federal-provincial conflict.

Through much of the twentieth century, Ottawa has used its spending power to ameliorate regional disparities and to influence public policy in areas of provincial jurisdiction. For most political leaders in Quebec, these federal "intrusions" are unacceptable since they effectively transfer decision-making authority in some areas from the *Assemblée nationale* in Quebec City to the English-Canadian dominated government in Ottawa. Nationalist politicians in Quebec believe that the division of powers developed in 1867 is already too centralist; for Ottawa to "invade" jurisdictions that are supposed to belong exclusively to the provinces is intolerable. For provinces such as Alberta and British Columbia, the intrusions of the federal government into areas of exclusive provincial jurisdiction (and the concomitant transfer of tax dollars from West to East) have become unacceptable as well. These two provinces are now dominated by an ideology of "alienation" and a view of provincial rights that suggests that their dissatisfaction with Canadian federalism is only slightly less than that of Quebecers.[1] Their sense of grievance against Central Canada is expressed in terms of demands that Ottawa remove itself from areas of provincial jurisdiction and that federalism take a more decentralized form in the future. In other words, Alberta and British Columbia have a perspective on Canadian federalism that is in some ways not all that different from the perspective of Quebec nationalists.

Yet there are powerful reasons why many Canadians steadfastly oppose the call for a more decentralized federal system. It is often argued that a strong federal presence in key provincial jurisdictions is essential for the defence of national standards of service in health care, welfare, and education. Many Canadians fear that if Ottawa retreats from these areas in order to satisfy the demands of regionalist politicians in British Columbia, Alberta, and Quebec, Canadians will end up with dramatically different levels of services in the different provinces. Those who live in rich provinces would receive first-class health care, for example, while those in the less prosperous provinces would have to settle for something substantially worse. According to opponents of decentralization, then, a federal retreat from provincial jurisdictions would make Canada less of a country and something more akin to a patchwork quilt.

---

1   See Doug Owram, "Reluctant Hinterland," *The Canadian Political Tradition: Basic Readings*, 2nd ed., ed. R.S. Blair and J.T. McLeod (Scarborough: Nelson Canada, 1993) 153-68.

The opponents of decentralization were able to carry the day in their fight against the Meech Lake and Charlottetown Accords. Those accords would have placed restrictions on new federal initiatives in areas of provincial jurisdiction and, in the case of Charlottetown, would have seen the federal government withdraw entirely from a number of the less important provincial jurisdictions. Oddly enough, however, today's federal system is perhaps becoming far more decentralized than anything contemplated in either of the accords. One of the catalysts for this transformation has been the near victory of the separatist side in the 1995 referendum on sovereignty in Quebec. Their close call with disaster has led our national politicians to take more seriously the traditional Quebec demands for limits to Ottawa's use of the spending power.

Under the 1999 **Social Union Framework**, for example, Ottawa agreed not to introduce any new shared-cost programs in provincial jurisdictions without first obtaining the approval of seven provinces which, taken together, have 50 per cent of the total Canadian population. Ottawa also agreed that any province that chooses not to participate in such a program will be provided with equivalent federal dollars to run a program of its own.

A second (and perhaps even more important) catalyst of decentralization has been the federal debt and deficit. The federal government now takes the view that it simply cannot afford to intervene in provincial jurisdictions on the scale that it used to. Federal funding for health, education, and welfare is being cut back significantly, and it is likely that the cuts in funding will lead to a decline in the federal government's influence on provincial policies and standards. A more decentralized federal system now seems inevitable.

Will this new trend to decentralization be sufficient to satisfy the politicians and voters in Quebec, Alberta, and British Columbia? On the other hand, will it be so strong that it unravels the fabric of Canadian nationhood? These sorts of questions reveal how Canada's future will, in large part, be tied to the development of our federal system. When we consider whether the present federal system works, how it might be reformed, and whether Canadians can ever agree on the constitutional changes required for such reforms, the fundamental issue of federalism comes to light: to what extent do Canadians believe there should be a powerful national government that rules them from the centre of the country and is controlled by a national majority, and to what extent do Canadians believe that Canada should become more of a confederation of ten largely independent provinces for whom the federal government is merely a coordinator, not a leader? Federalism is a system of divided loyalties: each of us is a citizen of both a province and a country, ruled by two different governments. Canadians are being forced to confront the question of which government they believe to be the most important and why.

Key Terms

federal

unitary

Sections 91 and 92

reservation

disallowance

quasi-federalism

centralized

decentralized

classical federalism

emergency federalism

cooperative federalism

executive federalism

fiscal federalism

direct tax

indirect tax

federal spending power

conditional grant

unconditional grant

equalization payments

bicameralism

social union framework

The Canadian Charter of Rights and Freedoms

5.1   What is a Charter of Rights?
5.2   The Adoption of the Charter
5.3   Opposition to the Charter
5.4   The Notwithstanding Clause
5.5   Section 1
5.6   The Political Impact of the Charter

5.1   What is a Charter of Rights?

With the adoption of *CA 1982*, Canada acquired a constitutionally entrenched charter of rights. For reasons that will become evident later in this chapter, the introduction of the Charter marked a profound transformation of the Canadian regime. But there are many other questions that must be addressed before we can discuss its impact. The first of these is the most obvious: what is a charter of rights?

The basic idea behind a charter of rights is best understood by thinking back to our discussion of Canada's regime principles in Chapter 1. Because Canada is a democracy, one of our regime's central principles is majority rule. Yet, because Canada is not just a democracy, but a *liberal* democracy, we may also say that our regime is devoted to the protection of fundamental rights. The great problem in liberal democracy is that these two fundamental principles—majority rule and rights—are not always in harmony. A majority of the people's elected representatives might decide to pass a law that violates the rights of some minority. For instance, since the vast majority of Canadians and their MPs are at least nominally connected to the Christian faith, Parliament might find it reasonable to declare Sunday a day sacred to the Lord and to prohibit shop-owners from doing business on that day. Yet a law that did so might be seen by non-Christians as an attempt to force them to follow

Christian rules. In other words, it could be seen as a violation of their right to freedom of religion.

The purpose of a charter of rights is to prevent democratic majorities from using political power[1] to violate rights, especially the rights of minorities. A charter does so by entrenching those rights in the text of the constitution. You will recall from Chapter 2 that *CA 1867* and *CA 1982* are the supreme law of the regime. It therefore follows that any statute which is inconsistent with the constitution can have no force or effect. Thus, a constitutional charter of rights will put rights beyond the reach of the majority and its elected representatives by incorporating them into the supreme law of the regime.

The institution that enforces the constitution is the judiciary. Just as it is our courts that determine whether the constitution puts a given matter under federal or provincial jurisdiction, then so, too, the courts decide whether specific statutes do or do not violate the rights protected in the Charter. Indeed, the constitution states this point explicitly in S. 24(1) of *CA 1982*:

> Anyone whose rights or freedoms, as guaranteed by this Charter, have been infringed or denied may apply to a court of competent jurisdiction to obtain such remedy as the court considers appropriate and just in the circumstances.

To see how the Charter works, it is useful to work through an example. One of the Supreme Court's first Charter decisions was the case of *Lawson Hunter v. Southam* (1984). This case involved a federal statute called the *Combines Investigation Act*. Combines are a form of monopoly, and the government normally regulates or even prohibits monopolistic practices because they often lead to exploitation of the consumer. The *Combines Investigation Act* established certain rules to govern investigations by the Department of Justice of monopolistic practices. Among

---

1 It is important not to confuse constitutional charters of rights with statutory **human rights codes**. A human rights code is a statute that protects rights in the private sphere. A human rights code provision prohibiting racial discrimination would thus prevent one private individual (a landlord) from discriminating against another private individual (a tenant) on the basis of race. A constitutional charter of rights, on the other hand, is meant to protect rights from violations in the public sphere, that is, violations by the government. A charter provision prohibiting racial discrimination would thus prevent a government from passing a law that was itself racially discriminatory (no welfare for Asians) or permitted others to behave in a discriminatory fashion.

other things, this legislation provided that agents of that department might search any premises (and seize any materials therefrom) which they suspected might contain evidence relevant to one of their investigations. The only limitation on this provision was that the agents conducting the search had to obtain a kind of warrant beforehand from a member of the Restrictive Trade Practices Commission.

In the early 1980s, the Combines Investigation branch of the Department of Justice was looking into the activities of the Thomson and Southam newspaper chains because it suspected that they had made a secret deal so that one chain would have a monopoly on the Winnipeg market while the other would have a monopoly on the Ottawa market. Pursuant to this investigation, an official of the Combines Investigation unit, Lawson Hunter, sent four of his agents to search the offices of *The Edmonton Journal*, a Southam paper, and to seize a number of the paper's files. In conformity with the law, the agents had obtained an authorization for the search from Dr. Frank Roseman of the Restrictive Trade Practices Commission before carrying out their mission.

Southam Press was unhappy about this search, and decided to take the Department of Justice to court. There was nothing illegal in the activities of Hunter and his agents; their search had been carried out in perfect conformity with the *Combines Investigation Act*. Yet what Southam argued was not that the law had been broken, but that the law was itself unconstitutional. Section 8 of the Charter stipulates that "Everyone has the right to be free against unreasonable search or seizure." The allegation made by Southam was that the search and seizure provisions of the *Combines Investigation Act*, which provided the legal authorization for Hunter's search of the *Edmonton Journal*, were "unreasonable." If Southam was right about this, the *Combines Investigation Act* would be in violation of a part of the constitution — the supreme law — and would thus be of no force or effect. Consequently, there would be no legal authority for the search that had taken place, and the items seized in that search would have to be returned to Southam.

But was Southam's allegation correct? When the Supreme Court heard this case, its task was obviously to decide how to define "reasonable" and "unreasonable" search and seizure laws. To do so, it began by suggesting that the purpose of the right entrenched in Section 8 is to ensure a sensible balance between the government's need to conduct searches and seizures for the prosecution of criminal cases and the public's right to privacy. The court went on to suggest that to ensure that such a balance is maintained, any legislation establishing search and seizure procedures must make those procedures conform to three conditions: the searchers must obtain prior authorization for their search, the official who grants that authorization must be impartial (that is, not a member of the organization conducting the search), and the probability that the search would in fact uncover important evidence must be high (in other words, no "fishing expeditions"). Applying these standards to the case at hand, the court ruled that the *Combines Investigation Act* was in violation of Section 8. The *Act* did meet the first condition — it required the agents of the Department of Justice to seek prior authorization for their search. But, because the official from whom they were to seek authorization for the search was himself an official of the Department of Justice, the *Act* did not meet the second condition; the official granting the authorization for the search was not sufficiently impartial. The court therefore ruled that the *Combines Investigation Act* was unconstitutional, and this meant that the Department of Justice no longer had any legal right to keep the files it had seized from *The Edmonton Journal*.

5.2   **The Adoption of the Charter**

It is sometimes suggested that the adoption of the Charter in 1982 marked the introduction or creation of a new set of rights. This suggestion is misleading. Although a number of the rights set down in it might be thought of as new, the Charter was primarily a new mechanism for the protection of rights that were already well established in the Canadian political tradition.

To see that the protection of rights does not necessarily depend on the existence of a charter of rights, it suffices to look at the example of Great Britain. Britain has never had a constitutionally entrenched charter of rights, but certain fundamental rights and freedoms have long been as well respected there as they are in regimes that have constitutional charters. In some cases, those rights have been codified in organic statutes, but for the most part they exist merely as traditions (or in some cases, as constitutional conventions). The British Parliament is legally entitled to pass legislation that violates those rights, but the inescapable necessity of keeping the support of the voters, coupled with the presence of an official opposition in the House of Commons, makes it difficult for any government to go very far in terms of violating rights.

For most of its life, the Canadian regime took the British approach to the protection of rights. Rights such as freedom of religion and freedom of speech were seen to be part of the liberal democratic tradition we inherited from Britain,[1] and Canadians generally thought it possible and desirable to trust our parliamentarians not to violate those rights.

On the whole, this approach worked reasonably well. Compared with most countries, Canada had an excellent human rights record. Yet there were important exceptions to this general trend. Provincial governments were sometimes not as careful about respecting rights as they should have been. In the 1930s, the Aberhart government in Alberta enacted legislation that clearly violated the right to freedom of speech. In the 1950s, the Duplessis government in Quebec passed a number of measures that were inconsistent with freedom of speech and freedom of religion.[2] In all of these cases, the offending measures were struck down by the Supreme Court, but only because the legislation in question was *ultra vires*: the court held that under the division of powers, only the federal government could regulate speech and religion so as to limit the right to free speech or religious freedom. Yet it was not clear that the federal government was entirely trustworthy on this matter either. During World War II, Ottawa had confined Canadians of Japanese origin in detention camps, alleging that their Japanese ancestry made them potential security threats. Though the government had widespread public support for this policy at the time, it was later recognized to have been a clear violation of the right to liberty and the right not to be arbitrarily detained or imprisoned. Finally, the records of both levels of government in observing and protecting the rights of Canada's aboriginal peoples are poor.

By the end of the 1950s, then, many Canadians came to be dissatisfied with our traditional approach to the protection of rights and freedoms. At that same time, the Supreme Court of the United States was just beginning to use that country's Bill of Rights to take bold steps

---

1 Some members of the Supreme Court of Canada flirted with the thesis that the reference to a constitution "similar in principle to that of the United Kingdom" in the preamble to *CA 1867* contained an "implied bill of rights" granting constitutional protection to all those rights that formed part of British constitutional traditions. See, for example, *Switzman v. Elbling* (1957). This thesis was never endorsed by a majority of the court.

2 The Aberhart government in Alberta passed a law requiring that province's newspapers to print government responses to all articles critical of the government. The Duplessis government in Quebec enacted legislation designed to suppress communist ideas and to curtail the activities of Jehovah's Witnesses.

in the fight for racial equality, striking down discriminatory legislation as unconstitutional. Rights activists in Canada began to argue that Canada should abandon its traditional British approach to the protection of rights and embrace the American idea of a constitutionally entrenched bill or charter of rights. The ground for such an innovation was already well prepared by our experience with federal judicial review; as a result of our interminable litigation over the division of powers, Canadians were quite used to the idea that courts might tell parliaments and legislatures what they were permitted to do and what they were not.

In 1960, the Diefenbaker government moved to address the human rights issue by adopting the **Canadian Bill of Rights**. This document recognized and declared the existence of a number of "human rights and fundamental freedoms" including freedom of religion, freedom of speech, freedom of assembly and association, the right to the enjoyment of property, and a number of procedural legal rights, such as the right to retain legal counsel upon arrest. But there was a fundamental flaw in this document: it was merely an organic statute. This created two problems. The first was that this Bill of Rights, as a *federal* statute, did not apply to acts of the provincial governments and legislatures. Moreover, it was not even clear that it could be used to annul federal legislation. Courts are able to strike down one type of law only by applying or appealing to some higher law. Since the Canadian Bill of Rights was itself merely a statute, however, there was no logical reason to give it precedence over any other statute. Thus, the Canadian Bill of Rights presented the courts with a constitutional dilemma, a dilemma they were never able to resolve. In the case of *The Queen v. Drybones*, a divided Supreme Court did use the Bill of Rights to invalidate a federal law that discriminated against aboriginal Canadians. But in the other cases it heard involving the Bill of Rights, the Supreme Court always found some reason for upholding whatever legislation was being challenged under the Bill.

By the 1970s then, human rights activists came to argue that what Canada needed was a constitutionally entrenched charter of rights—a charter that would apply to all levels of government and that would be manifestly superior in status to ordinary legislation. These activists found a keen ally in Prime Minister Trudeau, who saw a constitutional charter as an excellent device for entrenching his particular vision of a bilingual Canada. At Trudeau's insistence, the constitutional accord worked out at Victoria in 1971 contained a basic charter which provided for the entrenchment of bilingual language rights, as well as a number of fundamental civil liberties.

Although the Victoria proposal was never adopted, it did set the agenda for future constitutional development. Within a decade, Trudeau was able to succeed in sponsoring the adoption of a much broader document, the Canadian Charter of Rights and Freedoms. From the point of view of its development, the Charter may be said to have three elements. First, it entrenches, in expanded form, most of the basic rights that were included in the Canadian Bill of Rights.[1] It guarantees fundamental freedoms such as freedom of speech and freedom of religion (Section 2), basic democratic rights including the right to vote (Sections 3-5), basic legal rights like the right not to be subjected to any cruel or unusual punishments (Sections 7-14), and the right to non-discriminatory treatment under the law (Section 15). Second, the Charter includes a number of language rights which serve to entrench the Trudeau vision of a bilingual Canada (Sections 16-23). Beyond these first two elements, the Charter includes various specific provisions for which there was no precedent in the Canadian Bill of Rights. Section 6 creates a regime of "mobility rights," including the right to enter, remain in, and leave Canada, and the right to pursue the gaining of a livelihood in any province. Section 27 provides an explicit recognition of the "multicultural heritage" of Canadians. Sections 1 and 33 (each of which will be discussed in detail below) establish principles and mechanisms for limiting the application of the rights enumerated in the Charter.

5.3   **Opposition to the Charter**

From the day the Charter was adopted, an overwhelming majority of Canadian citizens has supported it enthusiastically. Indeed, many Canadians see it as the fullest and clearest expression of the moral foundations of our regime. Yet there has always been a powerful undercurrent of opposition to it. During the negotiations that ultimately produced *CA 1982*, Manitoba's Premier Stirling Lyon attacked the idea of an entrenched charter of rights as an unacceptable departure from the principle of parliamentary sovereignty. Lyon argued that in a parliamentary regime, the final responsibility for public policy should rest with the

---

1   One exception is the right to the "enjoyment of property," which is protected in Section 1a of the Bill of Rights but is not mentioned in the Charter.

democratically elected representatives of the people in Parliament. This, he feared, would no longer be true once the Charter gave the judiciary the power to invalidate federal and provincial legislation.[1] Though Lyon's criticisms did not de-rail the adoption of the Charter, they have been taken up by some of Canada's leading constitutional experts, and skepticism about the Charter remains strong in some academic circles.

At the heart of the matter is the question of democracy. Charter skeptics argue that the adoption of an entrenched charter has effectively transferred a great deal of political power to the judiciary (especially the Supreme Court of Canada). This transfer is said to be a profoundly undemocratic development since it means that an unelected and unaccountable judiciary can use the Charter to impose its own policies on the rest of the country in a host of areas, including matters such as abortion, Sunday shopping, euthanasia, capital punishment, and the use of marijuana.

Those who defend the Charter do not deny that it has certain undemocratic effects. Indeed, they retort, that is precisely the point of having an entrenched Charter of Rights. Canada is not simply a democracy. It is a *liberal* democracy. And this means that the democratic principle of majority rule must always be tempered by a respect for the rights of the minority. Yet, as the example of our treatment of Japanese-Canadians in World War II shows, the rights of the minority are sometimes subject to flagrant violation by Canada's democratically elected leaders. It is therefore not only reasonable but necessary to empower a judicial elite to correct the illiberal excesses of the democratic majority.

On its face, this rebuttal appears impressive, yet Charter skeptics claim that it loses its force when one looks at how the Charter is actually used by the courts in practice. Charter cases rarely, if ever, involve a

---

1   Lyon may, in some respects, have been trying to lock the barn door after the cows had left. The noted nineteenth-century English constitutionalist A.V. Dicey once wryly remarked that the drafters of the BNA Act should have said in its preamble that Canada was to have a constitution similar in principle to that of the United States. His point was that Canada's federal system, modelled on that of the United Sates, required a division of powers established in constitutional law. The adoption of a constitutional law logically meant that Canada's Parliament was not supreme for the courts would have to possess the authority to determine whether a particular matter was *intra vires* or *ultra vires*. To the extent that our courts have since Confederation been placing limits on the scope of Parliament's actions, parliamentary supremacy has always been something of a misnomer, and the step from judicial review on the basis of federalism to judicial review on the basis of a charter was not, conceptually, a difficult one.

blatant violation of clear-cut rights comparable to what happened in the case of the Japanese-Canadians.[1] The typical Charter case will focus instead on what Peter Russell has called the "periphery" of the rights it guarantees, the grey area where the precise meaning of the right is in doubt and where there can be reasonable differences of opinion as to what does or does not constitute a violation of the right.[2] Canadians agree, for example, that the right "not to be subjected to any cruel or unusual treatment or punishment" (Section 12) includes, at its core, the principle that punishment must be proportionate to the crime. We would therefore find it reasonable for a judicial minority to use Section 12 to overturn an act of a parliamentary majority imposing a minimum prison sentence of ten years on jay-walkers. But would a law permitting capital punishment for serial killers be a violation of Section 12? On a question like this there would be profound disagreement among Canadians, and it is not evident why the nine judges of the Supreme Court should have the final say on the matter. Their legal training provides them with no special expertise for deciding a moral-political question about capital punishment. Why, then, should they, a very tiny minority, have the right to impose their moral or political views on the democratic majority? In cases like this (which constitute much, if not most, of the courts' Charter work) was Stirling Lyon not right to insist that political matters should be decided by the elected representatives of the people in Parliament?

5.4 The Notwithstanding Clause

Though Lyon's objection to the Charter did not block the adoption of that document, it was not without impact. A number of the premiers supported his position, and Prime Minister Trudeau was able to get the Charter passed only by agreeing to an important concession: the inclusion of Section 33, the "**notwithstanding clause**."

Section 33 provides that Parliament or a provincial legislature may pass a law and declare it to be valid "notwithstanding" (that is, in spite

---

1 And even when they do, it is not clear that a Charter will make much difference. Charter skeptics often point out that the American Bill of Rights did not prevent the government of the United States from taking the same action against Japanese-Americans that our government took against Japanese-Canadians.

2 Peter Russell, "The Political Purposes of the Canadian Charter of Rights and Freedoms," in *The Canadian Bar Review* 61 (1983): 43-44.

of) the guarantees offered by Sections 2 and 7-15 of the Charter. Such a declaration renders the legislation immune to judicial review under those sections for a period of five years. At the end of that period, the declaration may be renewed for another five years, and Parliament or a legislature may renew such a declaration as many times as they wish.

The notwithstanding clause has vigorous partisans and equally vigorous detractors. For those who share Stirling Lyon's reservations about the Charter, Section 33 is a flexible instrument that allows us to combine judicial review with parliamentary supremacy: the courts may use the Charter to invalidate legislation, but in cases where Parliament or a legislature think the judges' decision is wrong, they may use Section 33 to reserve the final word for themselves. From the point of view of those who oppose the notwithstanding clause, however, Section 33 is a regrettable measure because it seriously compromises the efficacy of the Charter and thus weakens the protection of human rights in Canada. Brian Mulroney once expressed this view in its extreme form when he claimed that Section 33 meant that "the Charter is not worth the paper it's printed on."

Mulroney's claim is certainly an exaggeration. The historical record suggests that the notwithstanding clause has had little impact on the effectiveness of the Charter. Section 33 has been invoked only three times. In 1982, the Parti Québécois government of René Lévesque applied it to all Quebec legislation as a means of showing its disapproval of *CA 1982*, an act that Quebec has still not endorsed. Several years later, the government of Saskatchewan applied the notwithstanding clause to a piece of labour legislation. Then in 1988, after the Supreme Court declared the French-only sign provisions of Quebec's Bill 101 unconstitutional, the government of that province passed a new version of that legislation, Bill 178, and shielded it from judicial review by invoking Section 33.

The use of the notwithstanding clause in this third case met with hearty approval among francophone Quebecers, but many anglophone Canadians thought it scandalous that the Quebec government could use Section 33 to do something the Supreme Court had declared a violation of rights. Though English Canadians had been almost completely indifferent about the notwithstanding clause when it had been used by the government of Saskatchewan, they now came to see it as a serious defect in the constitution. As a result, it is now extremely difficult for a government to use Section 33 because Canadians (especially English Canadians) would tend to interpret such an act not as an assertion of parliamentary supremacy, but as a violation of their fundamental rights. For better or for worse, then, Canadians will likely see little of the notwithstanding clause, at least in the forseeable future.

5.5 Section 1

Canadians who are concerned about preserving the sanctity and integrity of Charter rights have relatively little to worry about in Section 33. A much more significant source of concern is **Section 1**:

> The *Canadian Charter of Rights and Freedoms* guarantees the rights and freedoms set out in it subject only to such reasonable limits prescribed by law as can be demonstrably justified in a free and democratic society.

Section 1 appears to be at odds with itself. It begins by "guaranteeing" the rights set down in the rest of the Charter, but it then concedes that the enjoyment of those rights shall be subject to such limitations as are "demonstrably justified in a free and democratic society." That concession has the effect of enabling the courts to permit exceptions to the rights supposedly guaranteed by the Charter, and experience has shown that the courts are willing to do this on a regular basis. One might therefore characterize Section 1 as a giant constitutional "loophole."

It may seem surprising that our Charter should have this kind of loophole in it, but the framers of that document had reasons for writing Section 1 the way they did. It is generally accepted that no right is absolute. Rights conflict, and decisions must be made about their order of value. Moreover, in any political order, rights must sometimes be limited for the sake of the common good. For instance, though we believe we have a right to freedom of speech, we recognize that in a free and democratic society it is perfectly reasonable to pass laws prohibiting speech of a libellous or slanderous character. We would therefore not want our Charter of Rights to entrench a freedom of speech so general or absolute as to make libel and slander laws unconstitutional. Section 1 was included in the Charter to resolve this type of problem for us.

Section 1 effectively turns most Charter cases into a two-stage process. In the first stage, the courts must decide whether the legislation in question violates one of the rights guaranteed by the Charter. If it does, the courts must then ask whether that violation might not be a reasonable limitation of the right in question under the terms of Section

1. If the Section 1 question is answered in the negative, then the legislation is deemed unconstitutional. If it is answered in the affirmative, however, the legislation is "saved" by Section 1, despite the fact that it violates a Charter right.

In the 1986 case of *R. v. Oakes*, the Supreme Court of Canada developed a systematic procedure for adjudicating Section 1 questions. A brief examination of *Oakes* will provide an excellent introduction to the meaning and significance of Section 1.

David Edwin Oakes was arrested by police officers who found eight one-gram vials of hashish oil in his possession. Section 8 of the *Narcotic Control Act* stipulated that once a court has determined that an individual was in possession of illegal narcotics, the burden of proof would then be on that individual to demonstrate that he or she was not in possession of them for the purpose of trafficking. Thus if Oakes could not prove that he had no plans to sell the narcotics found in his possession, he would have been found guilty not merely of possession, but of the far more serious offence of drug trafficking. Oakes protested that it should have been up to the Crown to prove him guilty and not up to him to prove his innocence. To make his case, he argued that Section 8 of the *Narcotic Control Act* was unconstitutional because it violated Section 11(d) of the Charter which guarantees the right to be "presumed innocent until proven guilty." The court had little trouble in concluding that Section 8 of the *Act* was in violation of Section 11(d) of the Charter, but was then obliged to consider whether the *Act* might not be "saved" as a reasonable limitation of Section 11(d) by virtue of Section 1.

In order to tackle this question rationally, the court began by establishing a general procedure for Section 1 questions. The court argued that a law in violation of some Charter right could be saved under Section 1 only if it met two tests. The first concerned the purpose or objective of the law: a law must be a response to a "pressing and substantial" problem in order to justify overriding a Charter right. The second concerned "proportionality," that is, the suitability of the means used to pursue the law's objective. The court said it would use three criteria when applying that test. First, are the means rational and non-arbitrary? Second, do the means impair the right in question as little as possible? Might there be other ways of achieving the same objective without limiting Charter rights? Third, is the good that will be achieved by these means sufficient to outweigh the deleterious effects they will have on those individuals or groups whose rights are being set aside?

With this framework in place, the court was able to consider Oakes's claim in a reasonable and systematic fashion. The judges easily concluded that Section 8 of the *Narcotic Control Act* met the first test. The purpose of the provision was to allow the government to suppress the drug trade, and the court accepted that this was a "substantial and pressing" concern, one of "sufficient importance to warrant overriding a constitutionally protected right."[1] When it came to the second test, however, they were not as indulgent. Writing for the majority, Chief Justice Brian Dickson argued that the means for fighting the drug trade contemplated in Section 8 of the *Narcotic Control Act* could not meet the first criterion of being rational and non-arbitrary. Innocent people who had no intention of trafficking might not be able to prove that fact. This could lead to erroneous convictions, with severe consequences for the accused. The court therefore concluded that Section 8 of the *Act* could not be saved under Section 1, and they declared it to be unconstitutional. Oakes was thus innocent of the charge of drug trafficking.

Although in *Oakes* the Supreme Court decided that Section 1 could not be used to save Section 8 of the *Narcotic Control Act*, the interpretive framework developed in that case has been applied in many others with the opposite result. A number of laws that violate some Charter right have been able to pass the **Oakes test** and have thus been upheld under Section 1 as "reasonable limitations" of the Charter. In the 2001 case *R. v. Sharpe*, for example, the Supreme Court held that although criminal code restrictions on the distribution of child pornography constitute a limitation of freedom of expression (Section 2b), most of the law could be upheld as a reasonable limitation on that section. Using the Oakes test, the court ruled that it is important to protect children from exploitation and that the measures in the law restricting distribution of child pornography were a suitable means for achieving that end.

5.6 The Political Impact of the Charter

The adoption of a constitutionally entrenched charter of rights has substantially altered the structure of the Canadian regime. The most obvious change is the fact that courts now decide many questions that were formerly decided by parliaments, governments, and legislatures. In other words, the Charter has made the courts more powerful and more active

---

1 *The Queen v. Oakes* (1986), *Federalism and the Charter*, ed. Peter Russell (Ottawa: Carleton University Press, 1989) 458.

political players. Numerous examples of this change could be cited. We shall limit ourselves here to a few of the most celebrated.

In 1988, the Supreme Court of Canada handed down what is perhaps its most famous Charter decision to date, *The Queen v. Morgentaler*. This case dealt with the politically explosive issue of abortion. Parliament had legislated what it thought was a compromise solution to the abortion issue: abortions were made an offence under the criminal code unless they were performed in accredited hospitals on the recommendation of a therapeutic abortion committee. The law was challenged by Dr. Henry Morgentaler, who sought an unrestricted right to perform abortions in his own clinics. In **Morgentaler**, the Supreme Court held by a 5-2 vote that Parliament's law was a violation of Section 7 of the Charter and that it could not be sustained under Section 1. It is interesting to note that the court's position was quite fragmented. Four separate opinions were written. One claimed that the law should be struck down on the grounds that Section 7 made it unconstitutional to restrict abortions, except, perhaps, in the latest stages of pregnancy. Two other opinions suggested that the law was unconstitutional, but only because its specific regulations were in one way or another procedurally unfair. Contrary to the first three opinions, the fourth claimed that the law should be upheld. In this opinion it was argued that the government had every right to regulate abortion and that the specific terms of the law in question were not tainted by a lack of procedural fairness.

Though the judges had difficulty agreeing on how to apply the charter to abortion law, there was no ambiguity about the effect of their decision: the law was struck down, and Dr. Morgentaler was free to perform abortions in his clinics. It is worth noting that the decision in *Morgentaler* did not preclude the introduction of a new abortion law, since the majority of the judges had indicated that they would not oppose a law that was "procedurally fair." The Mulroney government proposed to Parliament a bill it thought would satisfy the judges, but the bill was narrowly defeated in the Senate. The Supreme Court's decision in *Morgentaler* has thus turned out to be the decisive factor in the reversal of Canada's abortion law.

Our judges have had a significant impact on many other policy questions. In the 1988 case of *Quebec v. Ford*, the Supreme Court struck down Quebec's law prohibiting signs in languages other than French. The court's decision touched off a political storm, culminating in the adoption of Bill 178, and, some would say, the defeat of the Meech Lake Accord. In the 1985 case of *Singh v. Minister of Employment and Immigra-*

tion, the Supreme Court declared that Canada would have to change its policy on the handling of refugee claims, despite the fact that that policy had been praised by the United Nations as a model for the rest of the world. On the basis of Section 7 of the Charter, the judges held that all persons claiming refugee status must be given a full hearing. The federal government was forced to introduce new regulations to comply with this judicial order, thereby creating the most open and liberal procedures in the world for the handling of refugee applications. In the 1999 case of *M v. H*, the Court held that governments may not deny gay and lesbian couples benefits that are provided to heterosexual spouses. In the 2001 case of *United States v. Burns*, the court declared that prisoners may not be extradited to states that use the death penalty unless the minister of justice receives assurances that the death penalty will not be sought. In so doing, the court appears to have closed the door to any future reintroduction of capital punishment as a violation of Section 7 of the Charter.

These cases demonstrate how the adoption of the Charter has entailed a substantial transfer of policy-making power from elected bodies to the judges. The student of Canadian government is therefore compelled to pay ever closer attention to the role and conduct of our judiciary. For instance, some political scientists are raising questions about whether the arrangements we have made for the judiciary do not need to be changed now that the judges have a much more important role in the formulation of public policy. It is frequently suggested, for example, that we need to change our procedures for appointing the justices of the Supreme Court in order to provide for more democratic control over our policy-making judges.[1]

Other political scientists are asking what differences will follow from the fact that judges, as well as politicians, are now making policy decisions. Michael Mandel claims that the "legalization of politics" that follows from the adoption of the Charter will work to the advantage of big business rather than ordinary Canadians.[2] He notes that the first people to take advantage of the Charter were in fact corporations: Big M Drug Mart used the right to freedom of religion in order to win the right to make money on Sundays, and Southam Press used Section 8 to prevent the government from prosecuting it for monopolistic practices. For

---

1   See Chapter 8.5 below.
2   Michael Mandel, *The Charter of Rights and the Legalization of Politics in Canada* (Toronto: Wall and Thompson, 1989).

Mandel, it is likely that these early Charter cases will be indicative of the Charter's long-term impact, for Charter challenges are expensive, and it is big corporations that are best positioned to pay for them.

But still other political scientists believe that the Charter is more likely to work to the advantage of interest groups than big business. Rainer Knopff and Ted Morton speak of the emergence in our regime of a "Court Party." This Court Party is composed of legal and judicial elites, along with civil libertarians, "equality seekers" and social engineers, who all see the Charter as an opportunity to win through the courts changes they would be unlikely to win in the political arena. Knopff and Morton suggest that the judiciary has a natural interest in cooperating with these groups since the implementation of their agenda requires (and justifies) an expanded political role for the judges themselves.[1]

The adoption of the Canadian Charter of Rights and Freedoms has thus introduced a whole new range of questions for the student of Canada's regime to ponder.

Key Terms

human rights codes	Section 1
Bill of Rights	Oakes test
notwithstanding clause	Morgentaler

---

1 F.L. Morton and Rainer Knopff, *The Charter Revolution and the Court Party* (Peterborough, ON: Broadview Press, 2000).

Part three: Institutions

The Crown and Its Servants

6.1   The Crown

6.2   The Governor General

6.3   The Functions of the Governor General

6.4   The Cabinet

6.5   The Cabinet Committee System

6.6   The Prime Minister

6.7   Prime Ministerial Government?

6.8   The Civil Service

Canadians usually refer to those who exercise political power in this country as "the government." But "government" is a very imprecise term. For some, it appears to refer to a specific team of ministers—"the Mulroney government" or "the Chrétien government," for example. For others, the term "government" includes a large number of public servants, such as the person at the motor vehicle office who issues drivers' licences.

The source of the confusion here is the fact that "government" is an informal and unofficial term. Our constitution nowhere defines the meaning of "government" because, strictly speaking, there is no such institution in the Canadian regime. What Canadians loosely refer to as "the government" is in fact a complex web of independent, but inter-related institutions: the Crown, the prime minister, the cabinet, and the civil service. Our purpose in this chapter is to explain what those institutions are and how they are related.

6.1   The Crown

We have seen that the preamble to *CA 1867* stipulates that Canada is to have "a constitution similar in principle to that of the United Kingdom." This implies that in Canada, as in Britain, governmental power is technically in the hands of the "Crown," and that our head of state is the reigning queen or king. To understand this fact, it helps to keep in mind the peculiar evolution of British constitutional practice. Centuries ago, when Britain was a full-fledged monarchy, all governmental power was vested in the Crown. Over time, in response to the demands of their people for a more democratic regime, British monarchs began to "delegate" certain of their powers to other people or bodies. Legislative power was delegated to the body that came to be known as parliament. Today Parliament is the real seat of legislative power. Yet even today, Parliament's decisions do not have the force of law until they have received royal assent; this indicates that the legislative power is still technically a power of the Crown. The same is true of executive power. As early as the seventeenth century, British monarchs began to delegate the Crown's executive power to a prime minister and cabinet. Today, the prime minister and cabinet have virtually complete control of executive power. In principle, however, this power remains a power of the Crown, and those who exercise it are deemed to do so as servants of His or Her Majesty. Their executive decisions are, in principle, merely "advice" to the Crown and have no force or effect until they receive royal assent. The British regime is thus described as a **constitutional monarchy**, a regime which is monarchical by law, but democratic by convention. The Canadian constitution is very much like the British constitution on this point.

Section 9 of *CA 1867* stipulates that "The Executive Government and Authority of and over Canada is hereby declared to continue and be vested in the Queen." Of course, the Queen would no more exercise this executive power of government here in Canada than she does in Britain. By constitutional convention, she delegates her executive power to certain elected representatives of the people — the prime minister and cabinet. In law, however, the executive power of government is a power of the Crown. In other words, all executive decisions must have the assent of the Crown and must be carried out in the Crown's name. This explains why those who prosecute criminals in Canada are called "Crown Attorneys" and why the cases they prosecute have names like *The Queen v. Oakes*. Queen Elizabeth was not personally involved in the trial of David Oakes; rather, when the officials of the Department of Justice prosecuted Oakes, they were exercising executive power that had been delegated to the department by the Queen.

A similar pattern is evident in the way the Canadian constitution deals with legislative power. Section 17 of *CA 1867* establishes that

Canada shall have a Parliament consisting of "the Queen, an Upper House styled the Senate, and the House of Commons." The constitution does not spell out the role of each of these three elements in the legislative process; these are covered by the preamble's reference to the constitutional practice of the United Kingdom. In the case of legislative power, the Queen asks "Her" parliament to send Her bills for Her consideration. These bills do not become law until they have obtained royal assent and are "proclaimed" by the Crown. Royal assent is still necessary for any bill to become law, but in order to guarantee the triumph of the democratic principle, a convention has evolved stipulating that royal assent must never be withheld.

These constitutional arrangements appear to be exceedingly complicated. Yet, as we shall explain in Section 3, below, there are important reasons for constructing our regime this way.

6.2 The Governor General

The powers, rights, and privileges of the Canadian Crown are vested in the queen or king of Canada. Our monarch is by law the same person who serves as monarch of the United Kingdom, but it is important to note that this person is serving in two distinct positions. One might say that Elizabeth II wears a number of different crowns: a British crown, a Canadian crown, an Australian crown, and so on. She is a monarch with many dominions. The important point is that, with respect to Canada, she is the Queen of Canada.

Now because Canada's monarch is also a British monarch who resides principally in the United Kingdom, it is practically impossible for her to serve actively here in Canada. Therefore, Section 10 of *CA 1867* provides that she shall have a permanent representative in this country, the governor general.[1] Under the **Letters Patent** signed by King George VI in 1947, the governor general has the right to exercise "all powers and authorities lawfully belonging to Us [the Crown] in respect of Canada." The monarch may still occasionally exercise certain of these powers when she is in Canada—in 1957, for example, Queen Elizabeth II opened our parliament during the course of an official visit to Canada. In almost all respects, however,[2] the powers of the Crown are now exercised by the governor general.

---

1   The role of the governor general is played by the lieutenant-governors in the provincial governments.

2   There are some minor exceptions. See J.R. Mallory, *The Structure of Canadian Government* (Toronto: Gage Publishing, 1984), 37-38.

Given that the governor general is the Queen's representative in Canada, she is the one who appoints this official. The term of office is generally five to seven years. In the early years of Confederation, when Canada was not yet entirely independent of Great Britain, the governor general was seen as the British government's representative in this country. Our first governors general were therefore always British nobles, appointed by the queen or king on the recommendation of the British government. After the World War I, the advice of the Canadian prime minister was sought as well. Only in 1952, however, did the Crown begin to appoint Canadian citizens to the position. At first, our prime ministers recommended non-political figures such as the diplomat Vincent Massey (1952-1959) or distinguished military leaders such as Georges Vanier (1959-1967). In more recent times, the trend has been to appoint political figures. There are clear advantages to doing so: because the governor general is responsible for some potentially significant political decisions, it makes sense to appoint people with political experience. On the other hand, there are also some disadvantages to nominating politicians for the office. Three of our last four governors general—Jeanne Sauvé (1984-1989), Ramon Hnatyshyn (1989-1995) and Romeo Leblanc (1995-2000)—had all served as cabinet ministers with or under the prime minister who nominated them. The danger in such appointments is that they may be perceived as partisan, or even "patronage," appointments. Such a perception is dangerous to the dignity and independence of the office. The Queen's most recent appointment—Adrienne Clarkson—was a noted public affairs journalist prior to taking office as governor general. It will be interesting to see whether Clarkson's appointment marks a shift back to the earlier tradition of appointing individuals with no previous involvement in electoral politics.

6.3 The Functions of the Governor General

In terms of constitutional law, the governor general, as the Crown's representative in Canada, has very extensive powers. Yet Section 11 of *CA 1867* stipulates that the governor general shall have certain official "advisors"—the prime minister and cabinet. By constitutional convention, the governor general acts, for the most part, only on the "advice" of these democratically elected officials. Governors general accept the executive or legislative "advice" presented to them as a matter of course, so that in colloquial terms the office is sometimes referred to as a "rubber stamp." Yet it is not without importance.

Since cabinet decisions are in legal terms "advice" to the Crown, the governor general must always be kept well-advised of cabinet's activities and intentions. On behalf of the cabinet, the prime minister meets regularly with the governor general to keep him or her abreast of the government's plans. Although in theory it is the governor general who is being advised by the prime minister, it is sometimes true that the prime minister will take advantage of these sessions to privately seek advice on matters that cannot be discussed with cabinet colleagues or other advisors. As the Crown's representative in the regime, and one whose impartiality cannot be questioned, the governor general is occasionally a useful sounding board for a prime minister with a difficult problem. In addition to this role of occasional advisor, the governor general has two significant functions in our regime.

A)   *The reserve powers*

The first is the exercise of the so-called reserve powers. The primary responsibility of the governor general is to ensure that Her Majesty has a government that has the confidence of the House of Commons. While this responsibility rarely requires governors general to take action, there are four situations in which they must either ignore the advice they receive from their ministers or act on their own initiative. When they do so, governors general are said to be using their reserve powers.

The *first reserve power* is the power to name the prime minister. We have seen in Chapter 3 that, in a political order based on the principle of responsible government, the voters do not elect a prime minister; they merely elect members of Parliament. It is therefore essential to give someone the authority to name a prime minister; in Canada, that officer is the governor general. Because in this situation there is no prime minister or cabinet to advise governors general as to who should be chosen, they make this decision on their own initiative.

As was mentioned in Chapter 3, it is conceivable that parliamentary elections might produce a fragmented House of Commons, in which no party has a majority of seats and it is not evident which party is most likely to lead a minority government. In such a situation, the governor general's power to name the prime minister is of great significance. But such a situation has never yet arisen in Canada. For the most part, we have had so few significant political parties that our elections have always produced either a clear majority for one party, or a minority situation where there is only one party with any chance of winning the confidence of the House. Historically, then, this first reserve power has never been exercised in a way that required the governor general to use any personal discretion.

The *second reserve power* is the power to dismiss a prime minister who attempts to govern without the confidence of the House of Commons. This power has never been used at the federal level and has not been used by a lieutenant-governor at the provincial level since the beginning of the twentieth century. Still, the power does exist and is essential to the smooth functioning of responsible government. Without it, there would be no way of preventing a prime minister and cabinet from clinging to office when, under the rules of responsible government, they are supposed to resign or ask for elections.

The *third reserve power* is the power to make appointments, including appointments to the judiciary and to the Senate. Under normal circumstances, the governor general exercises this power on the advice of the prime minister, but there may be occasions when the governor general reserves the right to ignore such advice. Such an occasion occurred after Prime Minister Tupper's Conservative party lost its majority in the elections of 1896. Before turning power over to the new prime minister (Wilfred Laurier), Tupper tried to take advantage of his last few days in office to advise the governor general to appoint a number of prominent Conservatives senators or judges. The Earl of Aberdeen, the governor general at that time, refused the advice on the grounds that Tupper did not have the confidence of the House of Commons and therefore had no right to give such advice.

The *fourth reserve power* is the power to "dissolve" Parliament and call elections. Normally governors general follow whatever advice is given them by their prime minister, yet there have been occasions when such advice has been refused. In 1926, Prime Minister Mackenzie King, realizing that his minority government was about to be defeated on a motion censuring the government for corruption, asked Governor General Lord Byng to dissolve Parliament and call new elections. Byng refused, instead calling upon Arthur Meighen, the Conservative leader, to form a new ministry. There is a great deal of disagreement as to whether Byng's decision was a good one,[1] but there is no doubt that the governor general needs the reserve power to refuse dissolution in circumstances where elections have been held recently and there is a plausible alternative choice for prime minister in the House.

---

1 See J.R. Mallory, *The Structure of Canadian Government* (Toronto: Gage, 1984), 52–55.

Because these four reserve powers are rarely used, Canadians have little sense of either their existence or their importance. Yet our entire system of responsible government depends on them. It is true that prime ministers rarely try to govern or to make appointments when they no longer have the confidence of the House of Commons, but if the governor general did not have the power to prevent such abuses, they would likely become more frequent. The reserve powers are essential to the healthy operation of responsible government, and the fact that they are rarely needed is more a proof of their efficacy than of their irrelevance. If we did not have them, we would quickly learn how important they are.

B) *The ceremonial function*

While wielding the reserve powers is the most essential function of the governor general, the most common function of the office is ceremonial. As our head of state, the governor general represents the Crown in a number of ways. First, the governor general must preside over a number of important political ceremonies, such as the opening of Parliament, and represents Canada at a wide variety of events where official representation is necessary — welcoming certain foreign dignitaries, presenting awards, and attending state funerals in foreign countries.

The governor general's ceremonial work frees the prime minister to concentrate more fully on the business of governing. More important, however, is the symbolic value of having someone other than the prime minister serve as the highest representative of our regime. In his influential book *The Crown in Canada*,[1] Frank MacKinnon argues that the Crown strengthens democracy by keeping potentially arrogant politicians in their place: the ceremonial work of the governor general is a constant reminder to politicians that they are servants of the Crown (and hence servants of the people), rather than political masters. Because the office of governor general stands above party politics, it represents all the people of Canada, rather than just those who voted for the party in power. This gives the citizens of the regime a non-partisan focus for their loyalty. They can be loyal to the regime, as embodied in the governor general, without necessarily supporting the politicians who run the government at any given point in time. For these reasons, MacKinnon argues, the Crown is a useful institution for keeping our powerful politicians humble.

---

1 Frank MacKinnon, *The Crown in Canada* (Calgary: McClelland and Stewart, 1976).

6.4 The Cabinet

As we saw in Chapter 3, the real seat of government power in a system of responsible government is a body known as the "cabinet." In constitutional practice (as opposed to constitutional law) it is this cabinet that exercises executive power. The cabinet also has decisive control over legislative power, especially in situations of majority government. But what, exactly, is the cabinet, and what is the constitutional basis of its power?

To answer these questions, we must turn, once again, to the text of the constitution. Section 11 of *CA 1867* creates a body called **The Queen's Privy Council for Canada,** which is given the all-important right to "advise" the governor general in the exercise of his or her powers. As "advisors," the privy councillors are, strictly speaking, mere servants of the Crown. As we have seen, however, under the rules of responsible government, "advice" given to the governor general is the equivalent of an order. The Queen's Privy Council for Canada is thus a very powerful body, for it controls virtually all those powers granted by the constitution to the Crown or the governor general.

Section 11 states that the privy councillors are appointed by the governor general, but constitutional convention stipulates that the governor general will make these appointments on the "advice" of the person he or she has asked to serve as prime minister. Although the constitution does allow for the possibility that the governor general might "remove" a member of the Privy Council, appointments to that body are in practice appointments for life. This means that the Privy Council includes every living person who has ever been named to that body. Privy councillors nominated by former prime ministers Trudeau, Clark, and Mulroney are thus still members of the Privy Council.

Of course, in a democratic regime, it would be unthinkable to have privy councillors who had been nominated by a defeated government continue to exercise political power. We therefore have a convention stipulating that the power to "advise" the governor general will be exercised only by a small subset of privy councillors: those who have been nominated by (and have maintained the confidence of) the current prime minister. It is this subset of the Privy Council that we call the "cabinet," and we may therefore define the cabinet as those privy councillors who have the power to advise the Crown.

While it is technically correct to refer to the members of the cabinet as privy councillors,[1] it is more common to call them "ministers." This is because most members of the cabinet will spend most of their time "advising" the Crown on the work of one of its "ministries" or departments. For instance, the Minister of Energy and Natural Resources will spend most of her time developing new policy for that ministry and ensuring that existing policy is being executed effectively and efficiently. (More will be said about this work in Section 6.8 below.)

But the cabinet is much more than a collection of individual ministers. An essential element of our system of responsible government is the principle of **collective responsibility**—the idea that cabinet must function *as a team* to develop, implement, and take responsibility for public policy. This principle follows logically from the conventions of responsible government: it is not individual ministers who must maintain the confidence of the House or resign; it is the ministry as a whole. To the extent that it is the ministry that has the mandate to govern, rather than a collection of individuals, responsibility for the exercise of power must logically rest with the ministry as a team rather than with individual ministers.

The principle of collective responsibility means that whenever ministers have an idea for new legislation in their area, their proposal must win the approval of the cabinet before it can be taken to Parliament. It also means that certain important executive decisions (for example, which of several companies should be awarded a lucrative contract to build frigates for the navy) will be made by the cabinet as a whole rather than by the single minister in charge of that area. For reasons outlined in Sections 6.5 and 6.7, it is increasingly the case that executive and legislative decisions that require cabinet approval are in fact being made by cabinet committees, or even by the prime minister. Under the principles of responsible government, such practice is legitimate only to the extent that those making the decisions have a mandate to speak for the cabinet.

Under the doctrine of collective responsibility, any decision made by the cabinet as a whole must be defended by each and every one of its members; and by convention, a cabinet minister who is not prepared to defend a position taken by cabinet must resign. This explains why cabinet discussions must always be confidential and secret: ministers would

---

1   The technical term "Privy Council" explains why executive orders emanating from the cabinet are called **orders-in-council**. They are literally orders given by the "governor-in-council," that is, the governor general acting on the advice of his or her Privy Council.

not be able to defend a cabinet decision in public if it were revealed that they had spoken against it in the course of cabinet deliberations.

Because the cabinet plays such a central role in the exercise of political power, it is essential that it be as representative of the country as possible. By tradition, it will have at least one member from each of the country's ten provinces, with the possible exception of PEI. The various regions of the country are normally represented in some sort of proportion to their population, but deviations will occur if particular regions have elected few government members. There must be a representative number of French Canadians. It is also important to ensure strong representation for women and at least some representation for those Canadians who are visible minorities. The formation of the cabinet must, in the final analysis, take into consideration the way in which Canadians identify the fundamentally important political distinctions of provinces, regions, ethnicity, and gender.

6.5 The Cabinet Committee System

In Canada's first century, the cabinet could handle its business by meeting once a week (usually on Friday afternoons). By the 1960s, however, the growth of the welfare state had expanded the workload of governments dramatically. This was reflected in the fact that the cabinet had grown from 12 ministers under Sir John A. Macdonald to over 30 under Pierre Trudeau.[1] Because of the volume of business to be conducted, as well as the number of participants involved, the traditional cabinet meeting was no longer an adequate forum for making the kinds of decisions that it needed to make. For this reason, Prime Ministers Pearson and Trudeau developed a system of cabinet committees that revolutionized the way cabinet does its business.

Each prime minister has the authority to organize the cabinet committee system however he or she likes, and since the Pearson/Trudeau years, a number of substantially different models have been used. It therefore makes little sense to describe any particular model in detail; yet each of the systems we have seen thus far is characterized by a number of essential features.

The basic idea of the system is to divide the cabinet's work and assign it to a number of smaller groups (the cabinet committees). The cabinet's work is done more efficiently because five groups of six people can

---

1   The size of the cabinet reached its peak at 40 under Prime Minister Mulroney. The Chrétien cabinet is now down to 28 members.

do five times as much work in an hour as one group of 30 people. Most cabinet committee systems will be composed of between five and twelve such committees, which are usually organized around a particular policy area (for instance, economic development or social policy). Each committee will study all of the problems or questions that arise in its particular area and make recommendations to the full cabinet. For the system to work, the cabinet must normally approve a committee's recommendations without too much debate — otherwise, it would end up doing the committee's work all over again. Still, individual ministers who are not members of the committee have every right to raise questions and objections at the cabinet level and sometimes succeed in having questions sent back to the committee for further study.

Most cabinet committee systems have contained one "super-committee." A typical example was Trudeau's Priorities and Planning Committee, which was composed of the chairs of each of the other committees and was itself chaired by the prime minister. In the Trudeau cabinet, the Priorities and Planning Committee was responsible for determining the broad lines of government policy. It was also a body to which many recommendations from other committees were referred either prior to or instead of sending them to the full cabinet.

Prime Minister Chrétien has done away with a formal coordinating committee. He has organized the cabinet committee system to fit his government's priorities. There are currently five cabinet committees: Economic Union; Social Union; Treasury Board; Special Committee of Council; and Government Communications. The prime minister works to ensure that a consensus emerges at the full cabinet meeting, which reviews each committee's recommendations.

6.6 The Prime Minister

Canadians know that the prime minister is the most powerful political figure in our regime, yet very few of us understand the basis for this power. Our written constitution gives us little help in this regard. The office of prime minister is not mentioned in *CA 1867*, and it is mentioned only in passing in *CA 1982*. Thus, the powers of the prime minister are all based on constitutional convention. Let us think for a minute about the title of the office: the "prime" minister is literally the "first" minister. This title makes sense because, in seeking out a group of advisors, the governor general first names a prime minister, who then offers advice on the appointment of the other ministers.

It is this right to advise the Crown on the assignment of cabinet posts that constitutes the core of the prime minister's power. We have seen that in a regime based on responsible government, the cabinet is the centre of legislative and executive power. The office of prime minister carries with it no specific departmental responsibilities, and in the modern age, prime ministers rarely reserve a specific ministry for themselves.[1] The fact that they control the membership of the cabinet gives prime ministers a tremendous amount of influence over all the other members of that most powerful body. Ministers who prove to be a thorn in the side of their prime minister may well be demoted to a less attractive portfolio, or dropped from the cabinet altogether. Conversely, ministers who support the prime minister's views may improve their chances of promotion to a more important cabinet post. As a result, few ministers are willing to resist a prime minister when he or she has strong opinions on some question.

Prime ministers chair the meetings of the cabinet, and this provides them with an important opportunity to exercise their leadership. Because the cabinet has to act together as a team, its decisions must be based on consensus. One of the prime minister's great tasks is to cultivate this consensus. In order to succeed at this task, prime ministers need great skill; they must know when to postpone discussion and when to continue it; when to paper over disagreements and when to have them argued out; and above all, when and how to use their own influence to settle a particularly divisive question. Moreover, it is up to the prime minister to determine whether consensus has been reached (there is no formal voting in cabinet) and to define what the consensus is. This prerogative is another source of significant political influence.

The other major task of the prime minister is to serve as the leading spokesperson for the cabinet. Individual ministers take responsibility for public relations in most matters relevant to their particular departments. If the issue is a particularly important one, however, the prime minister will often be the person who makes the cabinet's case to the public. This is especially true during election campaigns, when the public's attention is focussed almost exclusively on the prime minister and the leaders of the opposition parties.

In addition to their right to advise the governor general on the composition of the cabinet, Canada's prime ministers wield a number of other specific powers. The most important of these are the right to

---

1   This was done frequently in the first century of Confederation. Sir John A. Macdonald, for example, was his own Minister of Justice.

advise the governor general on the dissolution of Parliament and the holding of elections; the right to advise the governor general on a number of key appointments, including appointments to the Senate and to the judiciary; and the right to organize the machinery of government (including the number and composition of departments and the nature of the cabinet committee system).

Prime ministers have a number of people who help them in the performance of their duties. First are the members of the **Prime Minister's Office (PMO)**. Originally, the PMO was a small secretariat that took responsibility for organizing the prime minister's schedule, answering mail, and other routine tasks. The office was greatly expanded by Prime Ministers Trudeau and Mulroney. Today's PMO has a staff of more than 100; it is responsible for monitoring the general political situation and giving the prime minister political advice. The members of the staff (led by the Principal Secretary) are for the most part partisan political activists rather than career civil servants.

Just the opposite is true of a second secretariat, the **Privy Council Office (PCO)**, which is staffed by non-partisan career civil servants. As its name suggests, the PCO serves as a secretariat to the cabinet, and is thus responsible to the chair of the cabinet, the prime minister. The PCO facilitates the collective work of the cabinet by organizing and providing logistical support for its meetings and its committees. It has also, since the Trudeau years, served as an agency that can give policy advice to the prime minister and cabinet (as distinct from the political advice that emanates from the PMO). The PCO is headed by the Chief Clerk of the Privy Council, who is the highest-ranking civil servant in the country.

Prime ministers are also assisted in their duties by a **deputy prime minister**, a member of the cabinet who has a portfolio of his or her own, but who also serves as a kind of second-in-command to the prime minister. Through most of our history, being deputy prime minister conferred little real power. At most, it meant filling in for the prime minister when he or she was absent or indisposed. More recently, however, the office seems to have become more important. Prime Minister Mulroney actually delegated much of his day-to-day work to his deputy, Don Mazankowski, in order to free himself to concentrate on two or three particularly important issues, such as the constitution and free trade. This arrangement appeared to work quite well, but it is still too early to tell whether it will become a permanent feature of Canadian politics.

It is sometimes argued that the Canadian regime is moving away from cabinet government and toward "prime ministerial" government.[1] There can be no doubt that the office of prime minister has grown more powerful in recent years. In this television age, the prime minister's role as the chief spokesperson for the government gives him or her a public profile that dwarfs the profile of the cabinet. Moreover, the decentralizing tendencies of the cabinet committee system have had the effect of fragmenting the collective power of the cabinet. To a large extent, it has been the prime minister, with the assistance of the PMO and PCO, who has stepped into the gap.

Still, one must not forget that prime ministers are not directly elected to their position by the people. Because they are ultimately dependent on the confidence of the House of Commons, they cannot afford to alienate key sources of support such as the cabinet. Indeed, it should not be forgotten that a united cabinet, through collective resignation, could probably force the resignation of any prime minister. Moreover, in most federal cabinets, there are some ministers whose support within their party (or with the general public) is so strong that they are not easily intimidated by a prime minister. Prime Minister Chrétien knows that his government would be in big trouble if a minister like Paul Martin were openly to break with it, and this gives Martin a certain amount of leverage over Chrétien.

In the final analysis, the "strength" of any particular prime minister will depend as much on political circumstances as on the rules of the constitution. The prime minister is invited to form a government because he or she is the leader of the party that is most likely to have the confidence of the House of Commons. The prime minister's power as prime minister will therefore be directly related to the control he or she has over that party. This control of the party will be influenced by a number of factors. One is the process used by the party to choose its leader.[2] Another is party unity: the prime minister will have trouble dominating the government if the party in power is divided into factions. The most important factor, however, is the prime minister's popularity with the voters. Popular prime ministers who are poised to lead

---

1   For a recent discussion of this thesis, see Donald Savoie, *Governing From the Centre: The Concentration of Power in Canadian Politics* (Toronto: University of Toronto Press, 1999).

2   This is discussed below in Chapter 10.

their party to victory will command great support in their party. On the other hand, prime ministers whose personal unpopularity threatens to lead to electoral defeat will have a difficult time keeping their cabinet and caucus in line.

6.8 The Civil Service

Section 9 of *CA 1867* invests the executive power of government in the Crown. We have seen that under the terms of responsible government, the Crown exercises its executive power on the advice of a small number of servants (its ministers) who are accountable to the elected representatives of the people. But the tasks associated with the exercise of executive power are too numerous and complex to be handled by such a small group of people. The Crown therefore needs many other servants to carry out its executive tasks. These people are known as the Crown's "civil" servants (as opposed to its military servants). As of 2000, the federal government employed about 150,000 of them. They are non-partisan professionals, hired on the basis of merit (rather than their political connections), in most cases by the politically neutral Public Service Commission.

The civil service may be divided into two branches. The majority work in what are known as **line departments**, ministries like Transportation, Health, or Foreign Affairs, which provide services of some sort to the general public. A smaller group are employed by the so-called **central agencies** such as the PCO or the Treasury Board.[1] These are bodies that engage in the coordination of government policy rather than in the delivery of particular services to the public. Many of these civil servants wield a substantial amount of power. The civil servants who work as officers for Canada Customs, for instance, have a good deal of authority when it comes to searching the cars of Canadians returning from visits to the United States. In order to prevent abuses of that power, it is essential to ensure that all civil servants will be accountable for the way in which they carry out their duties. Under responsible government, this accountability is achieved through the principle of **ministerial responsibility**.

According to this principle, the minister who heads each department must be accountable to the House of Commons for the conduct of each

---

1 The Treasury Board is a special committee of the cabinet, established by statute, which reviews all proposed expenditures and which serves as the official employer of the civil service.

and every civil servant working in that department. On the most basic level, such accountability implies that the ministers may be asked in the House to investigate allegations of incompetence or impropriety in their departments and to take appropriate measures. If the incompetence or impropriety is substantial and may be attributed to serious mismanagement by the minister, the convention of ministerial responsibility requires the minister to resign, but resignations for reasons of egregious mismanagement have rarely occurred at the federal level.[1] The most recent case occurred in 1985, when Fisheries Minister John Fraser was compelled to resign after it became known that he personally ordered officials in his ministry to approve the sale of tuna that departmental officials had deemed unsafe for human consumption.

It is common, in our parliamentary system, for opposition members to demand a minister's resignation for much less serious matters, or for matters where the minister was less directly implicated. One of our most famous controversies regarding ministerial responsibility took place in 1988 when the budget of Finance Minister Michael Wilson was leaked to the press the day before it was due to be released. The leaking of a budget is a serious problem because those who have advance knowledge of certain changes in the government's fiscal policy can take advantage of that knowledge to make substantial profits by buying or selling stocks, bonds, currencies, or other commodities. When Wilson's budget was leaked to the press, members of the opposition immediately called for the minister's resignation. Wilson refused to resign, arguing that he could not be held personally accountable for the actions of an unknown person or persons who may have leaked the budget for criminal or malicious reasons. Wilson's argument was a reasonable one: to take a more stringent view of the meaning of ministerial responsibility would make each and every minister the hostage of any disaffected civil servant who wanted to see the minister fired. Under the convention of ministerial responsibility, Mr. Wilson would have been required to resign had the leak occurred due to gross personal negligence on his part; but it is well-established that a minister cannot be required to resign for mistakes that are not his or her own. To be sure, ministers would be *politically* accountable to the House of Commons for such mistakes, i.e., they must ensure that appropriate discipli-

---

1 S.L. Sutherland, "Responsible Government and Ministerial Responsibility: Every Reform Is Its Own Problem," *Canadian Journal of Political Science* XXIV, 1 (March 1991): 100–05.

FIG. 6.1   **Ministerial Responsibility**

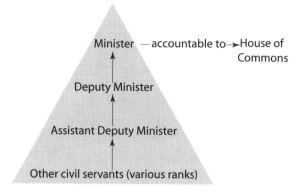

nary and corrective measures are taken, but they are not *personally* accountable for mistakes made by others.

Some observers argue that it is unrealistic or simplistic to say that ministers are in charge of their departments. The civil servants in each department are divided into various ranks. At the top of the ladder in each department is an official known as the deputy minister, a career civil servant who usually has advanced technical training and a good deal of civil service experience. In most cases, the deputy minister will know far more about the business of the department than will the minister. In theory, the deputy minister is merely the minister's chief advisor; in practice, however, the deputy's superiority in knowledge can lead to a situation where he or she is really the one who runs the department. This is particularly true in situations where one has a strong and experienced deputy working for a weak or inexperienced minister.

Key Terms

constitutional monarchy
Letters Patent
reserve powers
Queen's Privy Council for
    Canada
orders-in-council
collective responsibility

Prime Ministers Office (PMO)
Privy Council Office (PCO)
deputy prime minister
line department
central agencies
ministerial responsibility

Parliament

7.1   The Role of Parliament
7.2   The Parliamentary Calendar
7.3   The House of Commons: Membership and Officers
7.4   The Business of the House of Commons
7.5   The Rules of Procedure of the House of Commons
7.6   The Backbencher
7.7   House of Commons Reform
7.8   The Senate
7.9   Senate Reform

Under the heading "Legislative Power," Section 17 of *CA 1867* declares that Canada shall have a "Parliament" consisting of a House of Commons, a Senate, and the Queen. Since Canada's senators are appointed and the Queen has her position by heredity, only the House of Commons can claim to be a democratic institution. By constitutional convention, then, it is the House of Commons that takes the leading, indeed, almost exclusive role in the exercise of Parliament's powers. This is why it is common, in everyday speech, to equate "Parliament" with the House of Commons.

The constitution says relatively little about the structure, role, or powers of Parliament. Yet that lacuna does not leave us without guidance. The statement in the preamble of *CA 1867* stipulating that Canada is to have a constitution "similar in principle to that of the United Kingdom" establishes that, unless otherwise specified, our Parliament is to be a Canadian version of the British Parliament at Westminster. Of course, we have seen that the British constitution is one that is in continual evolution. This means that the place of Parliament in the British regime has changed greatly over the years. Before we begin to describe the specific workings of Canada's Parliament, it will be necessary to explain briefly the role of that institution in modern times.

7.1 The Role of Parliament

British constitutional history is the history of the development of parliamentary democracy. Originally, Parliament served as a body that advised the Crown in its exercise of legislative power. It was called a "parliament" (from the French word *parler*, to speak) because it was in essence a deliberative body, that is, a body designed to engage in speech about what should be done. Over time, Parliament's advice came to be understood as binding on the monarch, so that it was in effect in control of the legislative activity of government. As democratic ideas developed further, the British adopted the principle of responsible government—the idea that those exercising executive power must have the confidence of the people's representatives in Parliament. By the early nineteenth century, Parliament was in what is sometimes called its "golden age." With full control over legislative power, and a tight grip on those exercising executive power, Parliament was the most important political institution in British politics.

By the end of the nineteenth century, however, the power of Parliament had begun to wane because of the rise of highly disciplined political parties whose members could be counted on to vote in accordance with the wishes of their party leaders. In the "golden age" of Parliament, what was said or done in that body was of decisive importance. Great speeches might make or break legislative proposals, or force a cabinet to resign. But once Britain's parliamentarians had all joined parties that were able to control the way their members voted, real power was transferred to the cabinet; since the cabinet constituted the leadership of the party that had control of Parliament, it had effective control over that body. One might say that Parliament lost much of its influence because what was said there rarely affected what was done there. Party discipline guaranteed that the cabinet would always have enough votes to protect its own position in power, and to get its legislation adopted.

This is the situation that prevails in Canada. In the Canadian regime, it is Parliament that adopts legislation; and, formally, it is Parliament that determines whether a cabinet has the right to govern. But the existence of highly disciplined parliamentary parties means that Parliament rarely uses its power in these matters. When it adopts legislation, Parliament is in most cases merely ratifying legislative decisions that have in effect been made by the cabinet. Nor does Parliament often exercise much real power when it comes to determining whether a government should continue in office. For a cabinet backed by a party with a parliamentary majority, the "confidence" of the House of Commons is virtually guaranteed. And even in the case of minority government, when the House votes to withdraw confidence in a government, it is normally just formalizing a decision made by one of the opposition parties to force new elections.

In order to understand properly the role of Parliament in the Canadian regime, it is necessary to look at that institution in light of the changes that have followed from the emergence of disciplined political parties. Though Parliament is still a legislative body, and the House of Commons still has the power to make or break a government, the development of party discipline and the resulting transfer of parliamentary power to the cabinet have left Parliament with a new role. *The primary purpose of the modern parliament is to make the cabinet accountable for its actions to the public.* Parliament provides a forum in which opposition members can criticize the government and offer constructive alternatives. The opposition cannot prevent a cabinet from doing what it pleases, since the party in power will by definition be able to outvote the parties in opposition. But effective criticism of a government's policy in a high-profile setting such as Parliament can be very damaging to the governing party's chances in the next elections. By allowing opposition members to scrutinize and criticize the cabinet's conduct or policy, then, Parliament plays an essential role in keeping the government sensitive to the concerns of the voters.

7.2 The Parliamentary Calendar

To understand how Parliament works, one must begin with some basic information about the parliamentary calendar.

Parliament is not an institution that works on a permanent, ongoing basis. The parliamentary calendar divides the work of that body into distinct units called "parliaments." Each time general elections are held, the new contingent of MPs forms a new parliament. These parliaments are thus numbered in tandem with the country's elections. In 1867,

Canadians elected the first parliament. Our thirty-sixth parliament was elected in 1997 and lasted until the general elections of 2000, when the current parliament began.

Each parliament is broken down into smaller time units known as sessions. The session is its basic work unit. Any legislative work begun in one session (for instance, the adoption of new youth crime legislation) has to be completed in that session. If it is not, and those sponsoring the legislation wish to try again in a new session, they must start all over from scratch.

It is the governor general, on the advice of the prime minister, who decides when the session should begin. Similarly, it is the governor general, on the advice of the prime minister, who declares an end to the session (the technical term for this is **prorogation**). Thus, there is no set length of time for a parliamentary session; sessions will run until the prime minister is satisfied with what Parliament has accomplished. For most of our history, the average session ran for about a year. Since elections are normally held about every four years, this means that each parliament usually has four sessions. Recently, however, sessions are growing increasingly long. The first session of the thirty-second parliament, in which the Trudeau government proposed a number of controversial pieces of legislation (including the National Energy Policy and the plan for *CA 1982*), lasted almost four years.

Each session begins with a **Throne Speech**, delivered to the members of both the House and the Senate, assembled together in the Senate chamber. This speech is read by the governor general, but it is prepared by the prime minister's staff. The speech outlines the legislative program that the government intends to propose to Parliament. That program, and the government's general performance, are then debated for a few days in the House of Commons.

When the prime minister decides that it is time to terminate not only a session, but the parliament as well, he or she asks the governor general for a **dissolution** of Parliament. Dissolution automatically entails the holding of general elections to select another parliament.

7.3 The House of Commons: Membership and Officers

The House of Commons currently consists of 301 members of Parliament (or MPs). Each MP has been elected to represent one territorially-based constituency known as a **riding**. In general, ridings are constructed in accordance with the principle of representation by population, so that the percentage of "seats" each province has in the House will be roughly equivalent to its percentage of the national population. There are some minor, institutionalized deviations from this principle. Some of the smaller provinces (especially PEI) and the two territories are slightly over-represented in the House, while some of the larger provinces—notably Ontario and BC—are somewhat under represented. These deviations serve to improve dramatically the representation of the smaller partners in Confederation, yet do not seriously weaken the influence of the larger provinces.

The fundamental distinction among MPs is that some are "government members" (that is, they belong to the party that forms the cabinet) and the rest are members of the "opposition." Within the ranks of the opposition, there is a further distinction: the largest of the opposition parties becomes "Her Majesty's Loyal Opposition," or the "official Opposition," as it is sometimes called. Under parliamentary rules, this official Opposition is entitled to certain privileges that are not extended to the other opposition parties: its leader is appointed a privy councillor, is granted special speaking privileges in the House, and even has a special residence provided at taxpayers' expense (Stornaway). The conferral of these privileges and titles on a politician who, in effect, lost the election, is indicative of how vital a role the opposition plays in parliament. Because the central task of the modern parliament is to make the government accountable to the public, the opposition is an extremely important component of that body.

The most important officer of the House of Commons is the **Speaker**. The Speaker is an MP elected by the House at the beginning of each parliament to preside over its debates and to take responsibility for its administration. The person chosen as Speaker will, of course, have been elected to the House as a partisan politician—usually as an MP for the governing party. Once installed in office, however, Speakers must maintain a strict impartiality. They never intervene in parliamentary debate and are permitted to vote only when it is necessary to break a tie.

The House has a number of other officers. The **Clerk of the House**, who sits at a table in the middle of the floor directly in front of the Speaker, takes responsibility for doing the official paperwork of the House, and provides procedural advice to the Speaker when this is necessary. The **Sergeant-at-Arms**, usually a distinguished military figure, is responsible for the security of the House. Recording secretaries are also present in the House to keep an official record of its debates (commonly known as *Hansard*).

7.4 The Business of the House of Commons

The work of the House is complex and varied, but four main elements of its business may be identified.

The first, and most important business of the House, is the adoption of **bills**. Bills are legislative proposals. Any MP has the right to introduce a bill for the consideration of the House, but, for reasons discussed below in Section 6, **private members' bills**, though numerous, are rarely adopted. Most of Parliament's legislative activity is focused on **government bills**, legislative proposals presented to the House by a minister. These proposals have in most cases been generated by some combination of civil service, minister, and cabinet, and they are referred to as government bills because they normally will have received cabinet approval before they are brought to the House. Only a minister can introduce legislation that entails new taxes or the expenditure of public monies.

Parliament has an elaborate procedure for considering bills, but the complexities of the procedure are there for good reasons. A bill is adopted only after it has passed three "readings." In order to discourage hastiness, the rules stipulate that each of these readings must take place on different days.[1] Moreover, in order to facilitate an orderly consideration of bills, each reading has a distinct focus or purpose. The point of the **first reading** is merely to introduce the bill to the House and to give its members (and the public) a chance to acquaint themselves with its provisions. Some time later, the minister sponsoring the bill will move that it be given **second reading**. The second reading focuses on the basic purpose or principles of the bill. This gives the House an opportunity to endorse the general thrust of the proposal without getting bogged down in debate about details. Once a bill passes second reading it is sent to one of the House's committees for careful study of its specific provisions. At the **report stage**, the committee presents the House with the results of its study. The report normally includes proposals for amending some of the bill's provisions, and these amendments are voted on by the House. The bill is then presented to the House for final approval in

---

1 The House of Commons may, on occasion, vote to suspend this rule if it deems immediate action on a bill necessary.

a **third reading**. From here, the bill proceeds to the Senate, where it must go through the same stages. Once the bill has passed all three readings in the Senate, it is presented to the governor general for **royal assent**, which is a constitutional formality. Only at this stage may the bill be **proclaimed**, that is, transformed from a legislative proposal into a binding law or "statute."

A second type of business conducted in the House is the adoption of **resolutions**. A resolution differs from a bill in that it merely expresses the opinion of the House; it does not result in the adoption of a new law or policy. What, then, is the point of a resolution? Resolutions are essentially a means of allowing for public debate on issues. The opposition might move a resolution that "this House condemn the government's handling of the economy" in order to try to persuade the public that the government's economic policy is inadequate. The government, on the other hand, might propose a resolution designed to test the public's reaction to some course of action it is considering.

A third type of business conducted in the House is the **scrutiny of public expenditure**. This scrutiny comes in two stages, before and after the expenditure. Before any money is spent by a governmental department, the department must present its **estimates** (its proposed expenditures for the coming year) to whichever of the House's standing committees has jurisdiction in that area of government. This process presents MPs with an opportunity for a detailed examination of proposed government spending, and not a penny of public money may be spent by a department without prior approval by the House. Public expenditures are also scrutinized after the fact. The House's Public Accounts Committee, which is usually chaired by a member of the opposition, examines the books of each department to ensure that the public's money has been spent wisely. The committee is assisted in its efforts by a special officer of the House, the **Auditor-General**.

The fourth major type of business conducted in the House is the provision of information. In order to hold government accountable for its work, MPs must have access to relevant information. The procedures of the House allow members to submit written questions or requests for information. The government tables its responses to such questions or requests with the Clerk, and they are subsequently recorded in *Hansard*. MPs also have the chance to pose impromptu questions orally in the Question Period. As most Canadians will know, however, the questions asked in this forum are rarely asked in good faith. Opposition members ask questions that are designed not to elicit information, but to embarrass the government; indeed, the "questions" that are posed are often not questions at all, but barely camouflaged speeches. The ministers to whom the questions are directed therefore respond in kind: questions are frequently evaded or used as an opportunity to attack the opposition.

Many Canadians have a negative impression of Question Period because of the highly partisan and frequently hyperbolic character of the exchanges that take place during it. Yet while there are good reasons to be critical of some of the excesses of Question Period, no other forum allows for such intense and powerful criticism of government policy; it is no coincidence that almost all the footage of parliamentary debate one sees on the television news is drawn from that source. For all its faults, then, Question Period is an essential device for allowing Parliament to perform its crucial role of keeping the government accountable to the public.

7.5 The Rules of Procedure of the House of Commons

The proceedings of the House of Commons are governed by two types of rule. First, Parliament has codified basic regulations concerning the organization of its business and the conduct of its debates in a body of rules known as the **Standing Orders**. The House may amend these Standing Orders by a simple majority vote, and there have been numerous changes to them over the years. In addition to its Standing Orders, the House also recognizes a large number of rules that derive from British (or in some cases, Canadian) parliamentary tradition. It is useful to think of these rules as something like a parliamentary equivalent of constitutional conventions: while not carved in stone, they are respected because years of experience have shown them to be useful.

To the outside observer, many of the rules of procedure followed by the House may seem somewhat quaint. Yet rules that at first glance appear arbitrary or even whimsical often turn out, on closer inspection, to be both rational and valuable. The House of Commons is meant to be an adversarial chamber. In one way or another, most parliamentary rules are designed either to facilitate or to regulate the adversarial relationship between government and opposition. Notice, for example, how the seating arrangements in the House of Commons promote an adversarial mentality: government and opposition members are seated facing each other, ready to do battle like the offensive and defensive lines in a football game. At the same time, however, the House follows certain rules which are designed to ensure that the battle between the two sides remains civil: comments must always be addressed to the Speaker, rather than directly to one's opponent; and to prevent disagreements from becoming personal, colleagues are addressed as "the Honourable Member from X" rather than as Jane Doe.

Among the most important rules are those governing the use of House time. In the House of Commons, time is a precious commodity, for it takes a good deal of time for the government to get its program through the House. Though the opposition rarely has enough votes to block government measures, it can exert great pressure on the government by tying up House time and stalling the government's legislative agenda. The House therefore has a number of rules regarding the use of time which are carefully designed to strike a reasonable balance between the government's need to get its business through the House and the opposition's role as a check on the government. Speeches are normally limited to 20 minutes in length, and each member may speak only once on a given motion. Twenty minutes per member per motion is enough to allow the opposition members to cause substantial headaches for the government, but not enough time to stall legislation indefinitely. There is also a rule under the Standing Orders known as **closure**, which permits the government to cut off debate if it decides that the opposition is taking too much time. On paper, the closure provision would seem to deprive the opposition of a fair share in the control of the House's time. One must keep in mind, however, that closure is a suppression of debate. When the rule was first developed, it was assumed that governments would resort to it only in extreme cases, for suppressing debate might be perceived by the public as anti-democratic. Through most of the twentieth century, the closure rule was indeed used rarely, and often at great cost to the popularity of the government. More recently, however, it seems that a decline in public attention to Parliament has permitted governments to invoke closure more indiscriminately.

7.6 The Backbencher

In describing the roles of MPs, a distinction is often drawn between the "front benches" and the "back benches." The front benches on the government side of the House are taken by the members of the cabinet. The front benches on the opposition side of the House are occupied by the "shadow cabinet," members who have been assigned a responsibility for criticizing a particular minister. It is the members occupying the front benches who monopolize most of the responsibility, power, and publicity in Canadian politics. The "backbenchers," on the other hand, serve in relative anonymity. Indeed, they are often dismissed as "trained seals" whose only job is to vote when and how their leaders tell them to.

Yet it would be a great mistake to think that backbenchers are without influence. Parliament provides three major opportunities for them to voice their concerns. The first is the weekly caucus meeting. Whenever the House is in session, Wednesday mornings are reserved for meetings of the caucus—the MPs (and senators, if they wish) of each party. These meetings are held behind closed doors so that caucus members may speak frankly, but without damaging party unity. In opposition caucus meetings, the backbenchers wield a great deal of influence. In government caucus meetings, the backbenchers are less powerful; to a large extent, these meetings are used by cabinet as a means of informing the backbenchers what it has already decided to do. Still, the cabinet can remain in office only as long as it has the confidence of the House, and this gives the government backbenchers a certain amount of leverage; concerted opposition on their part to cabinet proposals will force the cabinet to reconsider.

A second venue in which backbenchers may exert influence is the House of Commons committees. Chief among these are the "standing" (that is, permanent) committees, each of which focuses on some particular area of public policy. The members of these committees, almost all of whom are backbenchers, may thus develop a certain expertise in that area. These committees are responsible for the clause-by-clause examination of bills that takes place after second reading and for the examination of departmental estimates. They may also take responsibility for carrying out studies or investigations on topics relevant to their jurisdiction, sometimes holding hearings across the country. These committees now have substantial budgets to support their work, and though their membership is constituted along party lines, party discipline is much less rigid there than it is in the House itself. This gives committee members an opportunity to exert some personal influence on the business of Parliament.

The third means for backbenchers to voice their concerns is the **private member's bill**. Any member of the House may introduce a bill for first reading on any topic, provided that the proposal does not require the expenditure of public money. The rules of the House allot very little time for the discussion of private members' bills, and few are ever adopted. But these bills do afford backbenchers an opportunity to put their ideas before the public, and it is not uncommon for some of those ideas to be picked up by the government and reintroduced later on in the form of a government bill.

7.7 House of Commons Reform

One of the most common complaints by Canadians about their government is that their elected representatives do not effectively represent them. MPs are routinely criticized for being too subservient to their party leaders. They seem to do a better job of representing the party in Parliament than of representing their constituents. This criticism has been the underlying cause for numerous attempts to reform the rules and structure of the House of Commons. Attempts at reform have focused on three areas in which the power of individual members might be increased: reforming the committee structure, private members' bills, and free votes.

It is important to understand that the House of Commons committees are staffed in numbers proportionally equal to the overall membership in the House. If one party has a majority in the House of Commons, it will also have a majority on each committee. This proportional representation ensures that the government party can control the outcome of committee legislation. But it also means that MPs are seen primarily as representatives of their party rather than as representatives of the interests of their constituents with respect to the legislation under consideration.

One possibility for reforming the House of Commons would be to increase the power and independence of legislative committees and thus increase the power of the backbenchers who make up those committees. More money and research staff would provide committees with the ability to put forward well thought out alternatives to government positions and ensure that the House of Commons more effectively holds the government accountable.

A second reform that is often discussed is the idea of allowing greater opportunities for the introduction and consideration of private members' bills. By providing more time for the debate of private members' bills, the power of individual MPs to bring forward issues relevant to their particular constituents would be increased.

Finally, it is proposed that MPs should be given more opportunity to vote against their own party. This freedom could be accomplished by relaxing the fairly strict rule governing confidence. One possibility would be that motions of non-confidence in the government would have to be explicit. No longer would defeat of government bills be tantamount to a motion of non-confidence, so government MPs would be able to vote against their party without fear that such a vote would bring down the government.

These reforms seem, at first glance, to be reasonable and workable. But each would also have some political "side-effects" that might make the cure worse than the disease. For example, allowing more time for private members' bills would take valuable time away from deliberation of government legislation. It is not clear that there is much time to spare. In the case of relaxing the confidence convention, one has to think about the effects that the reform would have on the government's ability to govern. Relaxing the confidence rule would encourage MPs from the government side to vote with the opposition. But it is unlikely that such a change would alter the way opposition MPs vote. We would therefore be confronted with the spectacle of an apparently divided government party and completely united opposition parties. This might turn out to be a recipe for weak government.

In the final analysis, one has to ask whether the defects of parliamentary government are not outweighed by its advantages. Parliamentary government runs smoothly and efficiently because it is, in the main, cabinet government and not government of 301 individual MPs. Cabinet government allows us to clearly establish who is responsible for government legislation and current public policy. The prime minister, the Cabinet, and, ultimately, the governing party will be held accountable by the electorate at the next elections. Parliamentary government may not be ideal in every respect, but its advantages should not be taken lightly.

7.8 The Senate

The purpose of the Senate is to serve as a chamber of "sober second thought," which reviews legislative proposals emanating from the House of Commons. It was originally hoped that in performing this function, the Senate would look at legislation from a perspective that differed from that of the House of Commons in two distinct ways. First, the Fathers of Confederation worried that a House of Commons elected on the democratic principle might fail to respect the rights of property; the poor majority might use its democratic power to despoil the rich minority. The Senate was meant to be a body that would stand up for property rights. This is reflected in the fact that Section 23 of *CA 1867* specifies that senators must possess assets, above and beyond their personal liabilities, in excess of $4,000. The sum of $4,000 does not seem like much today, but in 1867, a relatively small proportion of Canadians could have claimed to be that wealthy.

Secondly, the Senate was intended to pay special attention to the concerns of the less populous regions of the country. While the principle for allocating seats in the House of Commons was representation by population (making the larger provinces of Ontario and Quebec dominant in that body), the principle for allocating Senate seats was equality of the regions. *CA 1867* originally granted 24 seats to each of the three regions that first formed the country: Ontario, Quebec, and the Maritimes. The subsequent entry of other provinces into Confederation led to some minor deviations from the principle of regional equality, but Senate representation is still, in essence, based on that principle.[1]

In law, the powers of the Senate are almost the same as those of the House of Commons.[2] In practice, however, the Senate almost never makes full use of its powers. This is because senators are not elected.

---

1 The Senate currently has 105 seats. Ontario and Quebec have 24 each. The West has 24 seats (six per province). The Maritimes still have 24, but Nova Scotia and New Brunswick each gave up two to Prince Edward Island when that province entered Confederation in 1873. Newfoundland was granted six Senate seats when it joined Canada in 1949. This is the principal deviation from the principle of regional equality. The Yukon, Nunavut, and the Northwest Territories have one Senate seat each.

2 There are two exceptions. Section 53 of *CA 1867* specifies that the House of Commons is to take the leading role in the adoption of "money bills" (legislation raising or spending public funds). Section 47(1) of *CA 1982* specifies that the Senate has only a suspensory veto over constitutional amendments proposed by the House of Commons.

Section 24 of *CA 1867* provides that senators are to be "summoned" to that body by the governor general; in practice, this means that they are appointed by the prime minister. From the very beginning of Confederation, it was recognized that an appointed body like the Senate would have to defer to the leadership of the elected House of Commons. Over the course of our history, the prestige of the Senate has declined steadily, in part because Canadians, whose political ideas are increasingly democratic, have become less tolerant of non-elected officials. However, the decline is also a result of the fact that so many of the appointments made to the Senate by our prime ministers have been patronage appointments designed to reward service to the prime minister's party. By the middle of the twentieth century, it had become a convention of our constitution that the Senate must not oppose a bill that has the support of the House of Commons. Though senators still carried out their responsibilities for reviewing legislation, they restricted themselves to making recommendations for minor improvements to the bills sent to them by the House of Commons.

In recent times, however, the Senate has occasionally shown an uncharacteristic feistiness. When the Conservative government came to power in 1984, the Liberals had been in office for 16 years. In that period, the vast majority of Senate appointees had been card-carrying Liberals, and the Liberals thus had a comfortable majority there. When the Conservative-dominated House adopted a bill implementing the controversial Free Trade Agreement with the United States, the Liberal-dominated Senate refused to go along. By withholding their approval of the bill, the Liberal senators forced the Conservatives to call a general election, thereby giving the voters an opportunity to express their views on the issue. Shortly after the Conservatives won that election, they introduced legislation in the House to create the controversial GST. Again, after the legislation was passed by the House, the Liberal senators threatened to deny the bill their approval. Prime Minister Mulroney responded by using Section 26 of *CA 1867*, which gives the government the authority to appoint four or eight additional senators (one or two per region) when this is necessary to break a deadlock between the two houses of Parliament. Mulroney appointed eight new senators, all them Conservatives, and this was enough to ensure that the upper house passed the government's bill.

These episodes provide an interesting illustration of how constitutional conventions work. We saw in Chapter 2 that conventions depend for their enforcement on public reaction. In these cases, the Liberal senators gambled that public opinion would support them. They argued that their actions were consistent with the spirit, if not the letter, of the convention in question, for the purpose of the convention subordinating the Senate to the House of Commons was to ensure that power would be exercised democratically, and the polls indicated that the majority of voters wanted an election on free trade and the defeat of the GST. Whether the argument was good or not, the Liberals got away with it. The only way to enforce a convention is for the voters to punish those who violate it. In the 1993 elections, however, the voters gave the Liberals a strong majority.

7.9 Senate Reform

For years, Canadians have been dissatisfied with the Senate. **Senate reform** is thus a perennial theme of Canadian political discourse. It includes ideas about changing the way one becomes a senator, about the powers of the Senate, and about the relationship between the Senate and the House of Commons.

A substantial body of opinion suggests that the best way to reform the Senate is to abolish it. Many Canadians believe that senators do little or no productive work, and that the institution is nothing but a great waste of money. This is an overly simplistic view, but it is a popular one nonetheless. A more sophisticated case for abolition is made by those who point out that to the extent that senators have an influence on legislation, it is often an undesirable influence. The Senate was intended to be a body that would represent the interests of property. Although the vast majority of today's Canadians would be able to meet the Constitution's requirement that senators possess $4,000 in property, that body is still not representative of the socio-economic majority; even today, many (if not most) senators are very closely linked to Canada's business elite. Colin Campbell has argued that the Senate has operated has a "lobby" for big business, re-working legislation to the advantage of banks and other large corporations.[1] It is because of the close link between the Senate and corporate Canada that the NDP has traditionally supported Senate abolition.

Most advocates of Senate reform prefer to keep the Senate, but seek to restructure it so as to give more effective parliamentary representa-

---

1   Colin Campbell, *The Canadian Senate: A Lobby From Within* (Toronto: Macmillan and Co., 1978).

tion to Canada's less populous regions. The most common proposal along these lines is to transform the upper house into an elected legislative body. Drawing inspiration largely from the Senate of the United States, reformers argue that in a federal union, the legislative body of the national government should have one house based on representation by population, and a second, equally powerful house based on the principle of the equality of the provinces or regions of the country. On this view, the key to making Canada's Senate effective is to elect its members, so that they will have as much democratic legitimacy as the members of the House of Commons.

Other observers argue that the Senate should be left pretty much as it is. These analysts reject the proposal for electing senators on the grounds that it could lead to parliamentary paralysis in cases where the two chambers are dominated by different parties. They also reject abolition, arguing that the Senate is more useful than people realize: it cleans up errors or oversights in bills passed by the House of Commons; it serves as a source of cabinet ministers in cases where a prime minister has no MPs from a particular province;[1] and it serves as a convenient place to which a prime minister might "promote" cabinet ministers whose services are no longer required. Defenders of the status quo argue that since the operation of the Senate costs each Canadian only about a dollar a year, it would make more sense to make minor improvements to the institution than to abolish it.[2]

---

1 After winning the 1979 elections with almost no seats from Quebec, Prime Minister Clark used the Senate to strengthen his Cabinet's representation from that province. After the 1980 elections, which left incoming Liberals with no seats west of Winnipeg, Prime Minister Trudeau did the same thing.

2 Darcy Wudel, "A Job Description for Senators," *Policy Options* 7, 3 (April, 1986); J. Lemco and P. Regenstreif, "Let the Senate Be," *Policy Options* 6, 4 (May 1985).

Key Terms

prorogation
Throne Speech
dissolution
riding
Speaker
Clerk of the House
Sergeant-at-Arms
Hansard
bills
private members' bills
government bill
first reading
second reading
report stage

third reading
royal assent
proclamation
resolutions
scrutiny of public expenditures
estimates
Auditor-General
Standing Orders
caucus
closure
Senate reform

The Judiciary

8.1 The Role of the Judiciary
8.2 The Fundamental Principles of the Canadian Judiciary
8.3 Canada's Courts
8.4 The Supreme Court of Canada
8.5 The Politicization of the Judiciary

8.1 The Role of the Judiciary

The first thing that students of the constitution should notice about the provisions of *CA 1867* governing "the judicature" is the location of those provisions. As we have seen, the sections governing executive and legislative power occupy a prominent position close to the beginning of *CA 1867*. Judicial power, on the other hand, is not discussed until Part VII, three-quarters of the way through the *Act*. To some extent, this is a consequence of the fact that Canada's judicial system has a federal dimension to it, a fact that makes it reasonable to outline the provisions governing judicial power only after the provisions governing federalism have been laid down. But the relatively late discussion of judicial power is also a reflection of the fact that the Fathers of Confederation viewed judicial power as substantially less important than the legislative and executive powers.

Such a view would be untenable today, for the role of the judiciary has expanded far beyond its original limits. In 1867, most observers would have ascribed to the judiciary two basic tasks: the adjudication of legal disputes between private parties and the adjudication of cases in public law. Today's judges regularly engage in two additional activities: the direction of royal commissions of inquiry and judicial review of the Constitution. Judicial review, in particular, has magnified the importance of the judiciary far beyond anything the Fathers of Confederation had expected.

A) *Adjudicating legal disputes between private parties*

According to the liberal philosopher John Locke, the primary reason why human beings create political regimes is that they need someone to settle their disputes in an authoritative and impartial manner. Locke believed in certain universal and permanent principles of justice which he called natural laws, and he thought that all human beings could in principle understand the validity of those laws. But Locke doubted that human beings would respect those laws consistently. He also doubted their ability to apply and enforce them impartially. In their natural state of freedom, then, men would inevitably be drawn into an ever-escalating cycle of injustice and vengeance. Reasonable human beings are therefore willing to renounce their natural freedom and put themselves under the command of a political regime that will be able to resolve disputes before they turn violent.

In order to accomplish this objective, the political regime will adopt laws to govern the most common private disputes and establish courts to settle such disputes according to the principles laid down in those laws. The regime will still permit, and may even encourage, individuals to employ a number of private mechanisms to settle their disputes. The most common of these are negotiation, mediation (a process in which a third party is brought in to facilitate negotiations between the disputants), and arbitration (where the disputants agree to allow a third party to impose a settlement on them). But the effectiveness of these three mechanisms is largely dependent on the fact that disputants know that unresolved disputes can, and normally will, be taken to the courts for decisive resolution.

At the time of Confederation, it was deemed necessary to put responsibility for "private law" — laws governing matters such as property rights, contracts, and torts — in the hands of the provincial governments. Section 92.13 of *CA 1867* thus reserves "property and civil rights" as an exclusive jurisdiction of the legislatures of the provinces. The reason for this was that New Brunswick, Nova Scotia, and Ontario embodied their private law in one format while Quebec traditionally had used another.

Private law in Quebec is embodied in a statute called the civil code, a detailed and comprehensive compendium of all the rules governing matters of property and civil rights. This practice, used by most legislative jurisdictions in the world today, was one that Quebec had adopted when it was a French colony, and in 1774 the British government guaranteed Quebecers the right to retain their code. The other colonies, more British in heritage, had always followed the British practice of embodying much of their private law in a form known as "common law." Common law is judge-made law, as opposed to statutes adopted by legislative bodies. In late medieval England, royally-appointed judges slowly began to take control of what hitherto had been a patchwork system of justice. In order to impose some order and consistency on that system, they adopted the practice of deciding cases involving matters like property or contracts on the basis of **precedents** (previous judicial decisions on the same point of law). Where no precedent existed, judges were free to decide cases in the manner that seemed most consistent with the underlying principles of the case law that existed. By virtue of the principle of **stare decisis** ("to stand decided"), however, judges were required to respect any precedent that had been endorsed by courts of authority superior to their own. By following these basic rules, England's judges were able, over time, to develop a single system of private law "common" to the whole country.

B) *Adjudicating cases in public law*

Judges also have substantial authority in matters of "public law." The difference between public and private law is that while private law governs relationships between two or more private parties, public law creates and regulates relationships between private parties and the government. This difference is reflected in the names of the cases heard under each type of law: while a typical case in private law might be titled *Jones v. Smith*, cases in public law will feature the Queen, or some officer of the Crown, in their title: *Russell v. The Queen, Ford v. Attorney General of Quebec.*

The two main areas of public law are criminal law and administrative law. Section 91.27 of *CA 1867* declares criminal law to be an exclusive jurisdiction of Parliament (i.e., Ottawa). Our criminal law is contained primarily in the Criminal Code of Canada, which prohibits a wide variety of actions by declaring them to be criminal offences—assault, sexual assault, fraud, murder, and hateful speech, to name but a few. In addition to offering a legal definition of these crimes, the Criminal Code establishes appropriate ranges of punishment for each of them. It is the judges of Canada's courts, however, who decide on the specific sentence, and in most cases, the Criminal Code grants them a good deal of latitude. This constitutes a very substantial form of political power.

The term "administrative law" refers to any regulatory legislation that does not involve the application of criminal sanctions. Administrative law thus covers a very wide range of topics at both levels of government, from traffic regulations (a provincial matter) to old age pensions (a federal jurisdiction). Because of the tremendous number of administrative law decisions that need to be made by today's governments, a good deal of administrative law is now applied by administrative tribunals (for example, a Workers' Compensation Board) rather than courts. However, the judiciary still hears many types of administrative law cases, and will often have the power to overrule decisions made by administrative tribunals.

c) *Judicial commissions of inquiry*

In recent decades it has become increasingly common for governments to ask judges to take charge of royal commissions investigating either problematic areas of public policy or alleged misconduct in some part of the public sector. Judges have been asked to lead investigations into the deaths of dozens of babies at the Hospital for Sick Children in Toronto, into alleged racism in the justice system of Nova Scotia, into alleged illegal activities by the RCMP, and into Canada's medicare system, among other subjects. As a rule, the recommendations of these commissions carry a good deal of weight with the governments that create them. The individual judges who head such commissions are thus able to exert a substantial amount of influence on specific political issues.

Governments are not obligated to place the direction of royal commissions in the hands of judges. In fact, many such commissions have been led by non-judicial figures. There are two reasons why governments frequently look to the judiciary for their royal commissions: first, judges have professional experience in organizing hearings in which parties are able to present evidence in a procedurally fair manner.

Secondly (and probably more importantly), judges have a reputation for impartiality. Yet Peter Russell, a leading expert on the Canadian judiciary, argues that it is precisely because of their impartiality that judges should be spared from such work:

> The participation of judges in these commissions is bound to contribute to the politicization of the judiciary and will likely diminish the aura of impartiality — which is one of the reasons for appointing judges to royal commissions in the first place. If this resulted merely in fewer royal commissions or fewer judicial royal commissioners, there would be no serious loss; there are other means of conducting inquiries into government misconduct and public policy. The more serious danger is to the judicial branch of government itself and its capacity for effectively performing its essential function of adjudication.[1]

D) *Judicial review of the constitution*

We have seen in Chapter 2 that the terms of the constitution require interpretation and that it is the courts that take responsibility for that task. We have also seen, in Chapters 4 and 5, that this function of judicial review has given Canada's judiciary substantial political power. Judges now decide, or decisively influence, a number of important questions of principle and policy: how extensive are the powers of the federal government? Is it permissible for either level of government to restrict access to abortions? Are laws prohibiting the use of marijuana acceptable? These types of issues are now routinely decided by the courts rather than by legislatures.

It is important to note, however, that the judiciary does not become involved in such questions on its own initiative. Most of the time, judicial review of the Constitution is triggered by specific cases in private or public law where a ruling on the meaning of some part of the constitution is necessary for the adjudication of the dispute in question. Let us take as an example the case of *Big M Drug Mart v. The Queen, 1985*. In this case, Big M Drug Mart was charged with violating a federal statute, *The Lord's Day Act*, which prohibited commercial establishments like Big M from doing business on Sunday. In court, Big M did not deny that it was open on Sundays in violation of the law, but it argued that it

---

1 Peter Russell, *The Judiciary in Canada: The Third Branch of Government* (Toronto: McGraw-Hill Ryerson, 1987) 13.

should not be punished because the law itself was in violation of Section 2(a) of the Charter of Rights, which guarantees "freedom of religion." In order to determine whether or not Big M should be punished, the courts which heard this case (including, in the end, the Supreme Court of Canada) were required to make a ruling on the meaning of Section 2(a). Does the right to freedom of religion make it unconstitutional for governments to prohibit shopping on "the Lord's day"? If it does, Big M is innocent. If it does not, Big M must be punished in accordance with the law.

The second mechanism for triggering judicial review of the constitution is the **reference procedure**. When the federal government created the Supreme Court of Canada, it provided that the court could be called on to give its opinion on the constitutionality of specific decisions or statutes referred to it by the governor-in-Council. Originally, the government's intention was to use this reference procedure to help it decide whether specific provincial statutes should be disallowed. Eventually, however, the reference procedure came to be used as a means of obtaining quick rulings on the constitutionality of proposed legislation. (Waiting for the constitutionality of a law to be challenged by private parties and appealed through the judicial system might take as long as 10 years.) In the 1930s, for example, the government was able to refer the "New Deal" legislation proposed by R.B. Bennett to the courts and to learn in relatively short order that most of the legislation was *ultra vires*—beyond the jurisdiction—of the federal government. The provincial governments soon recognized the value of the reference procedure and established comparable mechanisms in their own courts. Today most judicial review of the constitution arises from the adjudication of cases rather than reference questions, but the reference procedure is the source of some of the more interesting and important cases—the *Patriation Reference*, for example (discussed on p. 42 above).

8.2　**The Fundamental Principles of the Canadian Judiciary**

There are three fundamental principles that govern the Canadian judiciary in its efforts to carry out the tasks described above: impartiality, independence, and equality before the law. Each of these principles has been inherited from the British judiciary. Indeed, it is plausible to argue that the authoritative status of these three principles is implied by the statement in the preamble to *CA 1867* that Canada is to have "a Constitution similar in principle to that of the United Kingdom." As we shall see, however, the Constitution entrenches these principles in other places as well.

A) *Impartiality*

Section 11(d) of the Charter of Rights and Freedoms guarantees that any person charged in Canada with some offence has a right to a "fair" trial before an "impartial tribunal." There is nothing surprising in this, for the requirement that judges be impartial is more or less implicit in the very concept of adjudication.

The general meaning of the principle of **impartiality** is relatively straightforward: judges must be free from prejudice for or against any party appearing before them. It may, of course, be impossible for human beings to refrain from showing at least some prejudice in their judgment about things, but our regime assumes that its judges will be reasonably impartial and for the most part leaves it up to individual judges to police themselves in this regard. It does, however, attempt to promote impartiality by means of three specific provisions.

The first is the right of parties to appeal a judge's decision to a higher court. The right of appeal promotes impartiality in two ways: knowing that their judgments may be subjected to the scrutiny of a higher court gives individual judges great incentive to be fair and objective, and parties who have been victims of judicial bias get a second hearing. It is important to note, however, that the right to appeal is not unlimited. In the first place, it is not automatic. One generally has to ask the court to which one seeks to appeal a decision for permission (or "leave") to appeal. Appeal courts will grant such leave only if they have serious doubts about the ruling of the lower court. Moreover, not every aspect of a case is subject to appeal. When judges adjudicate disputes, they engage in two distinct processes: they must first decide the facts of the situation in dispute — what exactly happened — and they must then determine what the law says about these situations. Appeal courts will grant leave to appeal if there appear to be problems in what a judge has said about the law, or perhaps if the judge has made procedural errors, but, as a rule, they do not hear appeals of a judge's decision about the facts of a case.

Another feature of Canada's judicial regime that serves to promote impartiality is its "adversarial" character. In many countries, judges will play a very active role in the judicial process, taking responsibility for fact-finding and then settling the disputes in accordance with their understanding of the law. Such arrangements are not consistent with our regime's suspicion of public power and its emphasis on individual liberty and responsibility. In Canada, we follow the British practice of giving judges a more passive role. We place the responsibility for establishing facts and presenting arguments with the adversaries themselves, and our judges serve as referees rather than inquisitors. Instead of seeking out facts and arguments, they restrict themselves to making rulings on the basis of the facts and arguments presented to them by individual litigants. This has the effect of minimizing judges' latitude for imposing their own views on the contending parties.

The third provision is the doctrine of political neutrality. This doctrine, which we also inherited from Britain, decrees that judges must keep silent about political matters. They may not be members of political parties, they may not speak on political topics, and they must not display public preference for any particular political views. The reason for this doctrine is not hard to see. Judges will often be called upon to hear cases in which they will make decisions of political importance. If they have taken a public stand on a particular issue—if, for instance, a judge proclaims herself to be an ardent opponent of abortion—it will be difficult to persuade the public that both sides in a case involving abortion will get a fair hearing from her. Moreover, as Peter Russell points out, if judges start attacking politicians, it is inevitable that politicians will fight back. This would only serve to undermine the authority and independence of the courts.[1]

In 1981, Canadians witnessed an interesting example of the doctrine of political neutrality. Justice Thomas Berger of the British Columbia Supreme Court publicly attacked the constitutional accord which formed the basis of *CA 1982* because it did not contain a veto for Quebec and because it did not entrench certain rights for aboriginal Canadians. A committee of the Canadian Judicial Council, which investigated Berger's conduct, reported that Berger's comments might serve to undermine the public's perception of the judiciary's impartiality:

> It is apparent that some of the native peoples are unhappy with s.35 of the Canadian Charter of Rights and Freedoms. If Justice Berger should be called upon to interpret that section, for exam-

---

1 Russell 88-89.

ple, the meaning to be given to the word "existing" in "the existing aboriginal and treaty rights of the aboriginal peoples of Canada," would the general public have confidence now in his impartiality? After Justice Berger spoke publicly on the necessity for
Quebec retaining a veto, his brother judges in Quebec were called
on to determine whether such a right existed.[1]

The committee found that Berger's remarks were sufficiently indiscreet
to justify removing him from the bench, but thought that a warning
would be more appropriate. Berger rejected these findings, but resigned
from his position a year later.

It is sometimes alleged that the judiciary is not truly impartial
because it tends, on the whole, to be moderate or even conservative in
its politics. Stephen Brooks, for example, complains that judges are
never "radical critics of society." He notes that they "rarely concern
themselves with the distribution of power in society," and are generally
"insensitive to the structural inequalities that exist in society and in the
economy." This, he argues, is due to a number of factors. One is that
judges tend to come from middle- or upper-middle-class backgrounds.
Another is that they are appointed by governments, which, as a rule, do
not want to see political radicals on the judicial bench. Most important,
however, is the fact that the law itself is riddled with inherently conservative premises such as "individualism" and property rights. This means
that anyone schooled in the law, as judges must be, will almost inevitably
have acquired conservative political prejudices.[2]

It is certainly important for students of Canadian politics to understand the political implications of judicial decision-making, and it is
possible to argue, as Brooks does, that the judiciary's political impact is
in a sense conservative. Yet to claim that this constitutes a lack of impartiality is unfair to our judges. In the Canadian regime, the primary task
of the judiciary is to apply the law, not to make it. In those cases where
they in effect "make the law" by giving concrete meaning to imprecise
legislative language, it is entirely reasonable to expect them to formulate
their interpretations in light of the basic principles of the existing
regime. It is perfectly legitimate for Canadians to seek modifications to
the existing regime by pressuring their politicians to introduce the
appropriate legislative changes, but it would be inconsistent with the

---

1 Cited in F.L. Morton, *Law, Politics, and the Judicial Process in Canada* (Calgary: The
   University of Calgary Press, 1990) 111.
2 Stephen Brooks, *Canadian Democracy: An Introduction* (Toronto: McClelland and
   Stewart, 1993) 196-97.

principle of democratic government to expect the judiciary to act as agents of radical political change.

B) *Judicial independence*

In addition to guaranteeing a right to a trial before an "impartial" tribunal, Section 11(d) of the Charter of Rights and Freedoms also guarantees that tribunal shall be "independent." While the terms "independent" and "impartial" sound alike, they do not mean the same thing. Strictly speaking, the principle of **judicial independence** is a kind of subset of the principle of impartiality.

When we say that the judiciary must be independent, we mean that it must be independent of the executive branch of the regime. The reason for this is quite simple. In many, if not most cases before the courts, the executive will be a party to the dispute. *Big M Drug Mart v. The Queen* is actually a dispute between Big M and the Attorney-General of Alberta (a member of the provincial executive) who, in taking Big M to court, is attempting to execute his duties under the law by prosecuting a party alleged to have violated a federal statute. The judiciary would have difficulty being impartial if it were subject to the control of an executive which, of necessity, frequently appears before it as a litigant. The principle of judicial independence thus entails certain conditions to guarantee that judges will be free of pressure from the political executive.

In a 1985 case entitled *Valente v. The Queen*, the Supreme Court of Canada had an opportunity to articulate those conditions in an authoritative fashion. The first is that judges must have security of tenure. In other words, the executive must not be able to fire judges merely because it dislikes their rulings. Secondly, the salaries of judges must be fixed by law, for if the judiciary is not financially independent of the executive, the executive might try to influence judges by increasing or decreasing their salaries. The third and final condition is that the judges must have control over those aspects of the administration of their courts which have an impact on judicial decision-making (the scheduling of cases, for example).

Using the Supreme Court's three conditions as a standard, it may be said that Canada's judiciary is highly independent. Section 99 of *CA 1867* explicitly guarantees the judges of our superior courts security of tenure until the age of 75 "during good behaviour." This is a traditional way of saying that judges may be removed from office only if they are physically or mentally incapable of performing their duties or if they have engaged in activities that might bring the administration of justice into disrepute (for example, selling drugs or driving under the influence of alcohol). In other words, judges may not be fired for making decisions which the executive does not like or even for making mistakes. The tenure of the judges of Canada's other courts is protected by similar provisions in the statutes creating those courts.

Section 100 of *CA 1867* entrenches the principle that the remuneration of the judges of our superior courts shall be fixed by law. This protects the salaries of individual judges from manipulation by the executive. Once again, the judges of our other courts are protected by similar provisions in the statutes creating those courts.

The third condition of judicial independence set down by the Supreme Court in *Valente* is not entrenched anywhere in the constitution. For the most part, however, Canada's judges have ample authority over those aspects of courtroom administration that are essential to their adjudicative work.

The importance Canadians attribute to the principle of judicial independence may be seen in an incident known as "The Judges Affair." In March 1976, the Chief Justice of the Quebec superior court, Jules Deschenes, wrote to the federal minister of justice to complain that on separate occasions three of Prime Minister Trudeau's cabinet ministers had contacted judges concerning cases they were hearing. None of the ministers resigned over the allegations, but the prime minister made it clear that similar conduct would not be tolerated in the future. Two years later, when it was reported that Labour Minister John Munro had contacted a judge to discuss the sentencing of one of his constituents, he was forced to resign. A decade later, Jean Charest was forced to resign from the Mulroney cabinet for having called a judge on behalf of a voter from his riding.

C) *Equality before the law*

The third fundamental principle of Canada's judicial regime is that everyone is equal before the law. This principle is explicitly entrenched in Section 15(1) of the Charter of Rights and Freedoms. It is also implicit in the preamble to the Charter, which stipulates that "Canada is founded on principles that recognize the supremacy of ... the rule of law." One aspect of "the rule of law" is the principle that the law must be applied to all people equally.

Though Canada's courts are in principle committed to such equality, problems arise from the fact that legal proceedings are often very costly for those engaged in them. Provincial governments maintain legal aid programs to ensure that defendants in criminal cases who cannot afford to pay a lawyer will be provided with one. In non-criminal cases, however, the assistance offered under such programs is spotty. As a result, people who are entitled to some kind of redress under the law often are not able to pursue their claims because they cannot afford to. Moreover, even those who can pay a lawyer may find that they cannot afford full justice. In a judicial system that relies almost exclusively on the adversarial process for the presentation of facts and the articulation of arguments, the quality of one's legal representation can make the difference between winning and losing one's case. It is often true that the more money one has for legal fees, the better one is represented. This is not simply because high-priced lawyers are sometimes more effective than less expensive lawyers. It is also a function of the fact that the litigants with more money can afford expensive legal research and can drag cases on so long with appeals or procedural disputes that their adversaries can no longer afford the fight.

8.3 Canada's Courts

At first glance, Canada appears to have a bewildering array of courts, some of which have odd, or even quaint, names. But there is a logic to the structure of Canada's court system which is easily understood if one keeps in mind a small number of basic principles.

The first of these principles is hierarchy. Court systems are almost by definition stratified into different layers with some courts deemed superior to others, and one court labelled "supreme." There are several reasons for this. One is the division of judicial activity into trials (where a case is heard for the first time) and appeals (where the decision reached in the trial stage is re-examined). Logic dictates that if an appeal court is going to have the authority to overturn a decision reached by a trial court, it will have to be of higher status. Moreover, if litigants are to have a right to appeal the decision of the appeal court, there must be a court of higher authority than the appeal court—hence, at some point, there must be a final court of appeal which is "supreme."

Another reason why court systems are organized in hierarchical fashion is that some subjects of adjudication are inherently more important than others. Murder cases are very important, for example, because those found guilty of murder are subject to very severe penalties. Cases of illegal parking, on the other hand, generally involve relatively light sentences and are thus not as important as murder cases. It therefore makes sense to divide a judicial system into "superior" courts, which will in theory have the most able judges, and "inferior" courts, which may have more informal procedures, depending on the type of case they handle.

One may thus sketch a simple, hypothetical hierarchy of courts something like the diagram in Figure 8.1. Here we find "inferior courts" specializing in traffic violations or small claims, "superior" trial courts to handle crimes like murder or assault and battery, a Court of Appeal to hear appeals from both the inferior and superior trial courts, and a "Supreme Court" to hear appeals from the Court of Appeal.

FIG. 8.1

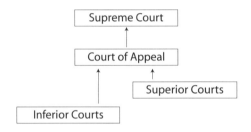

The second principle we must keep in mind in order to understand Canada's court system is federalism. The system sketched in Figure 8.1 would work well in a unitary regime like that of Great Britain. In a federal regime, however, the design of a court system becomes more complicated because one has to accommodate the claims of two layers of government. As we saw in Chapter 4, the United States was the first great model of a federal regime. In planning a judicial system for their federation, the Americans thought it best to create what is called a "dual" system. In this approach, there are two distinct networks of courts: a federal network for the adjudication of cases under federal law and a separate network in each state for adjudicating cases involving state law. The sole unifying feature in this dual system is that the Supreme Court of the United States sits in appeal of cases from both networks. Figure 8.2 provides a simple outline of the American "dual" system.

FIG. 8.2

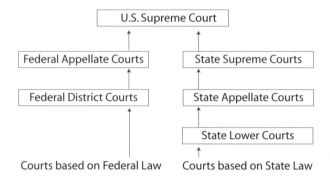

Courts based on Federal Law   Courts based on State Law

It is not surprising that the Americans opted for a dual system with a separate network of state courts, for their regime was originally designed to be a strongly decentralized federation with highly independent state governments. As we have seen, however, our Fathers of Confederation thought that the Americans had made a grave mistake in giving so much authority to their state governments. Accordingly, in planning Canada's judicial system, they sought an approach that would combine the diversity required by federalism and the uniformity that comes from a single, centralized system. This led them to create what Peter Russell has called an **integrated judicial system**: a single system under the joint custody of the two levels of government.[1] This system is outlined in Figure 8.3. It is more complex than the American one, but its structure can be easily understood if one looks at it in light of the basic rules set down in the Constitution.

FIG. 8.3

---

1   Russell ch. 3.

Section 92.14 of *CA 1867* stipulates that the provincial legislatures are to have jurisdiction over "the Administration of Justice in the Province, including the maintenance and organization of Provincial Courts, both of Civil and Criminal Jurisdiction." In other words, provincial governments have the power to create and run whatever courts they deem necessary for the operation of a fair and efficient judicial system. This includes **inferior courts** (often called "provincial courts") such as traffic, family, or small claims courts. It also includes the **superior courts** which, as we have noted, are either trial courts for more serious offences and disputes or appeal courts.

The reason for placing control over the administration of justice in the hands of provincial governments should be fairly obvious. The idea behind federalism is to permit local (that is, "provincial") control over matters that are best dealt with locally. The administration of justice is such a matter for a number of reasons. One is the difference between the civil code system of Quebec and the common law system in use in the rest of the provinces, a difference that might reasonably place different demands on their respective judicial systems. Another is that different provinces may find that situational factors as mundane as size could make a system appropriate for one province but inappropriate for another: while a large province might find it necessary to have "district" courts to give service to all areas of the province, such a system might be unnecessary in a small province. In any event, the colonies that united in 1867 to form Canada already had their own distinctive judicial systems in place, each of which was tailored to meet local needs, and there was no pressing reason to replace them.

There was, however, a need to modify the rules for appointing judges. While the federal principle requires local control over local matters, it also dictates that matters of national interest be handled nationally. The Fathers of Confederation decided that criminal law was a national matter (although the Americans had left it in the hands of the state governments) and should therefore be handled by the federal government. But the objective of having a single criminal law for all Canadians would have been undermined had its enforcement been left in the hands of a provincially controlled judiciary. Judges have a good deal of discretion when it comes to the sentencing of offenders, and courts in one province might have consistently imposed lighter or harsher sentences than judges in other provinces. In order to ensure that Canada's criminal law would be applied with some degree of consistency, it was stipulated in Section 96 of *CA 1867* that the federal government was to have the authority to appoint the judges of all *superior* courts (which would handle the most important aspects of criminal law). Further to this end, Section 100 provides that the salaries of those judges are to be set and paid by the federal parliament. While Canada's inferior courts are completely under provincial control, then, we have a network of superior courts under shared jurisdiction: the provinces create and maintain the courts according to local need, but Ottawa appoints and pays the judges to ensure national consistency of judicial decision-making. These two types of court are often referred to as **Section 92 courts** (inferior) and **Section 96 courts** (superior).

The constitution also provides for a third type of court: federally created courts with federally appointed judges. Section 101 of *CA 1867* grants Parliament the authority to establish special courts for "the better administration" of federal law, as well as a "General Court of Appeal for Canada." Parliament has made use of both branches of its powers under Section 101. In 1875 it created the Exchequer Court as a special court for the "better administration" of certain areas of federal law. In 1970, this court was significantly restructured and then re-named the Federal Court of Canada. The Federal Court hears cases in specialized areas of federal law (for example, maritime law and patent and copyright law) as well as appeals of decisions made by federal regulatory agencies and administrative tribunals.

In 1875, Parliament also used its powers under Section 101 to create the Supreme Court of Canada. The Supreme Court has the authority to hear appeals from provincial courts of appeal and from the Federal Court of Canada. The fact that this measure was not taken until seven years into the history of the Dominion does not mean that Canada was without a supreme court during that initial period. The Fathers of Confederation assumed that Canadians would use Britain's highest court, the Judicial Committee of the Privy Council (**JCPC**). The creation of the Supreme Court of Canada did not immediately change that practice: decisions of the provincial court of appeal could be appealed to the JCPC rather than to the Supreme Court. Indeed, the decisions of the Supreme Court could themselves be appealed to the JCPC. In short, the Supreme Court was at first not truly "supreme." One might say that it was the supreme court *in* Canada, but not the supreme court *for* Canada. It was not until after World War II that this quasi-colonial situation was terminated. In 1949, with the blessing of the JCPC itself,

Parliament abolished the right to appeal cases to the JCPC. Only then did the Supreme Court of Canada become truly supreme.

8.4 The Supreme Court of Canada

The Supreme Court now consists of nine judges, appointed by the prime minister. According to the terms of the *Supreme Court Act*, three of these judges must come from Quebec to ensure that the court will have at least three judges who are familiar with Quebec's civil law system. By tradition, at least one judge is always from Atlantic Canada, and a minimum of two must be from the West. Under normal circumstances, three of the judges will be from Ontario, although on occasion that province has had only two.

The court now hears about 100 cases a year. In some of these cases, the right to such a hearing is automatic (for example, in certain criminal cases where the appeal court has overturned the decision of the trial court). For the most part, however, the court is now in control of its own docket. Those who wish to appeal a case to it must persuade at least two members of a three-judge panel that the case deserves to be heard. The judges will want to hear a case if it appears there has been a serious error in the lower court's decision or if it raises an important legal or constitutional issue that needs to be settled by the country's highest court.

In order to avoid deadlock, cases are heard by odd-number panels of judges. There can be as few as five judges on a panel, though exceptionally important cases will be heard by all nine. Most, however, are heard by a panel of seven judges. After the case has been heard, the judges retire to discuss it. While in the Supreme Court of the United States it is the most senior judges who speak first in these discussions, in Canada it is customary to have the judges speak in reverse order of seniority. This is meant to ensure that the newer judges will not feel pressured to go along with the views of their more senior colleagues. In the vast majority of cases, the judges arrive at a unanimous verdict, and one of them is assigned to write a "decision" which explains the verdict and the reasons for it. When the court is not unanimous, one judge will author the **majority opinion** while another will write a **dissenting opinion**. Occasionally judges may agree on a verdict on the basis of different reasons. In such cases there will be a majority opinion but individual judges may write their own **concurring opinions**.

Perhaps the most peculiar feature of the Supreme Court is the fact that it exists by virtue of an organic statute—*The Supreme Court of Canada Act, 1875*—rather than a constitutional law. The amending formula set out in Section 41 stipulates that the "composition of the Supreme Court of Canada" may not be amended without the consent of Parliament and all 10 provincial legislatures. Apart from this, the structure, operation, and perhaps even the existence of the court depend on the will of the federal Parliament. Some observers have argued that a political institution as important as the Supreme Court should be entrenched in the constitution, and provision was made to do so in the Meech Lake and Charlottetown constitutional accords. The failure of those accords leaves the court a creature of organic statute.

8.5 The Politicization of the Judiciary

Canada's judiciary was designed to be professional and non-political. Our judges are not elected to their positions; they are appointed by the executive from the ranks of practising lawyers and legal specialists. Moreover, the principles of judicial independence and impartiality have served to keep our judges at arm's length from partisan politics.

Until recent times, the only movement for reform of the judiciary has been in the direction of making it even less political than it is. The target of reformers was the partisan character of the appointment process. It has always been the case that the party in power tends to appoint a disproportionate number of its own supporters to the bench. This tendency is less pronounced now than it was 50 years ago, but it is still significant. Reformers have not been able to eliminate the partisan character of judicial appointments, but they have managed to curb the most serious abuses. It is now generally the practice for the ministers of justice, who take responsibility for these appointments, to have their potential nominees screened by a non-partisan body of legal experts. These experts will designate as "unqualified" any candidates they think unsuited to the position, and it is very rare for a minister to appoint anyone so designated.

In recent times, however, the movement for reform has turned in the opposite direction. Observers of the judiciary are quick to point out that in many cases, especially cases involving judicial review of the Constitution, judges are making decisions that have significant political consequences. Moreover, as we saw in Chapter 5, it appears that many of these decisions are of necessity made on political (or moral–political) rather than legal grounds. This leads many observers to ask why a small number of unelected (and largely unknown) judges should have the power to make fundamental, and often irrevocable, political decisions for Canada. That in turn leads them to press for changes to the current judicial regime.

It has now been conceded by all relevant parties, for example, that provincial governments ought to have some input into the appointment of Supreme Court justices. As we saw in Chapter 4, those judges have to make rulings about the respective powers of the federal and provincial governments under Sections 91 and 92 of *CA 1867*. In the past it was assumed that Supreme Court judges were non-partisan professionals who could be trusted to make those rulings in an impartial manner, even though they owed their positions on the court to the federal government. Now, however, it is generally supposed that division of powers cases are at least to some extent inherently political rather than legal matters. This fact makes it necessary to alter a regime in which one of the parties to those cases — the federal government — has exclusive control over appointments to the court that has the final say on those cases. It was only logical that in both the Meech Lake and Charlottetown constitutional accords, it was agreed that Ottawa should share the power of Supreme Court appointments with the provincial governments. This process would allow each level of government to veto the appointment to the court of anyone whose views on federalism were unacceptable to it.

But it is the adoption of the Charter of Rights and Freedoms that has led to the most radical calls for politicizing the appointment of the judiciary. In Charter cases, judges have been compelled to decide whether Canada should have laws against euthanasia, whether Sunday shopping should be permitted, whether the government should be allowed to permit cruise missile testing, and other similar questions. Because these are questions to which there may be only political answers, it is now frequently suggested that the judges who make those decisions must somehow be politically accountable. The most radical means of achieving political accountability is to make the judges directly responsible to the voters by making their positions elected rather than appointed. This option has few supporters because it is generally recognized that an elected judiciary would have little independence from voters and would thus be less than fully impartial. A more common proposal is to copy the American practice of subjecting nominees for Supreme Court positions to examination by the legislative branch of the regime. In theory, this is meant to allow the public to find out ahead of time what political views the nominee would bring to the bench, and to block the appointment of nominees whose views are deemed undesirable.

There are a number of problems with such proposals. In the first place, it is not clear that parliamentarians will be able to find out exactly what a nominee's political views are. As the American experience indicates, potential judges are reluctant to commit themselves to specific positions in response to hypothetical questions, for they realize that this will compromise their ability to deal with particular cases in an impartial fashion. They therefore tend to be highly evasive when answering such questions before screening committees. Moreover, one has to consider how the American approach would work in the substantially different Canadian regime. The United States has a relatively weak party system in that Democrats will often vote for Republican proposals and vice versa. It is therefore common for the Supreme Court nominees of a Democratic president to be supported by Republican senators. In Canada's highly disciplined party system, on the other hand, MPs almost always vote according to a party line. Would this not lead to a partisan examination of Canadian Supreme Court nominees in which government members automatically vote for the nominee and opposition members automatically vote against? If so, what purpose would the process serve? Finally, one has to wonder if such a process would not serve to make the judges themselves highly partisan. After all, if Parliament has examined their political beliefs and found them acceptable, why should they feel any restraint about imposing those beliefs on Canadians when they make their rulings?

Key Terms

precedents
stare decisis
reference procedure
impartiality
judicial independence
integrated judicial system
inferior courts
superior courts

Section 92 courts
Section 96 courts
Section 101 courts
JCPC
majority opinion
dissenting opinion
concurring opinion

Part four: Participation

Elections

9.1 Elections and Representation
9.2 Canada's Electoral System
9.3 The Effects of SMP
9.4 Proportional Representation
9.5 Voting in Canada

9.1 Elections and Representation

We learned in Chapter 1 that the Canadian regime is not a direct democracy but a representative democracy. This means that the central democratic mechanism of our regime is elections. Section 3 of *CA 1982* entrenches the most important of our democratic rights in the following language:

> Every citizen of Canada has a right to vote in an election of members of the House of Commons or of a legislative assembly and to be qualified for membership therein.

To understand the significance of these rights, it is important to consider them in light of the basic principles of responsible government. We have seen that in responsible government, the regime obtains its democratic legitimacy by virtue of the fact that those who exercise political authority are in some way accountable to the citizens who form the electorate. Our members of Parliament are directly accountable to us in that they must be periodically re-elected in order to remain in office. The prime minister and cabinet are accountable to us indirectly in that they must always maintain the confidence of the House of Commons we have elected directly. Elections to the House of Commons thus constitute the democratic linchpin of the regime because they ensure that those who make political decisions will in some sense represent the will or interests of the electorate.

But how exactly do the politicians "represent" the voters? What exactly is meant by the term representation? It is important to consider these questions with some care if we are to understand properly the logic of our elections. In democratic theory, there are at least three main concepts of representation. According to the first view, elected representatives are seen as **delegates**, that is, spokespersons who faithfully transmit the views of the majority of the people who elect them. A second interpretation treats representatives as **trustees**, people to whom we "entrust" the responsibilities of government. In this view, our representatives are elected for their character and judgment and are free to decide for themselves how to vote on each issue. A third concept of representation emphasizes the role of the representative as a **party member**. According to this view, the task of our representatives is to be loyal supporters of the policies advocated by their party. It should be obvious that these three concepts of representation are to some extent contradictory. On any given issue, it is likely that an MP would vote one way as a loyal party member and a different way as a delegate speaking for his or her local constituents. Acting as a trustee and voting according to his or her conscience, the MP might favour yet another alternative.

Which of these models of representation do we use in Canada? This is a question for which there is no official answer. The Constitution is silent on the matter, and that perhaps explains why Canadians often seem confused about it. Some will tell you that they vote for the party (or perhaps the party leader), while others claim to vote based on the personal qualities of their local candidates. Still, consideration of the logic of responsible government will allow us to draw some general inferences about how our representatives are supposed to represent us.

We know that responsible government turns out, in practice, to be government by a cabinet that is accountable to the House of Commons. Because the cabinet is not elected directly by the voters, it is important that we elect the House of Commons in such a way as to draw the strongest link possible between the voters and the cabinet. This means that our representation must, for the most part, be party representation. The idea of party representation forms the basis of the concept of a **mandate**. If it is assumed that the voters elected their MPs primarily on the basis of party affiliation, then the party which is called on to form the government may reasonably infer that the electorate has endorsed the general line of policy that it proposed in the election campaign. The party may thus claim that it has a "democratic mandate" to carry out that line of policy. If our MPs were elected primarily as delegates or trustees, there would be no such mandate. The strongest link between the electorate and its government would be severed, leaving the government less accountable to the people than we think it should be.[1]

This is not to say, however, that there is no room for the delegate and trustee models of representation in Canada. It should not be forgotten that MPs have an opportunity for full and free debate on matters within the parliamentary caucus. Voters may therefore reasonably expect their MP to speak in accordance with his or her judgment (trustee model) or on behalf of the constituents (delegate model) in that setting. But they probably should not expect their MP to vote against a position taken by his or her party once the caucus has made up its mind.

Another issue that emerges when we consider the matter of representation is the question of who can represent us. According to the **microcosm** theory of representation, legislative bodies are fully representative *only* if the assembly is a microcosm of society as a whole. For example, if 51% of the population is female, then 51% of the representatives ought to be female. Similarly, if the population is composed of diverse ethnic groups, the assembly should reflect that diversity. The microcosm theory has always played some role in the Canadian regime. As we saw in Chapter 6, the prime minister is expected to form a cabinet that reflects our country's diversity not only in geographic terms, but also in terms of religion, ethnicity, language, and sex. The microcosm theory is also becoming increasingly influential in deciding who is to be selected to serve on the Supreme Court of Canada. In recent times, there has been some discussion of reforming our electoral system in order to have our Parliament mirror more closely the social composition of the regime. During the negotiations leading to the Charlottetown Accord, for example, it was proposed that half the seats in any elected Senate should be reserved for women.

---

1 We suggested, in Chapter 1, that the Fathers of Confederation would not have insisted on maintaining such a direct link between the voters and the government. It is obvious that Canadians' thinking on this point has evolved over time. While Canadians maintain a belief in the virtues of indirect (representative) government, we do insist that the government should be accountable to the electorate in a meaningful way.

There are, however, some serious questions to be raised about the microcosm theory of representation. First, who would decide what the politically relevant characteristics of society are? How do we determine which groups get special representation and which do not? Second, how is a system to be designed to ensure that those characteristics are indeed represented? It would be easy enough to ensure there is an equal number of men and women in Parliament; we could simply elect one of each in every riding. But what about other groups? Finally, there is a deeper philosophical question: is it true that the interests of various groups can be represented only by members of those groups?

9.2 Canada's Electoral System

Political institutions are not neutral. They affect the way politics is conducted. Electoral institutions, in particular, can play a substantial role in determining who wins and who loses an election, how strong different parties will be, and what types of party are likely to succeed. It is therefore important to understand what kind of electoral system Canada uses and to consider what impact that system might have on the country's political life. We take up the former point in this section and the latter in Section 9.3.

The design of an electoral system will depend on three main factors. The first is the question of electoral districts. Will the country be divided up into a number of electoral districts, or will the voters all vote in a single national election? Second is the number of representatives. What is the optimum number of representatives for the legislative body? If there are too few, that body may not be sufficiently representative of the population. If there are too many, it may become dysfunctional. (Imagine a House of Commons with 10,000 MPs!) Furthermore, if the electoral system is based on multiple districts, one has to ask if there will be one member elected per district or multiple-member districts. (One might want double-member districts to ensure that each district is represented by one man and one woman, for example, or by more than one party.) Finally, there is the question of the method of electing representatives. How is the actual voting to be structured? Does the person with the most votes (a **plurality**) win, or must the winner have a majority of votes? Does the elector simply choose one candidate, or does the voter rank the candidates in order of preference?

The preamble to *CA 1867* specifies that Canada is to have a constitution "similar in Principle to that of the United Kingdom." In addition to this Constitution, we also adopted the same type of electoral system. Like Great Britain, then, Canada has what is usually referred to as the single-member plurality **(SMP)** system. This is an electoral system in which the country is divided into a number of electoral districts (informally called **ridings** or **constituencies)**, each of which has one representative. That representative is elected by a plurality of votes rather than a majority. A winning candidate will therefore often have less than 50 per cent of the votes cast in the district. For this reason, the system is sometimes referred to as **first-past-the-post**.

Section 37 of *CA 1867* specifies how many MPs there will be from each province. By extension, this should tell us how many electoral districts there will be. But Sections 51 and 52 provide for a readjustment of these numbers after each decennial census of the population. The current distribution of seats/electoral districts is listed in Figure 9.1.

FIG. 9.1   **Distribution of Seats in the House of Commons**

Atlantic Canada		32
	Prince Edward Island	4
	Nova Scotia	11
	New Brunswick	10
	Newfoundland	7
Central Canada		178
	Ontario	103
	Quebec	75
Western Canada		88
	Manitoba	14
	Saskatchewan	14
	Alberta	26
	British Columbia	34
Northern Canada		3
	North West Territories	1
	Nunavut	1
	Yukon	1
Total:		301

In order to respect the democratic principle of "one-person, one vote," Canada's electoral districts are designed to be roughly equal in population. At the last redistribution of seats, the average electoral district had about 80,000 people. But it is impossible, and even undesirable, to insist that every constituency be exactly the same size. Notice, for example, that making the electoral districts equal in population will make them unequal in geographical size. One will find 80,000 people in a very small area in Toronto, but it may take the northern quarter of Saskatchewan to create a district with that population. A constituency that size may be too large for an individual MP to represent effectively. In order to keep the geographical size of constituencies reasonable, it is not uncommon to create electoral districts with smaller than average populations in remote areas. Deviations in the size of electoral districts are also imposed by Section 51A of *CA 1867*. Designed to provide protection for the smaller provinces, this section declares that no province shall have fewer MPs than its number of senators. Because of Section 51A, PEI is guaranteed four MPs (though in terms of population, it deserves only one). Similarly, New Brunswick must always have ten MPs, though its current population would warrant only seven.[1]

9.3   The Effects of SMP

Our use of a single-member plurality system has important consequences for electoral politics in Canada. SMP divides our voting into 301 separate elections. It then awards seats in the House of Commons only to those who come first in each of the electoral districts. These arrangements will generally produce results marked by a wide discrepancy between the distribution of votes and the distribution of seats.

To see how this may be so, let us consider a hypothetical example. Imagine a Canadian election with only three parties, Parties A, B, and C. Suppose that on voting day, Party A gets 34 per cent of the total votes in Canada, Party B gets 33 per cent, and Party C also gets 33 per cent. This would appear to be the closest election in Canadian history. But what happens if the overall ratio of support (34/33/33) is consistent right across the country? Under our SMP system, Party A would end up with all 301 seats (it would win each constituency 34-33-33) and Parties B and C would get none! Under SMP, then, one party could get

---

1   Note that the effect of the amended section 51 of *CA 1867* is to ensure that no province will ever have fewer seats in the House of Commons than it had in 1985, which is when this section came into force.

100 per cent of the seats in the House of Commons even though a large majority of the electorate (66 per cent) voted for someone else. Furthermore, the votes of those 66 per cent would, in a manner of speaking, be wasted.

The example cited above is an extreme one, but Canadian political history contains cases that are similar in principle. In the 1987 provincial elections in New Brunswick, for example, the Liberal Party under the leadership of Frank McKenna received about 60 per cent of the total vote. Because that support was relatively consistent across the province, the Liberals won all 58 seats in the New Brunswick Legislature. And despite winning almost 40 per cent of the votes, the Progressive Conservatives and the NDP got no seats at all.

The New Brunswick provincial election of 1987 demonstrates dramatically a characteristic that is typical, in lesser degree, of all Canadian elections. SMP systematically favours the leading national party with the widest distribution of voters. Such a party will almost always receive a larger percentage of seats than its percentage of the popular vote in the "winner-take-all" format of SMP. The historical record shows that since World War I, the leading national party generally obtains around 45 per cent of the votes. But thanks to our electoral system, 45 per cent of the vote consistently yields the leading party 60 or even 70 per cent of the seats. This is a significant fact, for it means that it is the SMP electoral system that is responsible for the creation of majority governments in Canada. Only three of the 24 elections since World War I have given a single party more than 50 per cent of the votes (1940, 1958, and 1984). Yet 16 of those elections have resulted in majority governments.

The impact of the SMP system is felt not only by the leading party. Obviously, if the leading party benefits from SMP, it does so at the expense of the other parties. But the other parties are not all treated the same way by SMP. Our electoral system favours small regional parties but works against the less popular national parties. A moment's reflection on the logic of SMP shows why. Because of SMP's "winner-take-all" approach, votes are wasted unless the party comes in first. This means that secondary parties will succeed only if their support is heavily concentrated in key areas. If their support is spread evenly throughout the country, they are unlikely to win many seats. The 1993 elections provide a good illustration of the point. The Bloc Québécois (BQ) received 14 per cent of the popular vote, but its support was concentrated entirely in the province of Quebec. As a result, the Bloc captured 54 seats—18 per cent of the total. The Progressive Conservatives, on the other hand, actually received more votes than the Bloc— 16 per cent of the total. Yet because the Conservatives' votes were spread right across the country, they rarely had enough support to win. Though they had more votes than the BQ, the Progressive Conservatives won only two seats—less than one twenty-fifth of the Bloc's total!

SMP strengthens regionalism in Canada not only by promoting regional parties; it also intensifies regional strengths and weaknesses within our broadly national parties. Because of its "winner-take-all" rules, SMP systematically underrepresents certain regions in each party caucus. In the 1980 election, for example, over 20 per cent of Westerners voted for Liberal candidates. Yet because the Liberal candidates consistently came in behind the Conservative or NDP candidates, the Liberals ended up with only two seats in the whole region (about 3 per cent). This made it difficult for the incoming Liberal prime minister, Pierre Trudeau, to give Western Canada adequate representation in his cabinet. During the 1970s and early 1980s, a similar pattern characterized electoral results in Quebec. There the Conservative Party routinely won a not insubstantial share of the vote, but almost no seats.

A look at the 2000 election results shows that the regionalization of party representation continues today. For example, the Liberals won 100 out of 103 seats in Ontario. This is obviously a far greater percentage of the seats than it is of the votes. The same holds true for the Canadian Alliance in Western Canada, which won 62 of the 82 seats. In both of these cases, the regionally dominant party had nowhere near such a commanding share of the popular vote. It was our SMP electoral system that transformed strong popular support into a near monopoly of House of Commons seats.

To summarize, we may say that the SMP electoral system has four major effects on electoral politics. First, it creates artificial majority governments by rewarding the largest national party with more seats than it "deserves." Second, it handicaps smaller national parties (for example, the NDP) by giving them a smaller share of seats than their share of the popular vote. Third, it encourages regionalism by fostering the growth of parties that focus on regional interests and concerns. Fourth, it encourages regionalism by magnifying the regional strengths and weaknesses of our national parties.

9.4 Proportional Representation

Political observers who are troubled by some of the effects of SMP have advocated the adoption of an alternative electoral system, called **proportional representation** (PR). Proportional representation is used in many liberal democracies. It exists in a variety of forms, some of them rather complicated. The one most commonly proposed for adoption in Canada is known as the **party list system**.

In this system, each party prepares a list of its candidates in rank order. Electoral districts are abolished, so that instead of holding 301 elections, we hold a single nation-wide election. In this single election, the electorate votes for parties, rather than candidates. When the results are tabulated, the number of seats each party wins is determined by the proportion of the vote it received. If, for example, Party A received 20 per cent of the vote, it would receive exactly 20 per cent of the seats available. On the assumption that we keep 301 seats, this would mean that Party A gets 60 seats. Those seats would then be awarded to the first 60 candidates on Party A's list.

Advocates of PR argue that this system is fairer than SMP. Parties get seats in proportions that mirror exactly the preferences indicated by the voters. As opposed to SMP, this electoral system does not "distort" the electorate's voting pattern by favouring certain types of parties and disadvantaging others. PR is also said to be fairer in that it eliminates the phenomenon of "wasted ballots." Under PR, every vote has an impact in shaping the composition of the House of Commons.

Another point raised by advocates of PR is that it provides for more diverse representation within each party caucus. We have seen that SMP tends to magnify the regional strengths and weaknesses of each party. PR offers a solution to this type of problem. Because parties are free to structure their lists as they like, each party can arrange its list to ensure that all regions will have adequate representation within the caucus. Similarly, the party leadership can use its control over the composition of the list to ensure adequate representation in the House of Commons for groups that are traditionally underrepresented there—women, for instance.

It should be noted, however, that PR also entails certain disadvantages. The charge most frequently levelled against it is that it leads to political instability. As we have seen, the Canadian electorate rarely gives any party a majority of votes. It is our SMP electoral system that is responsible for transforming a mere plurality of votes (nation-wide) into a majority of seats in the House of Commons. Precisely because PR gives each party seats based on its proportion of the overall vote, the adoption of PR would make majority governments extremely rare. Minority governments or coalition governments, which are generally less stable, would become the norm.

Connected with the problem of unstable government is the allegation that PR will lead to a more divisive politics by facilitating the emergence of small single-issue parties and parties with non-mainstream agendas. Such parties are generally shut out of the House of Commons by our SMP system, which awards seats only to those parties strong enough to come first in some riding. Under PR, however, it is likely that an anti-abortion party or an animal rights party — or even a frivolous group like the Rhinoceros Party — would be able to scrape together enough votes nation-wide to earn a seat or two in the House of Commons. In a minority government situation where the party in power is in danger of losing a vote, the government party might have to cut a deal with one of these minor parties in order to stay in office. The tail would then wag the dog as the minor party dictated its terms to the party in power.

A third major problem with PR is that local constituencies would no longer have an MP of their own. A well-structured party list might ensure that all regions have adequate representation, but it would not guarantee an MP for each of our electoral districts. Ontario, for example, would likely be dominated by representatives from Toronto. The province of New Brunswick might have two MPs from Moncton and three from Saint John, but nobody from the other two-thirds of the province. And even in those two cities, the link between the voters and the MPs would be much weaker than it is today, for the MPs would owe their positions in the House of Commons not to the support of the local electorate, but to the party bosses in Ottawa who put their names high on the party list. For these reasons, the adoption of PR would mean that Canadians would no longer be able to count on having a representative in Ottawa to listen to their concerns or to help them when they have problems with the government.

Although in constitutional law it is the governor general who dissolves Parliament and calls new elections, the governor general does so on the "advice" of the prime minister. If the prime minister's party controls only a minority of votes in the House of Commons, the House can force an election at any time by voting a lack of confidence in the government. Such a vote would compel the prime minister either to resign or, more likely, to advise the governor general to dissolve Parliament and call elections. In the more typical case of majority government, however, the prime minister has a free hand to determine the timing of elections, within certain limits. Section 4(1) of *CA 1982* stipulates that no parliament is to last longer than five years. Prime ministers rarely wait the full five years because there is a general expectation in Canada that elections ought to be held somewhere in the fourth year of a parliament. If a prime minister has waited five years to ask for a dissolution, that is usually a sign that the government is afraid to face the electorate. On the other hand, prime ministers are sometimes tempted to ask for a dissolution after less than four years if their government is particularly popular or the opposition is particularly weak.

Once the governor general dissolves Parliament, **general elections** follow immediately. (We speak of "general elections" to describe nationwide elections. A **by-election** is held in a single constituency to fill a seat vacated mid-way through a parliament by the death or resignation of an MP.) General elections are administered by a politically neutral civil servant called the **Chief Electoral Officer** who appoints a **Returning Officer** for each of the 301 electoral districts in Canada. Electoral districts are divided into smaller units called **polls**, each of which has about 250 voters. The returning officer for each electoral district will appoint a deputy returning officer and a couple of poll clerks to run the election at each poll.

The returning officer also appoints two **enumerators** for each poll; their task is to prepare the official voters' list for the poll. Under the Canada Elections Act, all citizens who are 18 years of age or older have the right to vote. (One notable exception is the Chief Electoral Officer, who has no vote. The returning officers are allowed to vote, but only in the case of a tie.) The preliminary voters' list must be ready 26 days before the election. Those who have been left off the list have 10 days to get their name added to it.

To have their names put on the ballot, candidates must present the returning officer with official nomination papers signed by 100 eligible voters from the constituency. (The candidates themselves do not have to be residents of the constituency, but it is generally a distinct liability to be a non-resident.) Candidates must also leave the returning officer a deposit of $1,000, a sum which is returned to all those who gain 15 per cent or more of the vote. The purpose of these two requirements is to discourage frivolous candidacies.

In order to minimize the influence that those with money might have on electoral outcomes, Canadian electoral laws place limits on the amount that a candidate may spend. They also provide substantial subsidies to those candidates who have won 15 per cent of the vote or more. The subsidies are not enough to pay for an entire campaign; candidates still need money from their national party, from local donations, and often from their own pockets, in order to mount an effective campaign. Still, these subsidies, combined with the legislated spending limits, serve to reduce the impact that candidates' private wealth (or the wealth of their supporters) might have on the electoral process.

A more complicated matter is the issue of third party advertising. The problem is well illustrated by the 1988 elections. It is widely believed that the victory of the Conservative Party, which backed free trade, was in some measure due to a massive advertising campaign conducted on its behalf by "big business." Parliament has attempted to limit this type of advertising. Its rationale has been that such advertising is inconsistent with the democratic principle of one person–one vote because it gives the wealthy more influence on elections than the less wealthy. Our courts have struck down Parliament's legislation, however, on the grounds that it violates Section 2 of the Charter.

Elections are normally held on a Monday. The polls are open for 12 hours in each of Canada's time zones. (The times are staggered to reduce the gap between the time the polls close on the East Coast and the time they close on the West Coast.) Lest the voters in the more Western time zones be influenced by the results of the voting in the East, our election laws forbid the broadcasting of any results in an area where the polls are still open. Due to advances in communication technology, however, this rule is becoming increasingly difficult to enforce.

Each party is permitted to have two **scrutineers** at the poll all day long to observe the process and to keep the candidates posted on whether known supporters have voted. Upon the closing of the poll, the votes are counted by the deputy returning officer while the scrutineers look on. The deputy returning officer then seals all the votes in the ballot box and sends them to the returning officer for an official count, which takes place over the next few days. But the deputy returning officer's unofficial count is immediately communicated to the returning officer, who passes the information on to the media. The unofficial results are thus generally known within approximately half an hour.

Key Terms

delegate model

trustee

party member

mandate

microcosm theory

plurality

SMP

riding

constituency

first-past-the-post

Proportional Representation

party list

general elections

by-election

Chief Electoral Officer

Returning Officer

poll

enumerators

scrutineers

Political Parties

10.1 Political Parties in the Canadian Regime

10.2 The Functions of Political Parties

10.3 Parties and Ideology

10.4 The Organization of Political Parties

10.5 The Canadian Party System

10.6 Canada's Federal Parties

10.7 Party Government and Party Politics

10.1 Political Parties in the Canadian Regime

Political parties are publicly organized groups of people who are motivated by some common set of political ideas and whose goal is to have their particular members win public office so that those ideas can be put into practice.

It is obvious to even the most casual observer that Canadian political life is dominated by political parties. Every Canadian parliament has been divided along party lines, and, except for a brief interlude during World War I, membership in every Canadian cabinet has been restricted to those who were members of the dominant political party at the time.[1] It is worth noting, however, that the dominant role of political parties is not something mandated by the constitution. *CA 1867* and *CA 1982* do not mention political parties. Nor could one claim that the role of political parties is a matter of constitutional convention: constitutional conventions are rules, and there is no rule requiring our MPs to be members of political parties. The truth of the matter is that the domi-

---

1 The "conscription crisis" of 1917 led to the formation of a "Union Government" that included all of the Conservative MPs and all of the Liberals who favoured conscription. Those Liberals who opposed conscription remained in opposition.

nant role of our political parties is simply a matter of need. We have political parties because they are useful (as we shall see in the next section) and because there is no law to prohibit them. One might compare the role of political parties in the Canadian regime to the role of the coach of a hockey team. There is nothing in the National Hockey League rule book that says a team must have a coach. Theoretically, a team could play without one. But, since every team finds that it is useful to have somebody directing the players, every team has a coach.

To be sure, fans will often think their team would be better off without its coach. So, too, do we often hear complaints to the effect that political parties constitute an impediment to reasonable, democratic, political life. The "party system" is accused of limiting our choices and stifling debate. It is blamed for focusing political deliberation on partisan advantage rather than the common good. Yet while Canadians often express frustration with the "party system," they almost never take advantage of their right to elect an "independent" candidate — a candidate with no party affiliation. It is well worth pondering why that is.

A lone MP in the House of Commons exercises little political power. While he or she may have a free hand to represent constituent interests, there is no party organization in the House that can wield the power necessary to effect, or at least influence, legislation. Our "independent" MP may be a noble lone voice in Ottawa, but he or she is unlikely to accomplish much within a political institution that runs on the principle of party discipline. An independent MP would be effective only in a House that actually banned party membership, yet a rule banning party membership would certainly be in violation of the right to freedom of association guaranteed by Section 2d of the Charter.

All things considered, the existence of political parties is a sign of a healthy democratic regime. Authoritarian and totalitarian forms of government usually move quickly to extinguish political opposition by means of outlawing opposition parties. They concentrate all power in the hands of the state by means of imposing a one-party state. In Frank Underhill's words:

> The acid test of freedom in a state is whether power and office can pass peaceably from one political party to another. "Her Majesty's Opposition" is just as necessary to free government as "Her Majesty's Government."[1]

---

1   Frank Underhill, *Canadian Political Parties* (Ottawa: The Canadian Historical Association Booklets, No.8, 1964) 3.

Liberal democratic party politics is workable because the parties agree on at least one thing: different political parties have a right to exist, and should one party win an election, it has a legitimate right to rule until the next election. Parties are "parts" of the regime. Party politics is, therefore, non-revolutionary: it works because every party agrees on the fundamental principles of the regime.[1]

10.2 The Functions of Political Parties

In their efforts to win political power, parties perform five valuable functions. First, they recruit people into the party as members and, sometimes, as candidates. This recruitment function is obviously crucial, for modern democracies are constantly imperilled by apathy and lack of civic participation. The dangers of what Alexis de Tocqueville described as "individualism"—where people tend to withdraw into their individual lives of work, family, and friends, and pay little attention to political affairs—are fairly obvious. Democracy means the rule of the people, and it is endangered when the people lose their taste for politics. The parties supply us with our political leaders through national leadership conventions, our candidates by means of constituency elections, and the vast number of campaign workers needed to run all the aspects of a modern election.

Second, parties raise money for their organizations and election campaigns. This is still, by and large, a private activity. It is regulated by election finance laws. It is worth considering that if we did not have political parties to raise much of the money for elections, the costs would have to be borne by the taxpayer.

Third, parties identify, represent, and balance the diverse interests of Canadians. This process, often referred to as **interest aggregation**, is crucial to the healthy functioning of a liberal democracy. It is rare that Canadian voters have a single common interest. In most cases, policy that is advantageous for one group ultimately comes at the expense of others. Fiscal transfers to have-not provinces are paid for by the more prosperous provinces; companies in Winnipeg compete with companies in Montreal for lucrative government contracts. If Canada had no political parties, our MPs would be free to vote for whatever was in the best interests of their own constituents. But this would ultimately mean that the most powerful political constituencies—Ontario and Quebec—

---

1   See Giovani Sartori, *Parties and Party Systems*, Vol.1 (Cambridge: Cambridge University Press, 1976).

would make all the rules to their own advantage. Because the major national political parties have to seek votes in all constituencies—French and English, men and women, East and West, business and labour—they are forced to hammer out compromise positions which offer a relatively fair deal to all the major categories of voters. If we did not have political parties to perform this process of interest aggregation, our regime would likely be much less successful in its pursuit of fair treatment for all Canadians.

In the process of attempting to aggregate interests and integrate them into a national whole, the parties formulate and influence public policy. Normally they design their policies at policy conventions, large gatherings of rank and file members who debate the current political issues and design or revise the party's main policies in light of these debates.

Finally, parties educate people about political life. Party membership provides an education in holding political office by means of providing elected offices within the party. Often a candidate has served as an elected member of a constituency organization before ever running for nomination. Parties meet to discuss policy and ideas and hold regular policy conventions. The educational function of parties thus extends beyond the party members to citizens at large, who benefit from media coverage and commercial advertising of party policy. It culminates in the way parties help to structure voter choice. The parties accomplish this by attempting to persuade voters to vote for them. One need only imagine an election without parties to see how essential their function has become.

10.3 Parties and Ideology

Parties are usually built on the basis of a loose set of fundamental political principles, commonly referred to as an **ideology**. Those principles are then used as the basis for generating ideas about the purposes of government, how it should be organized, and what public policies should be implemented.

Some might argue that this description is too "idealistic." They would instead emphasize that political parties are groups of people who are motivated primarily by the goal of winning public office so that they can obtain political power to serve their own interests. We would not disagree. Like most of us, those who enter directly into political life are rarely saints. And politics is inseparable from the desire for the benefits and honours that come with holding public office. In other words, democratic political parties are **pragmatic**. They are organizations designed to win elections, and they often compromise, if not design, their political principles to facilitate electoral success.[1]

The political parties in liberal democratic regimes are therefore best understood as attempts to serve both the ideal and the practical. They must steer a moderate, middle course between the extremes of powerless idealism on the one hand and the cynically unprincipled pursuit of power on the other. There is no point in pursuing ideals that are attractive to only a very few voters. Conversely, the public will soon sour on the party or politician that is perceived to be without principles, often labelling them opportunistic and cynical. What we seem to want most are practical and pragmatic politicians who have political principles. In other words, we demand that our parties constantly manage the tension between theory and practice, between high political principle and workable public policy.

Most ideological questions turn on the issue of preservation and change. On most issues, there will always be those who favour change and those who prefer the status quo to any proposed change. One almost always finds those who argue that conserving what we now have is the best course of action, versus those who argue that we can make progress and hence improve our present lot by following a different course. In other words, one almost always finds "conservatives" and "progressives" in any political arena.

This dichotomy between those who favour the present and those who favour change is best explained in terms of two factors. First, it seems to be a nearly universal human phenomenon that within any group you will find that some people are more inclined to have conservative dispositions than others. Some people value caution and prudence, while others are more daring and willing to take a chance. In other words, party politics seems to be rooted in the different dispositions of human beings. Second, it is often the case that there will always be those who have a vested interest in maintaining things as they are, as opposed to those whose interests would be best served by some new political arrangements. For example, it is hard to imagine professional

---

1   There are, of course, some parties that are uncompromisingly committed to a specific set of well defined political ideas. But where these parties do not hold power, they often forego political success by maintaining ideological purity. Where they do hold power, they often maintain ideological purity by refusing to tolerate any meaningful debate or dissent.

athletes being in favour of a law that would limit their income to the salary of the highest paid police officers.

In the years following Confederation, the chief ideological issue dividing the leading parties was federalism. The Conservatives, who were in power, favoured a strong national government. The Liberals, in opposition, espoused the idea of greater "provincial rights." In the last decades of the twentieth century this ideological difference between the parties remains. Oddly, however, the two parties have switched sides. The Conservatives are now the party of decentralization, while the Liberals stand for a strong federal government.

These days, the main ideological division between our parties is on socio-economic matters. The dominant ideology at the time of Confederation (an ideology shared by both the Liberal and Conservative parties) might best be described as classical liberalism. Classical liberals emphasize the importance of liberty (freedom from governmental interference) and a free market economy. They also value equality, but they understand it to mean primarily equality of opportunity. In Canada, people or parties are labelled "conservative" when they are inclined to conserve the original principles of classical liberalism. The term "progressive," on the other hand, usually applies to "socialists" who advocate not only equality of opportunity, but greater equality of condition. In the Canadian context, equality of condition is pursued mainly by the redistribution of wealth through the tax system and through state funding of social programs. Because the creation of greater equality of condition usually requires intervention by government, progressives are generally less concerned about "liberty" than are conservatives. In general, they favour public regulation or even ownership of natural resources and key industries, and of economic institutions like banks.

Over the years, the main source of "progressive" ideas in Canadian politics has been the New Democratic Party (NDP). The Progressive Conservative Party has been the party most closely identified with classical liberalism, but as its hybrid name suggests, even the Conservatives have embraced some of the progressive measures espoused by the NDP. The Liberal Party of Canada generally stands between the other two and often finds itself divided between a progressive wing and a conservative wing.

You will recall that a national election in Canada is really a collection of 301 separate, simultaneous elections in the various electoral constituencies. Political parties are therefore organized at the constituency level. Each of Canada's major national parties has local constituency organizations, which are set up for a number of purposes: attracting members into the party; raising money for the next election; choosing a candidate to run in the riding; and sending members to the provincial and national conventions to debate policy ideas, elect party officials, and choose the party leader.

Each constituency has its own party association, with a constitution and an executive charged with responsibility for the association's ongoing business. Between elections, the association's full membership may meet only once or twice a year. Constituency organizations become more active at times when they must select delegates to a national convention or when an election is approaching.

Because Canada's parties are designed primarily for winning elections, they are organized in a way that gives the party leadership the power to set election strategy. The party leader usually plays the key role in providing the campaign platform, choosing the campaign strategy, and setting the party's course for the election campaign. Thus, the leader is usually the one who gets the credit for electoral success and who usually pays the price for electoral defeat. It is not unusual that a major defeat will soon be followed by a re-organization of the party, which often includes a leadership convention.

How party leaders are chosen affects how much political power they wield over the party. At the turn of the century, the parties still chose their leaders in a caucus meeting. Those members who were elected to Parliament would meet and choose who would lead them. This process of caucus leadership selection left individual MPs with some power over their leader, since he owed his position to them.

With the advent of the party leadership convention, the power of party leaders has grown considerably. The leadership convention process is one in which the party sends a fixed number of delegates to a convention and they in turn elect a leader. Many delegates will be representatives of their constituency associations. Others may be delegates representing various party associations. Still others will be MPs, senators, and elected members from provincial assemblies. All told, there may be 4000 to 5000 delegates at a convention. By a process of secret ballot, they vote on a leader from among a number of candidates. The usual procedure is for successive votes in which the field is reduced by dropping the candidate who has the fewest votes from the ballot until one candidate wins a majority.

The convention model greatly increases the power of the party leader over his or her caucus. Because the party leader no longer owes her position to the caucus but to the party organization as a whole, she can speak for the party over and against the caucus members who speak only for their individual constituencies. This system has been the dominant mode of leadership selection for most of this century. Recently, however, a new and even more democratic process of selecting a leader has begun to be used: the all-member vote.[1] Instead of a convention in which delegates represent the views of all the party's members, parties have elections in which each member gets to vote directly for a leadership candidate. The all-member vote system thus marks a continuation of the trend toward making the leadership selection process more democratic. Whether this new process is more likely to produce better or more popular leaders remains to be seen.

Of the three levels of government—federal, provincial, and local—the only level where party politics does not dominate is the local. Even there, party politics has slowly crept in. In some cities, we now find slates of candidates running under the banner of a political party, and one often finds that there are close, behind-the-scene links between civic politicians and provincial parties.

For the most part, however, Canada's parties are organized at both the provincial and federal levels. In some parties, the organizational links between the federal and provincial parties are strong; in others the federal and provincial parties are completely independent of each other. It is also important to note that it is not unusual for a party to be politically successful in a provincial election, but not in a federal election even within the same province. Voters often distinguish between the provincial and federal wings of the same party and may at the same time like one and reject the other. In the 2000 federal election, for example, the Conservative party did not elect a single member in Ontario even though the Ontario Conservative party controls the provincial legislature.

---

1 In recent years, variations of this new method have been used by the Canadian Alliance and the Progressive Conservative parties.

At each level, the party organization consists of two component parts: the parliamentary wing and the extra-parliamentary wing. The former consists of all those party members who have a seat in Parliament; the latter is made up of the party executive at the constituency, provincial, and national levels (see Figure 10.1).

FIG. 10.1 **Party Organization**

Parliamentary Wing	Extra-Parliamentary Wing
Parliamentary Leader	Party President
Caucus	National Executive
	Constituency Association

In Canadian political parties, the parliamentary wing wields power that far exceeds its size. This disproportion is to be expected, for the elected MPs necessarily view the party's policies and public positions in terms of what is conducive to being re-elected. Moreover, they must respond to the ongoing political events in the House of Commons. Therefore, the parliamentary wing of the party is forced to formulate policies and take positions long before the next policy convention can decide party policy. Thus, while parties never cease discussing ways and means of making the parliamentary wing more responsive to the extra-parliamentary wing, such reforms will always be blunted by the reality of electoral politics. Canada's parties are electoral machines designed primarily for the purpose of winning elections. To the extent that the parliamentary wing of the party is best positioned to guide the party toward electoral success, it will continue to exercise a dominant role within the party.

10.5 The Canadian Party System

One of the distinguishing features of liberal democracies is that they allow, and in many ways encourage, the development of political parties. Liberal democratic regimes are based on the principles of freedom of thought, freedom of association, and political participation. Because they protect and promote a diversity of political opinion, liberal democracies are of necessity home to a diversity of political parties.

For these reasons, Canada has a **multi-party system** rather than a

single-party system. In many countries, only one political party is legally sanctioned. China, for example, allows no other political party than the Communist Party. The idea underlying such a system is that the public interest is best served by working out public policy within the party rather than allowing diverse parties to develop competing alternatives to public policy. Canada's multi-party system allows for the development of different parties that represent different ideological positions, represent very different political interests, and put forward different political agendas. This diversity was evident in our most recent elections. At the time of the thirty-seventh general elections in 2000, 11 political parties were legally registered by Elections Canada. Nine of these parties—including the Green Party, the National Party, and the Libertarian Party—were strong enough to run candidates in at least 50 constituencies.

Of course many of Canada's registered parties have little real importance; none of the three mentioned above has ever won a single seat in the House of Commons. In reality, Canadian politics has been dominated by two parties: the Liberals and the Progressive Conservatives. This domination is to a large extent the result of Canada's electoral system. As we saw in Chapter 9, Single-Member Plurality systematically over-rewards large national parties that have broad appeal. At the same time, it systematically thwarts new national parties and national parties with non-centrist ideologies. SMP thereby fosters a multi-party system dominated by two giant **brokerage** parties, parties that espouse similar middle-of-the-road ideologies and that try to appeal to every region, every ethnic group, and every social class.

In the early stages of Canadian history, the Liberals and the Conservatives were the only two parties in our multi-party system. In every election since World War I, some "third party" has tried to break the monopoly of the two old parties. The emergence of third parties has led to what is commonly called a "two-and-a-half party" phase in our multi-party system.

Regionally-based protest parties have had the greatest short-term successes as third parties (as one would expect under SMP). In the 1921 elections, for example, the Progressive Party actually won more seats than the Conservatives. But regional protest parties are by their very nature short-term phenomena. Because they are merely regional, they cannot hope to win a majority. Their supporters eventually realize that in a regime based on responsible government, it is not terribly useful to be constantly sitting on the opposition side of the House of Commons. Support for the Progressives declined dramatically over the next few elections. By 1935, they were unable to elect a single member, and the remnants of the party merged with the Conservatives a few years later. The 1935 elections marked the emergence of another "third party," the Commonwealth Cooperative Federation (CCF). The CCF was to some extent a regional protest party, but it was also a party with a distinctive ideology — democratic socialism. This party and its successor, the NDP, have been the major third party for much of the last 60 years. However, because of their non-mainstream ideology, they have never been serious contenders for national power, and their lack of popularity has been compounded by our SMP electoral system, under which they have always received a smaller proportion of parliamentary seats than their proportion of the vote.

Some observers believe that the 1993 elections may have marked the advent of a new phase in Canada's multi-party system. In those elections, one of the traditional brokerage parties (the Liberals) won a solid majority, but the other was handed a stunning defeat: the Progressive Conservatives came in fifth, winning a mere two seats. Two new parties had bolted ahead of the Conservatives. In second place was the Bloc Québécois with 54 seats, followed closely by the Reform Party with 52. The Conservatives again finished fifth in both the 1997 and 2000 elections. What do these results mean for the future of our party system?

Because responsible government and SMP place such a premium on victory, it is improbable that our multi-party system will settle in to a prolonged four- or five-party phase. It is more likely that the system is undergoing a short-term readjustment. The BQ is a regional protest party, and it is clear that, one way or another, it will not be a permanent fixture in Canadian politics. On the other hand, the Reform Party (now the Canadian Alliance) began as a regional protest party, but it aspires to replace the Progressive Conservatives as the national alternative to the Liberal Party. The question for the long term is whether the Canadian Alliance will be able to break out of its regional base. If it does, it will drive the Conservatives into extinction and take that party's place as the second national alternative. If it does not, it will inevitably go the way of the Progressive Party. In either case, it seems likely that our multi-party system will settle back into its two-and-a-half party phase in the near future.

The political parties in Canada began as colonial descendants of the British parliamentary tradition. By the early part of the nineteenth century, British politics had become dominated by the parties known as Whigs and Tories, soon to become the Liberals and Conservatives respectively. When Canada was granted responsible government in the 1840s, the colonial parliament soon divided into similar loose groupings: in English Canada we had the Reformers (or Clear Grits as they were sometimes called) and the Liberal-Conservatives; in French Canada one found the more democratic party known as the Rouges and the more traditional party favouring the interests of the wealthy oligarchy and the Church, called the Bleus. At Confederation, these groupings came together to form two new national parties.

A) *The Conservative Party*

One of these was the Conservative Party, which developed under Canada's first prime minister, John A. Macdonald. Macdonald was able to build his party out of a coalition of Liberal-Conservatives from Upper Canada and Bleu politicians from Quebec. Under Macdonald and his French-Canadian lieutenant George Etienne Cartier, the Conservative party dominated Canadian politics for the first 30 years after Confederation. The Conservatives put in place a "national policy" of protectionism against the United States, western expansion via the CPR, and strong central government. The party was not opposed to state intervention in the economy. Such intervention was seen as necessary for the development of Canada, and the party has therefore traditionally favoured state enterprises. In the 1940s, the Conservatives absorbed the remnants of the Progressive Party and adopted the somewhat paradoxical name, the Progressive Conservative Party. In recent years the Progressive Conservative Party has come to stand for less government control, a more decentralized federation giving more responsibility to the provinces, a stronger free-market economy, and a smaller government.

B) *The Liberal Party*

The second great party from the Confederation era was the Liberal Party. The Liberal Party emerged out of a coalition of Upper Canadian

Reformers and the Rouge politicians of Quebec. During the first years of Confederation, the Liberal party was united mainly by its opposition to the Macdonald Conservatives. It was not until Wilfred Laurier, Canada's first French-Canadian prime minister, that the Liberal party developed a coherent set of political ideas based on free trade and provincial rights. The Liberal Party has long been the national representative of the rights of French-Canadians and therefore developed the tradition of alternating its leadership between anglophones and francophones. The view that Canada was a compact between two nations — English and French — is one that has had far greater influence within the Liberal Party than the Conservative. The policies of official bilingualism and multiculturalism were instituted under the Liberal governments. In recent years, the Liberal Party has come to stand for the maintenance of a strong national government and welfare state. Like the Conservative Party, the Liberals favour global free trade and a strong free-market economy.

C) *The New Democratic Party*

Populism and regional protest have been permanent features of Canadian politics. The growth of protest parties in each of the country's regions has been a regular occurrence since Confederation. In Quebec, there was the Union Nationale, the Creditistes, and more recently the Bloc Québécois. The same holds true in Ontario, Western Canada, and, to a lesser extent, the Maritimes. The politics of regional protest led to the formation of the Progressives, Social Credit, and the Cooperative Commonwealth Federation (CCF). More recent developments are New Brunswick's Confederation of Regions Party (COR) and the national Reform Party. These protest parties have tended to be popular, grass-roots parties. They have emphasized greater party democracy and listening to the voices of ordinary citizens who feel they have been shut out of the major parties. But the politics of regional protest has had both egalitarian and libertarian expressions. Its egalitarian expression has been the major source of socialism in Canada.

The NDP is Canada's only important democratic socialist party. It originated in the regional protest politics of the CCF, which began in reaction to the collapse of the prairie economy in the 1920s, for which capitalist interests, located mainly in central Canada, were held responsible. The reaction against free-market capitalism and liberalism was therefore long associated with the concern that Canada was a country run by central Canada to serve the interests of central Canada. The Liberals and the Progressive Conservatives were thought to represent the interests of the ruling elite or capitalist class, as opposed to the working class of industrial workers and farmers. The CCF was formed as a party to represent the interests of the working class.

In 1961, the NDP was formed by combining the organizations of the CCF and the Canadian Labour Congress (CLC), Canada's most important labour organization. Uniting farmers and unionized labour, and having representation from all regions of the country, the NDP has since had moderate electoral success. It elected a high of 43 members in the 1988 election. It has formed the government in four provinces and the official Opposition in others.

D) *The Canadian Alliance*

Canada's newest major political party, the Canadian Alliance, was initially very successful. Founded by Preston Manning in the 1980s as the Reform Party, it began as a Western protest party based on the criticism that Canada's national political institutions systematically disadvantage that region. The party was, therefore, a strong advocate of Senate reform, which would give the four Western provinces a much stronger voice in Ottawa. Similarly, it advocated a restructuring of the federal division of powers, less redistribution of wealth by Ottawa, and less government regulation of the economy.

The Canadian Alliance was founded in 1998 as an attempt to unite the conservative political forces, split between Reform and the Progressive Conservative parties. The Alliance has taken over the old Reform policies and remains ardent in its desire for greater fiscal conservatism in government, particularly lower taxes.

Unlike the other major national parties, the Alliance seeks to win seats only in the national government. It further seeks to distinguish itself from what it often refers to as the "old-line parties" by its emphasis on the constituent responsibility of its members. This delegate view of representation is based on the idea that its elected members are primarily responsible to the people who elected them. They are expected to represent the views of their constituents and not simply the party. If they must vote against the views of the party and its leadership, so be it. Needless to say, this view has caused some difficulties for its current leader, Stockwell Day, in maintaining party discipline and hence unity.

E) *The Bloc Québécois*

The Bloc Québécois is an unusual political party in that it is dedicated to achieving independence for Quebec and hence to its own disappearance as a political party in Canadian politics. It came into existence after the failure of the Meech Lake Accord, when a handful of Quebec MPs quit the Conservative and Liberal caucuses and joined together to form a new party. The 1993 election transformed the Bloc from a small group of disaffected MPs into a major political party, with 54 seats in Quebec. Because it had won more seats than any other opposition party, it became "Her Majesty's Loyal Opposition," a somewhat ironical outcome.

One point that should not be overlooked is that the Bloc is in one way a typical regional political party. Because the electoral system rewards regional party strength disproportionately, the Bloc was able to transform what is a small amount of the national popular vote into a relatively large number of seats. Like all regional political parties in Canada, it is in part a creation of the electoral system.

Finally, it should be noted that it is Quebec nationalism rather than ideology that unites the members of the Bloc into a political party. While some of its members are socialists and others are pro-business, nationalist sentiment overrides the ordinary political divisions within the BQ caucus.

10.7 Party Government and Party Politics

Parliamentary government is party government, and Canadian politics is party politics. While we may, from time to time, complain about this, it is probably both necessary and good that it is so, for it is the clear division of MPs into parties that allows us to determine easily who has won a national election and will form the next government. The governor general's obligation—to ensure that Canada has a workable government in Parliament—is thus easy to discharge. Political parties provide us both with clear outcomes to elections as well as with the parliamentary leader who will become the prime minister. One need only imagine, for a moment, a scenario in which this was all undetermined. The public would have no way of telling who the prime minister would be, and it is likely that without party discipline governments would come and go with problematic frequency. Party leadership and party discipline are what make for stable parliamentary government. One is left to conclude that the only thing worse than party politics would be parliamentary government without parties.

This is not to say that party politics is simply good. Almost any observer of Canadian politics will soon notice troubling instances where party interests appear to take priority over national interests. Is the government of the day, which consists of the leadership of a particular political party, not always looking out for its future electoral interests at least as much as it is for the national interest?

A further question is the power of party leaders, both in and out of Parliament. Within Parliament, the party leader has the power to determine cabinet positions within the government. In the opposition parties, the leader has the power to assign the "shadow cabinet" positions, the high profile positions of critics who follow issues of particular government departments. An MP with such a position has a chance for frequent national media exposure as well as the opportunity to build up a specialized expertise in an area of public policy. It is not unusual for a finance critic to become a finance minister should the critic's party win the next election.

Have the party leaders become too powerful in Canadian politics? They certainly dominate both Parliament and the public view of political life, often leaving us with the impression that politics is a kind of struggle between three or four individuals (and their personal advisors). But it is important to remember that the political power of party leaders ultimately depends on public opinion. Can the leader lead the party to success, however that is conceived, in the next election? A leader's power, even a prime minister's, quickly begins to decline when those in the party begin to sense defeat. While the liberal democratic regime is not a direct democracy, the political power of its parties and leaders ultimately rests on the votes, and therefore the opinions, of the people.

Key Terms

political party

interest aggregation

ideology

pragmatic party

multi-party system

single-party system

brokerage party

Interest Groups, Public Opinion, and Democratic Citizenship

11.1 Forms of Political Participation

11.2 Interest Groups

11.3 Women in Politics

11.4 Public Opinion

11.5 The Media

11.6 The Question of Public Opinion Polls

11.7 Civic Education and Democratic Citizenship

11.1 Forms of Political Participation

The liberal democratic regime aims at the ideal of "government of the people, by the people, and for the people." Those who are elected to office and serve in the government are ordinary citizens like you and me. They are responsible to the people as a whole to do what is in the public interest. For the regime to have a reasonable chance of working well, there must therefore be a substantial amount of political participation on the part of its citizens. People must be willing to run for public office or take part in other aspects of electoral politics. Most importantly, all citizens must have an education in politics that allows them to make reasonable judgements about who should hold public office and what constitutes good public policy. Democracy requires well-informed political participation.

What, then, are the forms of political participation in a liberal democracy? First and foremost is running for public office. Those who seek election help to generate a new political agenda; those who win participate directly in the process of making law and public policy. The second is involvement in a political party: going to party meetings, fund-raising, campaigning for the party's candidate, working on election day, and so on. Thousands of Canadians are involved in this fashion. A third, and even more widespread form of participation is through interest groups. Almost all of us belong to various interest groups — unions, lobby groups, volunteer organizations, community leagues, associations — all of which participate in the political process. Finally there is the ongoing process of politics — the ways in which we relate individually to government and our elected officials. We read newspapers, watch public affairs programs, attend political and civic meetings, discuss politics, write letters to editors and public officials, take part in public opinion polls, and ultimately vote in elections. The Internet and electronic mail are making many forms of participation even easier. Whether they will lead to greater or more informed participation remains to be seen.

11.2 Interest Groups

An **interest group** may be defined as an association of people sharing a common interest. This interest may be directly political, such as a desire for free trade or a wish to legalize marijuana, or it may be a less obviously political, such as belonging to a boat club or a society for showing dogs. What one soon discovers, however, is that even the least obviously political associations almost always become politically involved at some point — the point at which they attempt to preserve or promote their particular interest. An association becomes an interest group when it attempts to exert political influence to further its own interest.

One might, for example, belong to a sailboat club–a private organization with no obvious political ties. Its various members may belong to a number of different political parties or not belong to any. Some may be politically active, while others have no interest in politics whatsoever. The members may come from different socio-economic classes, have different ethnic backgrounds, and share no common religious affiliation. The interest they share may be nothing more than a simple love of sailing boats. And yet one can well imagine that the club is likely to have a strong position on specific environmental issues, perhaps to the point of lobbying government and attempting to exert influence on how such issues might be decided. The same could be said of boating licences, government safety regulations, navigation laws, the maintenance of inland waterways, zoning regulations in the area of the club, and so on. One can well imagine that meetings of the boat club would often involve discussions of political problems and ways to lobby the various levels of government to promote the group's interests. An interest group differs from a political party in two important respects. First, the interest that unites the group is much narrower than that which unites the members of a party. The Canadian Manufacturers' Association, for example, is a large interest group with members from many different sectors of the economy. The association may have positions on a wide variety of economic issues, ranging from pay equity to tax law, protective tariffs, and monetary policy. But it is unlikely that it will have a position on capital punishment or seatbelt legislation. Political parties must take into account a far broader spectrum of interests than an interest group. Parties attempt to accommodate as many different interest groups as possible.

Second, an interest group seeks to influence government; a political party seeks to occupy the elected offices of government. Whereas the former seeks only to influence the government, the latter seeks to exercise authority. Political parties thus become the means by which interest groups often operate. The latter try to influence government by offering support to parties or by threatening to withdraw support in favour of a competing party.

Interest groups often seek to influence politics by means of **lobbying** government. Lobbying is the attempt to influence government officials, elected and otherwise, to secure a favourable decision on a public policy or a political appointment. This often involves direct meetings with MPs or government bureaucrats. (In fact, the process is called "lobbying" because it originally took place in the members' lobbies located outside most legislative chambers.) One might best understand lobbying as a form of bargaining: the lobby group seeks the MP's support with respect to its particular interest; in return, the MP often seeks electoral support from the lobby group. Support might come in the form of campaign endorsement, campaign funds, or simply public acknowledgment from the group for the actions of the MP.

A good example of lobbying would be the recent federal legislation regarding gun control. A wide variety of interest groups — those concerned about public safety and violence, police associations, sport shooters, gun collectors, firearms dealers — wrote letters to the leaders of the various political parties, to their MPs, to government officials, and to newspapers. In some cases, they took out advertisements, hired media consultants, and perhaps even hired a professional lobbyist. They organized public meetings, protests, and marches and attempted to win over public opinion in a wide variety of ways. All of these activities are part of what interest groups normally do — anything to influence the course of politics to serve their interest.

Interest groups are obviously significant actors in Canadian politics and present a special problem. While they serve to inform and enliven political debate and policy-making, they are essentially acting to serve their own interests. Theodore White once said that the first rule of politics is that every individual and every group will want more than they deserve and demand more than they want. Interest groups are formed to serve the interests of members of a particular group. The question always remains: are those interests compatible with the public interest? Today the terms lobbying and special interests have strong negative connotations in the public mind. We are suspicious when legislators and government officials take actions that are based on secret meetings and that seem to be in the interest of a specific group rather than the public as a whole. We often wonder what the lobbyists have promised, and whether we can trust our government.

Yet lobbying is not simply a problem; it must be understood that interest groups play a useful role in our liberal democratic regime. Democratic government means government that is responsive to the needs and demands of the people, at least insofar as those demands are lawful and prudent. The government must be responsive to the general will as it manifests itself through public opinion. But how is the government to know what the general will is at any given moment? And how are the people kept informed about current issues and given the necessary information so that they might have an informed opinion? Interest groups establish an essential link between the government and the people. Elected officials, political parties, and government bureaucrats all interact with various interest groups on a regular if not constant basis. Interest groups play a crucial role in both providing government with a strong indication of public opinion and in providing the public with information on specific issues.

Still, interest groups pose a number of serious problems. First, they promote the idea that politics is simply a process of rewarding electoral support. A political party puts forward certain policies, an interest group supports the party, the party wins the election thanks in part to that support, and the party pays off the group by making public policy that furthers the group's interests. This cynical scenario makes politics look like nothing more than a competition of private interests in which the strong rule the weak. All idea of the public interest or common good disappears.

Second, interest groups, by seeking to exert political influence, strengthen our already strong propensity to look to government for solutions to our problems. Perhaps most important of all, they have the ability to dominate the political agenda and set public policy priorities. The problem that arises is that there are obviously some important interests in society which may be poorly organized and far less economically powerful than others. How powerful is an interest group representing the homeless or the mentally ill likely to be in comparison to the Business Council on National Issues or the National Action Committee on the Status of Women?

How, then, do we deal with the problem of interest groups and powerful political lobbies? There is no easy answer. We cannot outlaw such groups; for as long as we have the rights to freedom of speech and association, people will form associations to further their interests. The best we can do is to keep their power within acceptable limits. One means to accomplish this is through legislation that regulates the amount of money interest groups can contribute to political parties and candidates, that provides for the registration of professional lobbyists, and that requires the full disclosure on the part of politicians of the rewards they receive from such groups.

A second and more successful way to control the power of interest groups is to encourage their growth. This was the solution of one of the chief architects of the liberal democratic regime in the United States — James Madison. Madison argued that the real danger of politics was that a single interest might grow powerful enough to control the government to further its own narrow and private goals. The way to prevent such a danger from being realized, he argued, was to encourage the growth of a **multiplicity of interests** so that no single interest might ever be powerful enough to control the government.[1]

Finally, government can itself create and promote the growth of public interest groups. This is particularly helpful when it comes to ensuring a competition of interests that will serve to debate the issues and provide for a more informed public. Thus we find that the Canadian government supports a wide variety of interest groups with respect to the arts, education, the rights of women, multiculturalism, and so on.

---

1   Alexander Hamilton, John Jay, James Madison, *The Federalist Papers*, no. 51.

On average, Canadian citizens are not terribly active participants in politics. Only 55 per cent of eligible citizens vote in national elections, and less than 5 per cent ever belong to a political party or run for public office. And while men and women have equal rights to all forms of political participation—voting, belonging to interest groups and political parties, serving on juries, running for and holding public office, and so on—it is evident that politics remains an activity in which men participate to a greater extent than women. Why this is so is complex, and there is probably no simple answer. Tradition, societal pressures, economic disparities, career differences, prejudice—a host of causes are no doubt at work. Whatever the answer, it is clear that the equal participation of men and women in Canadian politics remains more the ideal than an accomplished fact.

In terms of two of the primary forms of political participation—holding public office and organizing interest groups—women are now more of a visible force in politics than ever before. Going into the 1993 election, two of the leaders of the national parties were women—one of them Prime Minister Campbell. Over the past two decades, women have been elected leaders of major provincial political parties in most provinces. Two women have held the office of premier.

This trend toward greater participation at the level of holding public office is also visible in the House of Commons. Consider the following statistics showing the number of women elected to Parliament and the percentage of MPs that are women:

1980	15	(5%)
1984	27	(10%)
1988	39	(13%)
1993	54	(18%)
1997	62	(20.5%)
2000	62	(20.5%)

Nonetheless, while the number of women directly participating in politics has increased substantially in the past three decades, women remain under-represented in terms of their proportion of the population. Why should women not constitute 50 per cent of the MPs? A woman has yet to be elected prime minister, and only one woman—Katherine

Callbeck in Prince Edward Island—has been elected provincial premier.

This continuing under-representation has led to calls for reforming the electoral system to increase the likelihood of women seeking and winning election to public office. A system utilizing multi-member electoral districts, for example, would likely have this effect. Political parties might then seek to balance their slate of nominees by having a man and a woman nominated in each constituency.

The participation of women in politics has also increased through the formation of women's interest groups. The terms "women's issues" and "women's groups" have become part of everyday political discourse. We are now likely to assume that, like other interest groups, women should associate in voluntary organizations to pursue their interests, and that the normal process of interest group politics works to deal with their political demands. This assumption obviously has some validity. But it raises an interesting question: are "women's groups" interest groups in the same way as the Canadian Manufacturers' Association or the Canadian Wildlife Association? And can we identify, in some objective and authoritative fashion, a list of "women's issues" and "women's interests"?

The National Action Committee on the Status of Women (NAC) is perhaps the most well known "women's group" in Canada. NAC claims to speak for the interests of all Canadian women. It works to advance those interests by changing public opinion, by pressuring governments to change legislation and public policy, and by providing organizational assistance to other women's groups. But NAC is not without its critics, some of whom are women. Such critics deny that one organization can speak for all women because women's interests are just as diverse as men's. And while one response to this criticism would be that it is in the interest of all women to be treated equally with men, there remains the question of what precisely constitutes equal treatment. Does equality require affirmative action, pay equity legislation, and compensatory public policies to redress past actions? Women remain divided on these questions.

On one view, then, women have a set of issues and interests that can be objectively defined and politically advocated for the sake of all women. The problem posed by such a view is how women who disagree with the positions advocated by "women's groups" are perceived and treated. Often they are dismissed as prisoners of a "patriarchal mind set" or a "false consciousness." The alternative view is that women's interests are as diverse and politically volatile as men's. From this point of view, the proper focus for reform should be electoral politics, not interest group politics: by increasing the participation of women in electoral politics, the ideas and concerns of women will come to have an impact equal to those expressed by men.

11.4 Public Opinion

In the final analysis, the power of both political parties and interest groups depends on their ability to influence public opinion. Democratic politicians are not usually willing to support manifestly unpopular causes, for they are usually not long in office afterwards if they do. Political parties are in the business of winning elections, and their policies must have some measure of popular support.

The idea that public opinion is an essential element of democratic politics seems obvious, but the issue of democratic public opinion becomes complex upon thoughtful consideration. First, who is the "public" in public opinion? And how do we know what the public opinion is on any particular issue? In what ways is the public opinion determined by "opinion makers"? How does the process of studying public opinion affect it? Does the public have an informed and educated opinion, or is it based more on emotion and perhaps even mere prejudice?

When we speak of public opinion, we often assume we know what is meant by the term "public." But who do we mean? Do we mean all people living in Canada? All citizens? All eligible voters? Only those who vote? Only those with an opinion? Perhaps we mean simply the people that have an interest in a particular issue. The possibilities are numerous.

In fact, when we speak of public opinion we usually mean the reactions of a specific group of people to particular issues, events, and personalities. We are concerned with opinions about the important events surrounding government and politics. What we discover is that the "public" having an opinion on one issue may be a different "public" from the group formed around a different issue. I could have a strong opinion about free trade, for example, but no interest or opinion about fisheries. The opinion groups forming the "public" have an opinion that changes with the issue in question, and it is thus somewhat misleading to think of public opinion as one entity. In sum, public opinion is a convenient but somewhat misleading generalization.

When we study public opinion, we must first ask *who* has an opinion on the issue in question, and *what* their opinion is. In other words, we must inquire into the *content* of public opinion. Second, we must assess the *political importance* of the issue in question to those whose opinion we study. And third, we must ascertain the *intensity* with which people hold these opinions. These three factors can be intertwined in a variety of ways, and a moment's reflection reveals how complex the question of public opinion is.

Consider the following example: the federal government is considering major changes to its policies regarding how universities are to be funded. What is the public opinion on this issue? The first thing we discover is that many people have no interest or opinion on the matter. We can simply ignore this fact and move on to consider the opinions of those who are interested. But are we not ignoring the fact that many people have the opinion that this is not an important enough issue to command their attention? Or are they merely ignorant of what is at stake and as a result have no opinion?

Let us leave this first point aside and forge ahead. We find that while there are many who have an opinion, some care very passionately about the issue, and others are not concerned. One thus has to distinguish between **opinion preference** or content and the **intensity of the opinion**. You will not learn much if you do not know both the preference and the intensity of the opinion. If we were merely to ascertain public preference without ascertaining both how important the public thinks the issue is and how intensely the public holds its opinions, we would have little meaningful direction for action.

The question of the passion with which an opinion is held raises a further question: how well informed is the person holding the opinion? Is the passion a product of their being informed, or is it a product of their being uninformed? We have all experienced both, and we all know that passion ought not be confused with prudence. If we stick with our example about federal funding for universities, we could ask how many members of the public understand the way the federal funding programs now work, how proposed changes might affect those programs, and what alternatives the federal government might have given its current fiscal difficulties.

Political science of necessity must be interested in more than just an empirical description of public opinion. To the extent that political science attempts to make a reasoned evaluation of democracy's claim to be the best regime, it must consider how rational and well-informed public opinion is. Authority in a democracy is not based merely on consent, but on informed consent. When we analyze public opinion, perhaps the most important question of all is the question of how well informed the public is and upon what basis they have formed an opinion. Like a doctor examining a patient, political scientists are measuring the health of the liberal democratic regime when they examine the basis of public opinion.

The sources of public opinion are diverse. Our parents, family life, religion, schooling and education, peer group, advertising, government, the laws, political parties, interest groups, and the media all play important parts. The influence of the media is, today, a particularly controversial issue. Fears that public opinion is now routinely manipulated and controlled by the media are widespread and well known. But perhaps the most important source of public opinion is now public opinion itself. This may sound strange at first, but what is really at work is the phenomenon of conformism—the ways in which individuals come to conform with public opinion. This was de Tocqueville's observation about democratic society:

> The smallest reproach irritates its sensibility, and the slightest joke which has any foundation in truth renders it indignant; from the form of its language up to the solid virtues of its character, everything must be made the subject of encomium. No writer, whatever be his eminence, can escape paying this tribute of adulation to his fellow-citizens. The majority lives in perpetual utterance of self-applause....[1]

De Tocqueville argued that the power of democratic society to get its citizens to conform to public opinion is perhaps its greatest danger. The mass media only serves as the means, albeit an ever more powerful means, to the end of mass democratic conformism.

11.5 The Media

Is conformism more of a problem now than it was in the past? We would like to think not, given that the growth of the mass media has increased both the amount of, and access to, politically relevant information. Mass circulation newspapers and magazines, radio and tele-

---

1 Alexis de Tocqueville, *Democracy in America* (Markham, ON: NAL, 1956) 119.

vision, and more recently the Internet make a huge volume of information readily available to every citizen. Citizens in contemporary Canadian society have the ability to keep up on politics — to follow live debates and even committee hearings from the legislatures, press conferences, daily media interviews, and nightly news reports on the day's major political events. In addition, they can use the Internet to access newspapers, radio, television, and magazines from across the country, and, in most cases, this access is free. For those who wish to follow politics carefully, there has probably never been a time when so much information was so easily available to so many.

Nonetheless, informed opinion remains divided. There is a high degree of skepticism, if not cynicism, about the relationship between the mass media and political opinion. One reason for this skepticism is the problem of media ownership and control. In Canada, the media is by and large privately owned. While they are regulated by government, most of the media are business ventures owned by large corporations. (The major exceptions are the publicly owned and controlled radio and television networks.) Therefore, we should never forget that the media in Canada must always be viewed in the context of their role in bringing in advertising revenue. News reporting is one thing, among many things, that attracts readers' and viewers' attention and hence boosts sales or ratings.

The impact of this is clear: political news is one part of news reporting in general, and the media provides much more than news. Political news reporting is, in fact, a small part of what the media supplies. Most of what it supplies is entertainment. The net effect of this situation is that political news reporting runs the risk of becoming a small part of the overall entertainment package. Where the nightly news ends and the evening's entertainment news segment begins may not always be easily distinguishable. The fact that the news must be what sells is a problem, for what is most interesting may not always be what is most important. The implications of recent changes in government policy on trade, or the outcome of Supreme Court decisions, are likely to be of much greater political importance than a scandal in an MP's office or whether the prime minister fell asleep at a long political ceremony overseas. But the evening news often tends to focus on these spicier tidbits than deeper issues.

The focus and content of media coverage of political news has been roundly criticized in recent decades, and there is no shortage of criticism in this regard. A more interesting question, however, is whether the media should be held solely responsible for this situation. The media sells the news like any other product, so news reports are very sensitive to consumer preferences. If the media is accused of sensationalizing or dumbing-down the news, who is to blame? If the average media consumer is freely voting with his or her channel changer, who can fault the media for giving the people what they want? They would not be in business long if they did not.

There is, however, the question of the publicly owned media. The main public broadcaster in Canada is the CBC. It operates extensive media in French and English throughout the country. This helps to provide balance and competition for the private media. But while Canadians are often cynical about the private media, they are no less sceptical about media owned and controlled by government. The idea of government controlled media supplying citizens with the news about the government has always raised the spectre of bias in the media. Will public media provide us with a truly critical account of government activity? Should the funding of public media come from the government, how could they not be affected by a concern to maintain favour with those who fund them?

11.6 The Question of Public Opinion Polls

The issue of conformism is also at the heart of the long and heated controversy over the value and place of public opinion polls. Polling by political parties, private corporations, the media, and governments goes on constantly and has become a pervasive aspect of our lives. Polls inform us about everything from the important to the trivial, from Canadian opinions about major policy issues to how many people believe that Elvis is still alive. The interesting question is why they have become so pervasive.

One reason is that they are a useful tool of mass marketing. Mass marketing techniques for determining market demand and advertising can be successfully used in democratic politics. Interest groups, government departments and agencies, and political parties all use opinion polls in order to determine what issues are important to the public and whether a particular idea, policy, or personality could prove popular. One could thus argue that public opinion polling is an important resource in modern democracy. If governments and political parties are there to serve the people, they need to know what the people are thinking. Politicians can get a better read of public opinion and thus can give the people what they want by means of public opinion polls.

On the other hand, polls contribute to conformism by promoting the view that something is good simply because a majority in a public opinion poll think it to be good. Public opinion can easily change, especially on an emotionally charged political issue. A few grisly murders and the polls may show Canadians strongly in favour of capital punishment. Moreover, we are left to wonder how well informed the public may be on a particular issue and hence, to put the matter bluntly, what is the value of knowing their opinion. One might ask 1,001 Canadians whether the Bank of Canada should lower its interest rate. How would they know what the reasons and repercussions of changes to the bank's policy are?

Polls thus exacerbate a danger that is unique to the democratic regime — granting a kind of superior status to the opinion of a majority. De Tocqueville described the problem in the following terms:

> The moral authority of the majority is partly based upon the notion, that there is more intelligence and wisdom in a number of men united than in a single individual, and that the number of the legislators is more important than their quality.[1]

The danger is that we come to believe something is either true or good because a majority of people believe it so. Such a danger has been all too often realized with respect to issues of racial and religious tolerance.

The most common debate about public opinion polls concerns their possible effects on elections. Many argue for a ban on publication of pre-election opinion polls that attempt to measure and predict voter preference. Their argument is that in the weeks between the time Parliament is dissolved and the election takes place, Canadians should be left to make up their own minds without the "benefit" of polls.

Those who propose that the publication of public opinion polls be prohibited in the period immediately preceding an election argue that such polls undermine the electoral process in two important ways. First, the publication of pre-election polls turns elections into the equivalent

---

1 De Tocqueville 113.

of horse races: election coverage in the media often focuses more on who is ahead in the latest poll than on what the issues are. Politics is thus treated as the equivalent of a sporting event and to a great extent trivialized, with voters paying more attention to who is winning than who ought to win.

A second problem caused by pre-election polls is their effect on voting behaviour. Political parties and candidates who are shown to be badly trailing are often written off by voters, who then switch their votes to one of the two leading contenders. Often a **bandwagon effect** is created by voters who want to ensure that the winning candidate in their riding is from the party that is most likely to form the government. Whether voters switch their votes to the second-place or first-place party, the effect is the same: the SMP system's tendency to make it difficult for third parties to elect their candidates is magnified. If elections are supposed to be the average citizen's main opportunity for intelligent, public-spirited political participation, then the publication of election polls seems inconsistent with healthy democracy.

The issue of election polls points to a fundamental question for liberal democratic politics. To prohibit the publication of opinion polls would almost certainly be a violation of some of our most important rights—freedom of the press, for example. Yet if it can be established that polls diminish thoughtful participation in politics, then polls would arguably be anti-democratic. In the final analysis, the question of public opinion polls reveals the deep tension that sometimes exists between our devotion to liberalism and our devotion to democracy.

11.7   **Civic Education and Democratic Citizenship**

The question of how we create a well informed public and hence intelligent public opinion necessarily brings us to the problem of political education. How should we educate people to be citizens in a liberal democracy? What kind of citizen does the liberal democratic regime require if it is to remain healthy? What sort of education is most likely to produce intelligent citizens who care about politics, understand the important political issues, can make prudent decisions in their electoral choices, and ultimately can be told the truth rather than merely be flattered?

One of the keystones in such an education is the right to free speech and the freedom of the press. The free exchange of ideas is essential in a liberal democracy. Only when we hear and listen to ideas being debated can we begin to make any sort of intelligent judgement on a particular issue. Only when citizens have the right to debate political issues in an atmosphere of toleration and respect, and use that right to do so, can the liberal democratic regime be sure that public opinion is reasonably well informed.

Such debate must go beyond the issues of the day, although it must surely include those issues. It must include the ongoing controversies that surround the very principles of the liberal democratic regime itself: equality, liberty, rights, obligations, the rule of law, constitutionalism, federalism, and so on. Only when we are capable of debating the strengths and weaknesses of these principles, of understanding the competing interpretations of them, and of seeing how these principles are often at odds with one another do we approach the education needed of the citizen of the liberal democratic regime. For only then can the citizen separate those issues that go to the question of the continued health of the regime from those that are merely transitory and ephemeral.

Finally, political education in a liberal democracy must aim to encourage political participation. Citizens are far less likely to participate if they do not understand either the important political issues or the main institutions of politics. The reason for this is that without such an understanding we tend to underestimate the value of participation. Often we hear people ask: "what difference does one vote in thousands make?" or "how can you fight the establishment?" An education in the history of Canadian politics reveals that the establishment can change very rapidly, that individuals can come out of nowhere and rise rapidly to prominence in politics, and that the political landscape is often remade within months. In 1984, the Progressive Conservative Party won the greatest electoral victory in Canadian history. Nine years later, the party was virtually destroyed, and its future as a national party now appears questionable. The powerful political figures of the last decade have almost all disappeared from public life. Such changes are wrought by the actions of thousands of ordinary citizens, who belong to political parties and interest groups, write letters, and generally act as though their actions have consequences. Political participation is thus encouraged by a strong sense that we have an obligation to take part in government, that our actions make a difference, and that we benefit both ourselves and our country when we do participate.

An education in politics reveals that these beliefs are, by and large, well-founded.

Key Terms

interest group
lobbying
multiplicity of interests

opinion preference
opinion intensity
bandwagon effect

Appendix:
The Constitution Acts 1867 to 1982

A Consolidation (August 17, 1995)
DEPARTMENT OF JUSTICE CANADA

Constitution Act, 1867

30 & 31 Victoria, c. 3 (UK)
(Consolidated with amendments)
An Act for the Union of Canada, Nova Scotia, and New Brunswick,
and the Government thereof: and for Purposes connected therewith.

(*29 March, 1867*)

Whereas the Provinces of Canada, Nova Scotia and New Brunswick
have expressed their Desire to be federally united into One Dominion under the Crown of the United Kingdom of Great Britain and
Ireland, with a Constitution similar in Principle to that of the United
Kingdom:

And whereas such a Union would conduce to the Welfare of the
Provinces and promote the Interests of the British Empire:

And whereas on the Establishment of the Union by Authority of
Parliament it is expedient, not only that the Constitution of the Leg-
islative Authority in the Dominion be provided for, but also that the
Nature of the Executive Government therein be declared:

And whereas it is expedient that Provision be made for the eventual
Admission into the Union of other Parts of British North America:

I. Preliminary

This Act may be cited as the *Constitution Act, 1867*.   *Short title*

1 Repealed.   *[repealed]*

2 ### II. Union

3 It shall be lawful for the Queen, by and with the Advice of Her   *Declaration of Union*

Majesty's Most Honourable Privy Council, to declare by Proclamation that, on and after a Day therein appointed, not being more than Six Months after the passing of this Act, the Provinces of Canada, Nova Scotia and New Brunswick shall form and be One Dominion under the Name of Canada; and on and after that Day those Three Provinces shall form and be One Dominion under that Name accordingly.

Construction of
Subsequent
Provisions of Act

4 Unless it is otherwise expressed or implied, the Name Canada shall be taken to mean Canada as constituted under this Act.

5 Canada shall be divided into Four Provinces, named Ontario, Quebec, Nova Scotia and New Brunswick.

Four Provinces

Provinces of Ontario
and Quebec

6 The parts of the Province of Canada (as it exists at the passing of this Act) which formerly constituted respectively the provinces of Upper and Lower Canada shall be deemed to be severed, and shall form Two separate Provinces. The Part which formerly constituted the Province of Upper Canada shall constitute the Province of Ontario: and the Part which formerly constituted the Province of Lower Canada shall Constitute the Province of Quebec.

Provinces of Nova
Scotia and New
Brunswick

7 The Provinces of Nova Scotia and New Brunswick shall have the same Limits as at the passing of this Act.

Decennial Census

8 In the general Census of the Population of Canada, which is hereby required to be taken in the Year One thousand eight hundred and seventy-one, and in every Tenth Year thereafter, the respective Populations of the Four Provinces shall be distinguished.

III. Executive Power

Declaration of
Executive Power in
the Queen

9 The Executive Government and Authority of and over Canada is hereby declared to continue and be vested in the Queen.

Application of
Provisions referring
to Governor

10 The Provisions of this Act referring to the Governor General extend and apply to the Governor General for the Time being of Canada, or other Chief Executive Officer or Administrator for the Time being carrying on the Government of Canada on behalf and in the Name of the Queen, by whatever Title he is designated.

11 There shall be a Council to aid and advise in the Government of *Constitution of* Canada, to be styled the Queen's Privy Council for Canada; and the *Privy Council for* Persons who are to be Members of that Council shall be from Time *Canada* to Time chosen and summoned by the Governor General and sworn in as Privy Councillors, and Members thereof may be from Time to Time removed by the Governor General.

12 All Powers, Authorities and Functions which under any Act of the *All Powers under* Parliament of Great Britain, or of the Parliament of the United King- *Acts to be exercised* dom of Great Britain and Ireland, or of the Legislature of Upper *by Governor* Canada, Lower Canada, Canada, Nova Scotia, or New Brunswick, are *General with Advice* at the Union vested in or exerciseable by the respective Governors or *of Privy Council, or* Lieutenant Governors of those Provinces, with the Advice, or with *alone* the Advice and Consent, of the respective Executive Councils thereof, or in conjunction with those Councils, or with any Number of Members thereof, or by those Governors or Lieutenant Governors individually, shall, as far as the same continue in existence and capable being exercised after the Union in relation to the Government of Canada, be vested in and exerciseable by the Governor General, with the Advice, or the Advice and Consent of or in conjunction with the Queen's Privy Council for Canada, or any Member thereof, or by the Governor General individually, as the Case requires, subject nevertheless (except with respect to such as exist under the Acts of the Parliament of Great Britain or the Parliament of the United Kingdom of Great Britain and Ireland) to be abolished or altered by the Parliament of Canada.

13 The Provisions of this Act referring to the Governor General in *Application of* Council shall be construed as referring to the Governor General act- *Provisions referring* ing by and with the Advice of the Queen's Privy Council for *to Governor General* Canada. *in Council*

14 It shall be lawful for the Queen, if Her Majesty thinks fit, to autho- *Power to Her* rize the Governor General from Time to Time to appoint any Per- *Majesty to authorize* son or any Persons jointly or severally to be his Deputy or Deputies *Governor General to* within any Part or Parts of Canada, and in that Capacity to exercise *appoint Deputies* during the Pleasure of the Governor General such of the Powers, Authorities, and Functions of the Governor General as the Governor General deems it necessary or expedient to assign to him or them, subject to any Limitations or Directions expressed or given by the Queen; but the Appointment of such a Deputy or Deputies shall not

affect the exercise by the Governor General himself of any Power, Authority or Function.

Command of Armed Forces to continue to be vested in the Queen	15	The Command-in-Chief of the Land and Naval Militia, and of all Naval and Military Forces, of and in Canada, is hereby declared to continue and be vested in the Queen.
Seat of Government of Canada	16	Until the Queen otherwise directs, the Seat of Government of Canada shall be Ottawa.

IV. Legislative Power

Constitution of Parliament of Canada	17	There shall be One Parliament for Canada consisting of the Queen, an Upper House Styled the Senate, and the House of Commons.
Privileges, etc., of Houses	18	The privileges, immunities, and powers held, enjoyed, and exercised by the Senate and House of Commons, and by the Members thereof respectively, shall be such as are from time to time defined by Act of the Parliament of Canada, but so that any Act of the Parliament of Canada defining such privileges, immunities, and powers shall not confer any privileges, immunities, or powers exceeding those at the passing of such Act held, enjoyed, and exercised by the Commons House of Parliament of the United Kingdom of Great Britain and Ireland, and by the members thereof.(*8*)
First Session of the Parliament of Canada	19	The Parliament of Canada shall be called together not later than Six Months after the Union.
[Repealed]	20	Repealed.

The Senate

Number of Senators	21	The Senate Shall, subject to the Provisions of this Act, consist of One Hundred and five Members, who shall be styled Senators.
Representation of Provinces in Senate	22	In relation to the Constitution of the Senate Canada shall be deemed to consist of *Four* Divisions: 1. Ontario 2. Quebec 3. The Maritime Provinces, Nova Scotia and New Brunswick, and Prince Edward Island;

4. The Western Provinces of Manitoba, British Columbia, Saskatchewan, and Alberta;

which Four Divisions shall (subject to the Provisions of this Act) be equally represented in the Senate as follows: Ontario by twenty-four senators; Quebec by twenty-four senators; the Maritime Provinces and Prince Edward Island by twenty-four senators, ten thereof representing Nova Scotia, ten thereof representing New Brunswick, and four thereof representing Prince Edward Island; the Western Provinces by twenty-four senators, six thereof representing Manitoba, six thereof representing British Columbia, six thereof representing Saskatchewan, and six thereof representing Alberta; Newfoundland shall be entitled to be represented in the Senate by six members, the Yukon territory and the Northwest Territories shall be entitled to be represented in the Senate by one member each.

In the Case of Quebec, each of the Twenty-four Senators representing that Province shall be appointed for One of the Twenty-four Electoral Divisions of Lower Canada specified in Schedule A. to Chapter One of the Consolidated statues of Canada.

23   The Qualifications of a Senator shall be as follows: *Qualifications of*

(1) He shall be of the full age of Thirty Years;   *Senator*

(2) He shall be either a natural-born Subject of the Queen naturalized by an Act of the Parliament of Great Britain, or of the Parliament of the United Kingdom of Great Britain and Ireland, or of the Legislature of One of the Provinces of Upper Canada, Lower Canada, Nova Scotia, or New Brunswick, before the Union, or of the Parliament of Canada, after the Union:

(3) He shall be legally or equitably seised as of Freehold for his Own Use and Benefit of Lands or Tenements held in Free and Common Socage, or seised or possessed for his own Use and Benefit of Lands or Tenements held in Franc-alleu or in Roture, within the Province for which he is appointed, of the Value of Four Thousand Dollars, over and above all Rents, Dues, Debts, Charges, Mortgages, and Incumbrances due or payable out of or charged on or affecting the same:

(4) His Real and Personal Property shall be together worth Four Thousand Dollars over and above his Debts and Liabilities:

(5) He shall be resident in the Province for which he is appointed:

(6) In the case of Quebec he shall have his Real Property Qualification in the Electoral Division for which he is appointed, or shall be resident in that Division.

Summons of *Senator*	24	The Governor General shall from Time to Time, in the Queen's Name, by Instrument under the Great Seal of Canada, summon qualified Persons to the Senate; and, subject to the Provisions of this Act, every person so summoned shall become and be a Member of the Senate and a Senator.
[Repealed]	25	Repealed.
Addition of *Senators in certain* *cases*	26	If at any Time on the Recommendation of the Governor General the Queen thinks fit to direct that Four or Eight Members be added to the Senate, the Governor General may by Summons to Four or Eight qualified Persons (as the Case may be), representing equally the Four Divisions of Canada, add to the Senate accordingly.
Reduction of Senate *to normal Number*	27	In case of such Addition being at any Time made, the Governor General shall not summon any Person to the Senate, except upon a further like Direction by the Queen on the like Recommendation, to represent one of the Four Divisions until such Division is represented by Twenty-Four Senators and no more.
Maximum Number *of Senators*	28	The Number of Senators shall not at any Time exceed One Hundred and thirteen.
Tenure of Place in *Senate*	29	(1) Subject to subsection (2), a Senator shall, subject to the provisions of this Act, hold his place in the Senate for life. *Retirement upon attaining age of seventy-five years* (2) A Senator who is summoned to the Senate after the coming into force of this subsection shall, subject to this Act, hold his place in the Senate until he attains the age of seventy-five years.
Resignation of Place *in Senate*	30	A Senator may by Writing under his Hand addressed to the Governor General resign his Place in the Senate, and thereupon the same shall be vacant.
Disqualification of *Senators*	31	The Place of a Senator shall become vacant in any of the following Cases: (1) If for Two consecutive Sessions of the Parliament he fails to give his Attendance in the Senate: (2) If he takes an Oath or makes a Declaration or Acknowledgement of Allegiance, Obedience, or Adherence to a Foreign Power, or does

an Act whereby he becomes a Subject or Citizen, or entitled to the Rights and Privileges of a Subject or Citizen, of a Foreign Power:

(3) If he is adjudged Bankrupt or Insolvent, or applies for the Benefit of any Law relating to Insolvent Debtors, or becomes a public Defaulter:

(4) If he is attainted of Treason or convicted of a Felony or of any infamous Crime:

(5) If he ceases to be qualified in respect of Property or of Residence; provided, that a Senator shall not be deemed to have ceased to be qualified in respect of Residence by reason only of his residing at the Seat of the Government of Canada while holding an Office under that Government requiring his Presence there.

32 When a Vacancy happens in the Senate by Resignation, Death, or otherwise, the Governor General shall by Summons to a fit and qualified Person fill the Vacancy.

Summons on Vacancy in Senate

33 If any Question arises respecting the Qualification of a Senator or a Vacancy in the Senate the same shall be heard and determined by the Senate.

Questions as to Qualifications and Vacancies in Senate

34 The Governor General may from Time to Time, by Instrument under the Great Seal of Canada, appoint a Senator to be Speaker of the Senate, and may remove him and appoint another in his Stead.

Appointment of Speaker of Senate

35 Until the Parliament of Canada otherwise provides, the Presence of at least Fifteen Senators, including the Speaker, shall be necessary to constitute a Meeting of the Senate for the Exercise of its Powers.

Quorum of Senate

36 Questions arising in the Senate shall be decided by a Majority of Voices, and the Speaker shall in all Cases have a Vote, and when the Voices are equal the Decision shall be deemed to be in the Negative.

Voting in Senate

The House of Commons

37 The House of Commons shall, subject to the Provisions of this Act, consist of two hundred and ninety-five members of whom ninety-nine shall be elected for Ontario, seventy-five for Quebec, eleven for Nova Scotia, ten for New Brunswick, fourteen for Manitoba, thirty-two for British Columbia, four for Prince Edward Island, twenty-six

for Alberta, fourteen for Saskatchewan, seven for Newfoundland, one for the Yukon Territory and two for the Northwest Territories.

Summoning of
House of Commons

38 The Governor General shall from Time to Time, in the Queen's Name, by Instrument under the Great Seal of Canada, summon and call together the House of Commons.

Senators not to sit
in House of
Commons

39 A Senator shall not be capable of being elected or of sitting or voting as a Member of the House of Commons.

Electoral districts of
the four Provinces

40 Until the Parliament of Canada otherwise provides, Ontario, Quebec, Nova Scotia, and New Brunswick shall, for the Purposes of the Election of Members to serve in the House of Commons, be divided into Electoral Districts as follows:

1. Ontario

Ontario shall be divided into the Counties, ridings of counties, Cities, Parts of Cities, and Towns enumerated in the First Schedule to this Act, each whereof shall be an Electoral District, each such District as numbered in that Schedule being entitled to return One Member.

2. Quebec

Quebec shall be divided into Sixty-five Electoral districts, composed of the Sixty-five Electoral Divisions into which Lower Canada is at the passing of this act divided under Chapter Two of the Consolidated Statutes of Canada, Chapter seventy-five of the Consolidated Statues for Lower Canada, and the Act of the Province of Canada of the Twenty-third Year of the Queen, Chapter One, or any other Act amending the same in force at the Union, so that each such Electoral Division shall be for the Purposes of this Act an Electoral District entitled to return One Member.

3. Nova Scotia

Each of the Eighteen Counties of Nova Scotia shall be an Electoral District. The County of Halifax shall be entitled to return Two Members, and each of the other Counties One Member.

4. New Brunswick

Each of the Fourteen Counties into which New Brunswick is divided, including the City and County of St. John, shall be an Electoral District. The City of St. John shall also be a separate Electoral District. Each of those Fifteen Electoral Districts shall be entitled to return One Member.

41 Until the Parliament of Canada otherwise provides, all Laws in force in the several Provinces at the Union relative to the following Matters or any of them, namely,—the Qualifications and Disqualifications of Persons to be elected or to sit or vote as Members of the House of Assembly or Legislative Assembly in the several Provinces, the Voters at Elections of such Members, the Oaths to be taken by Voters, the Returning Officers, their Powers and Duties, the Proceedings at Elections, the Periods during which Elections may be continued, the Trial of controverted Elections, and Proceedings incident thereto, the vacating of seats of Members, and the Execution of new Writs in case of Seats vacated otherwise than by Dissolution,— shall respectively apply to Elections of Members to serve in the House of Commons for the same several Provinces. *Continuance of existing Election Laws until Parliament of Canada otherwise provides*

Provided that, until the Parliament of Canada otherwise provides, at any Election for a Member of the House of Commons for the District of Algoma, in addition to Persons qualified by the Law of the Province of Canada to vote, every Male British Subject, aged Twenty-one Years or upwards, being a Householder, shall have a Vote.

42 Repealed. *[Repealed]*

43 Repealed. *[Repealed]*

44 The House of Commons on its first assembling after a General Election shall proceed with all practicable Speed to elect One of its Members to be Speaker. *As to Election of Speaker of House of Commons*

45 In case of a Vacancy happening in the office of Speaker by Death, Resignation, or otherwise, the House of Commons shall with all practicable Speed proceed to elect another of its Members to be Speaker. *As to filling up Vacancy in Office of Speaker*

46 The Speaker shall preside at all Meetings of the House of Commons. *Speaker to preside*

47 Until the Parliament of Canada otherwise provides, in case of the Absence for any Reason of the Speaker from the Chair of the House of Commons for a Period of Forty-eight consecutive Hours, the House may elect another of its Members to act as Speaker, and the Member so elected shall during the Continuance of such Absence of the Speaker have and execute all the Powers, Privileges, and Duties of Speaker.

Quorum of House *of Commons*	48	The Presence of at least Twenty Members of the House of Commons shall be necessary to constitute a Meeting of the House for the Exercise of its Powers, and for that Purpose the Speaker shall be reckoned as a Member.

Voting in House of Commons

49 Questions arising in the House of Commons shall be decided by a Majority of Voices other than that of the Speaker, and when the Voices are equal, but not otherwise, the Speaker shall have a Vote.

Duration of House of Commons

50 Every House of Commons shall continue for Five Years from the Day of the Return of the Writs for choosing the House (subject to be sooner dissolved by the Governor General), and no longer.

Readjustment of representation in Commons

51 (1) The number of members of the House of Commons and the representation of the provinces therein shall, on the coming into force of this subsection and thereafter on the completion of each decennial census, be readjusted by such authority, in such manner, and from such time as the Parliament of Canada from time to time provides, subject and according to the following rules:

Rules

1. There shall be assigned to each of the provinces a number of members equal to the number obtained by dividing the total population of the provinces by two hundred and seventy-nine and by dividing the population of each province by the quotient so obtained, counting any remainder in excess of 0.50 as one after the said process of division.

2. If the total number of members that would be assigned to a province by the application of rule 1 is less than the total number assigned to that province on the date of coming into force of this subsection, there shall be added to the number of members so assigned such number of members as will result in the province having the same number of members as were assigned on that date.

Yukon Territory and Northwest Territories

(2) The Yukon Territory as bounded and described in the schedule to chapter Y-2 of the Revised statutes of Canada, 1985, shall be entitled to one member, the Northwest Territories as bounded and described in Section 2 of chapter N-27 of the Revised statutes of Canada, 1985, as amended by section 77 of chapter 28 of the Statutes of Canada, 1993, shall be entitled to one member, and Nunavut as bounded and described in section 3 of chapter 28 of the Statutes of Canada, 1993, shall be entitled to one member.

51A Notwithstanding anything in this Act a province shall always be entitled to a number of members in the House of Commons not less
than the number of Senators representing such province.

*Constitution of
House of Commons*

52 The Number of Members of the House of Commons may be from
Time to Time increased by the Parliament of Canada, provided that
the proportionate Representation of the Provinces prescribed by this
Act is not thereby disturbed.

*Increase of Number
of House of
Commons*

Money Votes; Royal Assent

53 Bills for appropriating any Part of the Public Revenue, or for imposing any Tax or Impost, shall originate in the House of Commons.

*Appropriation and
Tax Bills*

54 It shall not be lawful for the House of Commons to adopt or pass any
Vote, Resolution, Address, or Bill for the Appropriation of any Part
of the Public Revenue, or of any Tax or Impost, to any Purpose that
has not been first recommended to that House by Message of the
Governor General in the Session in which such Vote, Resolution,
Address, or Bill is proposed.

*Recommendation of
Money Votes*

55 Where a Bill passed by Houses of the Parliament is presented to the
Governor General for the Queen's Assent, he shall declare, according
to his Discretion, but subject to the Provisions of this Act and to Her
Majesty's Instructions, either that he assents thereto in the Queen's
Name, or that he withholds the Queen's Assent, or that he reserves
the Bill for the Signification of the Queen's Pleasure.

*Royal Assent to
Bills, etc.*

56 Where the Governor General assents to a Bill in the Queen's Name,
he shall by the first convenient Opportunity send an authentic Copy
of the Act to One of Her Majesty's Principal Secretaries of State, and
if the Queen in Council within Two Years after Receipt thereof by
the Secretary of State thinks fit to disallow the Act, such Disallowance (with a Certificate of the Secretary of State on the Day on
which the Act was received by him) being signified by the Governor
General, by Speech or Message to each of the Houses of the Parliament or by Proclamation, shall annul the Act from and after the Day
of such Signification.

*Disallowance by
Order in Council of
Act assented to by
Governor General*

Signification of *Queen's Pleasure on* *Bill reserved*	57	A Bill reserved for the Signification of the Queen's Pleasure shall not have any Force unless and until, within Two Years from the Day on which it was presented to the Governor General for the Queen's Assent, the Governor General signifies, by Speech or Message to each of the Houses of the Parliament or by Proclamation, that it has received the Assent of the Queen in Council.

An Entry of every such Speech, Message, or Proclamation shall be made in the Journal of each House, and a Duplicate thereof duly attested shall be delivered to the proper Officer to be kept among the Records of Canada.

V. Provincial Constitutions

Executive Power

Appointment of *Lieutenant Governors* *of Provinces*	58	For each Province there shall be an Officer, styled the Lieutenant Governor, appointed by the Governor General in Council by Instrument under the Great Seal of Canada.
Tenure of Office of *Lieutenant Governor*	59	A Lieutenant Governor shall hold Office during the Pleasure of the Governor General; but any Lieutenant Governor appointed after the Commencement of the First Session of the Parliament of Canada shall not be removable within Five Years from his Appointment, except for Cause assigned, which shall be communicated to be in Writing within One Month after the Order for his Removal is made, and shall be communicated by Message to the Senate and to the House of Commons within One Week thereafter if the Parliament is then sitting, and if not then within One Week after the Commencement of the next Session of the Parliament.
Salaries of Lieutenant *Governors*	60	The Salaries of the Lieutenant Governors shall be fixed and provided by the Parliament of Canada.
Oaths, etc., of *Lieutenant Governor*	61	Every Lieutenant Governor shall, before assuming the Duties of his Office, make and subscribe before the Governor General or some Person authorized by him Oaths of Allegiance and Office similar to those taken by the Governor General.

62 The Provisions of this Act referring to the Lieutenant Governor extend and apply to the Lieutenant Governor for the Time being of each Province, or other the Chief Executive Officer or Administrator for the Time being carrying on the Government of the Province, by whatever Title he is designated.

Application of Provisions referring to Lieutenant Governor

63 The Executive Council of Ontario and of Quebec shall be composed of such Persons as the Lieutenant Governor from Time to Time thinks fit, and in the first instance of the following Officers, namely,—the Attorney General, the Secretary and Registrar of the Province, the Treasurer of the Province, the Commissioner of Crown Lands, the Commissioner of Agriculture and Public Works, within Quebec the Speaker of the Legislative Council and the Solicitor General.

Appointment of Executive Officers for Ontario and Quebec

64 The Constitution of the Executive Authority in each of the Provinces of Nova Scotia and New Brunswick shall, subject to the Provisions of this Act, continue as it exists at the Union until altered under the Authority of this Act.

Executive Government of Nova Scotia and New Brunswick

65 All Powers, Authorities, and Functions which under any Act of the Parliament of Great Britain, or of the Parliament of the United Kingdom of Great Britain and Ireland, or of the Legislature of Upper Canada, Lower Canada, or Canada, were or are before or at the Union vested in or exerciseable by the respective Governors or Lieutenant Governors of those Provinces, with the Advice and Consent of the respective Executive Councils thereof, or in conjunction with those Councils, or with any Number of Members thereof, or by those Governors or Lieutenant Governors individually, shall, as far as the same are capable of being exercised after the Union in relation to the Government of Ontario and Quebec respectively, be vested in and shall or may be exercised by the Lieutenant Governors of Ontario and Quebec respectively, with the Advice or with the Advice and Consent of or in conjunction with the respective Executive Councils, or any Members thereof, or by the Lieutenant Governor individually, as the Case requires, subject nevertheless (except with respect to such as exist under Acts of the Parliament of Great Britain, or of the Parliament of the United Kingdom of Great Britain and Ireland), to be abolished or altered by the respective Legislatures of Ontario and Quebec.

Powers to be exercised by Lieutenant Governor of Ontario or Quebec with Advice, or alone

Application of Provisions referring to Lieutenant Governor in Council	66	The Provisions of this Act referring to the Lieutenant Governor in Council shall be construed as referring to the Lieutenant Governor of the Province acting by and with the Advice of the Executive Council thereof.
Administration in Absence, etc., of Lieutenant Governor	67	The Governor General in Council may from Time to Time appoint an Administrator to execute the Office and Functions of Lieutenant Governor during his Absence, Illness, or other Inability.
Seats of Provincial Government	68	Unless and until the Executive Government of any Province otherwise directs with respect to that Province, the Seats of Government of the Provinces shall be as follows, namely,—of Ontario, the City of Toronto; of Quebec, the City of Quebec; of Nova Scotia, the City of Halifax; and of New Brunswick, the City of Fredericton.

Legislative Power

1. Ontario

Legislature for Ontario	69	There shall be a Legislature for Ontario consisting of the Lieutenant Governor and of One House, styled the Legislative Assembly of Ontario.
	70	The Legislative Assembly of Ontario shall be composed of eighty-two Members, to be elected to represent the Eighty-two Electoral Districts set forth in the First Schedule to this Act.

2. Quebec

Legislature for Quebec	71	There shall be a Legislature for Quebec consisting of the Lieutenant Governor and of Two Houses, styled the Legislative Council of Quebec and the Legislative Assembly of Quebec.
Constitution of Legislative Council	72	The Legislative Council of Quebec shall be composed of twenty-four Members, to be appointed by the Lieutenant Governor, in the Queen's Name, by Instrument under the Great Seal of Quebec, one being appointed to represent each of the Twenty-four Electoral Divisions of Lower Canada in this Act referred to, and each holding Office for the Term of his Life, unless the Legislature of Quebec otherwise provides under the Provisions of this Act.

73 The Qualifications of the Legislative Councillors of Quebec shall be the same as those of the Senators of Quebec.

Qualification of Legislative Councillors

74 The Place of a Legislative Councillor of Quebec shall become vacant in the Cases, *mutatis mutandis*, in which the Place of Senator becomes vacant.

Resignation, Disqualification, etc.

75 When Vacancy happens in the Legislative Council of Quebec by Resignation, Death, or otherwise, the Lieutenant Governor, in the Queen's Name, by Instrument under the Great Seal of Quebec, shall appoint a fit and qualified Person to fill the Vacancy.
Questions as to Vacancies, etc.

Vacancies

76 If any Question arises respecting the Qualifications of a Legislative Councillor of Quebec, or a Vacancy in the Legislative Council of Quebec, the same shall be heard and determined by the Legislative Council.

Questions as to Vacancie etc.

77 The Lieutenant Governor may from Time to Time, by Instrument under the Great seal of Quebec, appoint a Member of the Legislative Council of Quebec to be Speaker thereof, and may remove him and appoint another in his Stead.

Speaker of Legislative Council

78 Until the Legislature of Quebec otherwise provides, the Presence of at least Ten Members of the Legislative Council, including the Speaker, shall be necessary to constitute a Meeting for the Exercise of its Powers.

Quorum of Legislative Council

79 Questions arising in the Legislative Council of Quebec shall be decided by a Majority of Voices, and the Speaker shall in all Cases have a Vote, and when the Voices are equal the Decision shall be deemed to be in the Negative.

Voting in Legislative Council

80 The Legislative Assembly of Quebec shall be composed of Sixty-five Members, to be elected to represent the Sixty-five Electoral Divisions or Districts of Lower Canada in this Act referred to, subject to Alteration thereof by the Legislature of Quebec: Provided that it shall not be lawful to present to the Lieutenant Governor of Quebec for Assent any Bill for altering the Limits of any of the Electoral Divisions or Districts mentioned in the Second Schedule to this act,

Constitution of Legislative Assembly of Quebec

unless the Second and Third Readings of such Bill have been passed in the Legislative Assembly with the Concurrence of the Majority of the Members representing all those Electoral Divisions or Districts, and the Assent shall not be given to such Bill unless an Address has been presented by the Legislative Assembly to the Lieutenant Governor stating that it has been so passed.

3. Ontario and Quebec

[Repealed] 81 Repealed.

Summoning of
Legislative
Assemblies

82 The Lieutenant Governor of Ontario and Quebec shall from Time to Time, in the Queen's Name, by Instrument under the Great Seal of the Province, summon and call together the Legislative Assembly of the Province.

Restriction on
election of Holders
of offices

83 Until the Legislature of Ontario or of Quebec otherwise provides, a Person accepting or holding in Ontario or in Quebec any Office, Commission, or Employment, permanent or temporary, at the Nomination of the Lieutenant Governor, to which an annual Salary, or any Fee, Allowance, Emolument, or Profit of any Kind or Amount whatever from the Province is attached, shall not be eligible as a Member of the Legislative Assembly of the respective Province, nor shall he sit or vote as such; but nothing in this Section shall make ineligible any Person being a Member of the Executive Council of the respective Province, or holding any of the following Offices, that is to say, the Offices of Attorney general, Secretary and Registrar of the Province, Treasurer of the Province, Commissioner of Crown Lands, and Commissioner of Agriculture and Public Works, and in Quebec Solicitor General, or shall disqualify him to sit or vote in the House for which he is elected, provided he is elected while holding such Office.

Continuance of
existing Election
Laws

84 Until the legislatures of Ontario and Quebec respectively otherwise provide, all Laws which at the Union are in force in those Provinces respectively, relative to the following Matters, or any of them, namely,—the Qualifications and Disqualifications of Persons to be elected or to sit or vote as Members of the Assembly of Canada, the Qualifications or Disqualifications of Voters, the Oaths to be taken by Voters, the Returning Officers, their Powers and Duties, the Proceed-

ings at Elections, the Periods during which such Elections may be continued, and the Trial of controverted Elections and the Proceedings incident thereto, the vacating of the Seats of Members and the issuing and execution of new Writs in case of Seats vacated otherwise than by Dissolution,—shall respectively apply to Elections of Members to serve in the respective Legislative Assemblies of Ontario and Quebec.

Provided that, until the Legislature of Ontario otherwise provides, at any Election for a Member of the Legislative Assembly of Ontario for the District of Algoma, in addition to Persons qualified by the Law of the Province of Canada to vote, every Male British Subject, aged Twenty-one Years or upwards, being a Householder, shall have a Vote.

85 Every Legislative Assembly of Ontario and every Legislative Assembly of Quebec shall continue for Four Years from the Day of the Return of the Writs for choosing the same (subject nevertheless to either the Legislative Assembly of Ontario or the Legislative Assembly of Quebec being sooner dissolved by the Lieutenant Governor of the Province), and no longer. *Duration of Legislative Assemblies*

86 There shall be a Session of the Legislature of Ontario and of that of Quebec once at least in every Year, so that Twelve Months shall not intervene between the last Sitting of the Legislature in each Province in one Session and its first Sitting of the next Session. *Yearly Session of Legislature*

87 The following Provisions of this Act respecting the House of Commons of Canada shall extend and apply to the Legislative Assemblies of Ontario and Quebec, that is to say,—the Provisions relating to the Election of a Speaker originally and on Vacancies, the Duties of the Speaker, the Absence of the Speaker, the Quorum, and the Mode of Voting, as if those Provisions were here re-enacted and applicable in Terms to each such Legislative assembly. *Speaker, Quorum, etc.*

4. Nova Scotia and New Brunswick

88 The Constitution of the Legislature of each of the Provinces of Nova Scotia and New Brunswick shall, subject to the provisions of this Act, continue as it exists at the Union until altered under the Authority of this Act. *Constitutions of Legislatures of Nova Scotia and New Brunswick*

5. Ontario, Quebec, and Nova Scotia

[Repealed]   89   Repealed.

6. The Four Provinces

Application to
Legislatures of
Provisions respecting
Money Votes, etc.

90   The following provisions of this Act respecting the Parliament of
Canada, namely,—the Provisions relating to Appropriation and Tax
Bills, the Recommendation of Money Votes, the Assent to Bills, the
Disallowance of Acts, and the Signification of Pleasure on Bills
reserved,—shall extend and apply to the Legislatures of the several
Provinces as if those Provisions were here re-enacted and made
applicable in Terms to the respective Provinces and the Legislatures
thereof, with the Substitution of Lieutenant Governor of the
Province for the Governor General, of the Governor General for the
Queen and for a Secretary of State, of One Year for Two Years, and
of the Province for Canada.

VI. Distribution of Powers

Powers of the Parliament

Legislative Authority
of Parliament of
Canada

91   It shall be Lawful for the Queen, by and with the Advice and Consent of the Senate and the House of Commons, to make Laws for
the Peace, Order and Good Government of Canada, in relation to all
Matters not coming within the Classes of Subjects by this Act
assigned exclusively to the Legislatures of the Provinces; and for
greater Certainty, but not so as to restrict the Generality of the fore-
going Terms of the Section, it is hereby declared that (notwithstanding anything in this Act) the exclusive Legislative Authority of the
Parliament of Canada extends to all Matters coming within the
Classes of Subjects hereinafter enumerated; that is to say,

1. Repealed.
1A. The Public Debt and Property.
2. The Regulation of Trade and Commerce.
2A. Unemployment insurance.
3. The Raising of Money by any Mode or System of Taxation.
4. The borrowing of Money on the Public Credit.
5. Postal Service.

6. The Census and Statistics.

7. Militia, Military and Naval Service, and Defence.

8. The fixing of and providing for the Salaries and Allowances of Civil and other Officers of the Government of Canada.

9. Beacons, Buoys, Lighthouses, and Sable Island.

10. Navigation and Shipping.

11. Quarantine and the Establishment and Maintenance of Marine Hospitals.

12. Sea Coast and Inland Fisheries.

13. Ferries between a Province and any British or Foreign Country or between Two Provinces.

14. Currency and Coinage.

15. Banking, Incorporation of Banks, and the Issue of Paper Money.

16. Savings Banks.

17. Weights and Measures.

18. Bills of Exchange and Promissory Notes.

19. Interest.

20. Legal Tender.

21. Bankruptcy and Insolvency.

22. Patents of Invention and Discovery.

23. Copyrights.

24. Indians, and Lands reserved for the Indians.

25. Naturalization and Aliens.

26. Marriage and Divorce.

27. The Criminal Law, except for the Constitution of Courts of Criminal Jurisdiction, but including the Procedure in Criminal Matters.

28. The Establishment, Maintenance, and Management of Penitentiaries.

29. Such Classes of Subjects as are expressly excepted in the Enumeration of the Classes of Subjects by this Act assigned exclusively to the Legislatures of the Provinces.

And any Matter coming within any of the Classes of Subjects enumerated in this Section shall not be deemed to come within the Class of matters of a local or private Nature comprised in the Enumeration of the Classes of Subjects by this Act assigned exclusively to the Legislatures of the Provinces.

Exclusive Powers of the Provincial Legislatures

92 In each Province the Legislature may exclusively make Laws in relation to Matters coming within the Classes of Subject next hereinafter enumerated; that is to say,

1. Repealed.

2. Direct Taxation within the Province in order to the raising of a Revenue for Provincial Purposes.

3. The borrowing of Money on the sole Credit of the Province.

4. The Establishment and Tenure of Provincial Offices and the Appointment and Payment of Provincial Officers.

5. The Management and Sale of the Public Lands belonging to the Province and of the Timber and Wood thereon.

6. The Establishment, Maintenance, and Management of Public and Reformatory Prisons in and for the Province.

7. The Establishment, Maintenance, and Management of Hospitals, Asylums, Charities, and Eleemosynary Institutions in and for the Province, other than Marine Hospitals.

8. Municipal Institutions in the Province.

9. Shop, Saloon, Tavern, Auctioneer, and other Licences in order to the raising of a Revenue for Provincial, Local, or Municipal Purposes.

10. Local Works and Undertakings other than such as are of the following classes:

(*a*) Lines of Steam or other Ships, Railways, Canals, Telegraphs, and other Works and Undertakings connecting the Province with any other or others of the Province, or extending beyond the Limits of the Province;

(*b*) Lines of Steam Ships between the Province and any British or Foreign Country;

(*c*) Such Works as, although wholly situate within the Province, are before or after their Execution declared by the Parliament of Canada to be for the general Advantage of Canada or for the Advantage of Two or more of the Provinces.

11. The Incorporation of Companies with Provincial Objects.

12. The Solemnization of Marriage in the Province.

13. Property and Civil Rights within the Province.

14. The Administration of Justice in the Province, including the Constitution, Maintenance, and Organization of Provincial Courts,

both of Civil and of Criminal Jurisdiction, and including Procedure in Civil Matters in those Courts.

15. The Imposition of Punishment by Fine, Penalty, or Imprisonment for enforcing any Law of the Province made in relation to any Matter coming within any of the Classes of Subjects enumerated in this Section.

16. Generally all Matters of a merely local or private Nature in the Province.

92A *Non-Renewable Natural Resources, Forestry Resources, and Electrical Energy*

(1) In each province, the legislature may exclusively make laws in relation to

    (*a*) exploration for non-renewable natural resources in the province;

    (*b*) development, conservation and management of non-renewable natural resources and forestry resources in the province, including laws in relation to the rate of primary production therefrom; and

    (*c*) development, conservation and management of sites and facilities in the province for the generation and production of electrical energy.

Laws respecting non-renewable natural resources, forestry resources and electrical energy

(2) In each province, the legislature may make laws in relation to the export from the province to another part of Canada of the primary production from non-renewable natural resources and forestry resources in the province and the productions from facilities in the province for the generation of electrical energy, but such laws may not authorize or provide for discrimination in prices or supplies exported to another part of Canada.

Export from provinces of resources

(3) Nothing in subsection (2) derogates from the authority of Parliament to enact laws in relation to the matters referred to in that subsection and, where such a law of Parliament and a law of a province conflict, the law of Parliament prevails to the extent of the conflict.

Authority of Parliament

(4) In each province, the legislature may make laws in relation to the raising of money by any mode or system of taxation in respect of

    (*a*) non-renewable natural resources and forestry resources in the province and the primary production therefrom, and

Taxation of resources

(*b*) sites and facilities in the province for the generation of electrical energy and the production therefrom,

whether or not such production is exported in whole or in part from the province, but such laws may not authorize or provide for taxation that differentiates between production exported to another part of Canada and production not exported from the province.

Primary production

(5) The expression "primary production" has the meaning assigned in the Sixth Schedule.

Existing powers or rights

(6) Nothing in subsections (1) to (5) derogates from any powers or rights that a legislature or government of a province had immediately before the coming into force of this section.(*49*)

Education

Legislation respecting Education

93 In and for each Province the Legislature may exclusively make Laws in relation to Education, subject and according to the following Provisions:

1. Nothing in any such Law shall prejudicially affect any Right or Privilege with respect to Denominational Schools which any Class of Persons have by Law in the Province at the Union:

2. All the Powers, Privileges, and Duties at the Union by Law conferred and imposed in Upper Canada on the Separate Schools and School Trustees of the Queen's Roman Catholic Subjects shall be and the same are hereby extended to the Dissentient Schools of the Queen's Protestant and Roman Catholic Subjects in Quebec:

3. Where in any Province a System of Separate or Dissentient Schools exists by Law at the Union or is thereafter established by the Legislature of the Province, an Appeal shall lie to the Governor General in Council from any Act or Decision of any Provincial Authority affecting any Right or Privilege of the Protestant or Roman Catholic Minority of the Queen's Subjects in relation to education:

4. In case any such Provincial Law as from Time to Time seems to the Governor General in Council requisite for the due Execution of

the Provisions of this Section is not made, or in case any Decision of the Governor General in Council on any appeal under this Section is not duly executed by the proper Provincial Authority in that behalf, then and in every such Case, and as far only as the Circumstances of each Case require, the Parliament of Canada may make remedial Laws for the due Execution of the Provisions of this Section and of any Decision of the Governor General in Council under this Section.(50)

Paragraphs (1) to (4) of section 93 do not apply to Quebec.

Uniformity of Laws in Ontario, Nova Scotia and New Brunswick

94 Notwithstanding anything in this Act, the Parliament of Canada may make Provision for the Uniformity of all or any of the Laws relative to Property and Civil Rights in Ontario, Nova Scotia, and New Brunswick, and of the Procedure of all or any of the Courts of Those Three Provinces, and from and after the passing of any Act in that Behalf the Power of the Parliament of Canada to make Laws in relation to any Matter comprised in any such Act shall, notwithstanding anything in this Act, be unrestricted; but any Act of the Parliament of Canada making Provision for such Uniformity shall not have effect in any Province unless and until it is adopted and enacted as Law by the Legislature thereof.

Legislation for Uniformity of Laws in Three Provinces

Old Age Pensions

94 The Parliament of Canada may make laws in relation to old age pensions and supplementary benefits, including survivors' and disability benefits irrespective of age, but no such law shall affect the operation of any law present or future of a provincial legislature in relation to any such matter.

Legislation respecting old age pensions and supplementary benefits

Agriculture and Immigration

95 In each Province the Legislature may make Laws in relation to Agriculture in the Province, and to Immigration into the Province; and it is hereby declared that the Parliament of Canada may from Time to Time make Laws in relation to Agriculture in all or any of the Provinces, and to Immigration into all or any of the Provinces; and

Concurrent Powers of Legislation respecting Agriculture, etc.

any Law of the Legislature of a Province relative to Agriculture or Immigration shall have effect in and for the Province as long and as far only as it is not repugnant to any Act of the Parliament of Canada.

VII. Judicature

Appointment of
Judges

96 The Governor General shall appoint the Judges of the Superior, District, and County Courts in each Province, except those of the Courts of Probate in Nova Scotia and New Brunswick.

Selection of Judges
in Ontario, etc.

97 Until the laws relative to Property and Civil Rights in Ontario, Nova Scotia and New Brunswick, and the Procedure of the Courts in those Provinces, are made uniform, the Judges of the Courts of those Provinces appointed by the Governor General shall be selected from the respective Bars of those Provinces.

Selection of Judges
in Quebec

98 The Judges of the Courts of Quebec shall be selected from the Bar of that Province.

Tenure of office of
Judges

99 (1) Subject to subsection two of this section, the Judges of the Superior Courts shall hold office during good behaviour, but shall be removable by the Governor General on Address of the Senate and House of Commons.

Termination at age
75

(2) A Judge of a Superior Court, whether appointed before or after the coming into force of this section, shall cease to hold office upon attaining the age of seventy-five years, or upon the coming into forces of this section if at that time he has already attained that age.

Salaries, etc., of
Judges

100 The Salaries, Allowances, and Pensions of the Judges of the Superior, District and County Courts (except the Courts of Probate in Nova Scotia and New Brunswick), and of the Admiralty Courts in Cases where the Judges thereof are for the Time being paid by Salary, shall be fixed and provided by the Parliament of Canada.

General Court of
Appeal, etc.

101 The Parliament of Canada may, notwithstanding anything in this Act, from Time to Time provide for the Constitution, Maintenance, and Organization of a General Court of Appeal for Canada, and for the Establishment of any additional Courts for the better Administration of the Laws of Canada.

VIII. Revenues; Debts; Assets; Taxation

102 All Duties and Revenues over which the respective Legislatures of Canada, Nova Scotia, and New Brunswick before and at the Union had and have Power of Appropriation, except such Portions thereof as are by this Act reserved to the respective Legislatures of the Provinces, or are raised by them in accordance with the special Powers conferred on them by this Act, shall form One Consolidated Revenue Fund, to be appropriated for the Public Service of Canada in the Manner and subject to the Charges in this Act provided.

Creation of Consolidated Revenue Fund

103 The Consolidated Revenue Fund of Canada shall be permanently charged with the Costs, Charges, and Expenses incident to the Collection, Management, and Receipt thereof, and the same shall form the First Charge thereon, subject to be reviewed and audited in such Manner as shall be ordered by the Governor General in Council until the Parliament otherwise provides.

Expenses of Collection, etc.

104 The annual Interest on the Public Debts of the Several Provinces of Canada, Nova Scotia, and New Brunswick at the Union shall form the Second Charge on the Consolidated Revenue Fund of Canada.

Interest of Provincial Public Debts

105 Unless altered by the Parliament of Canada, Salary of the Governor General shall be Ten thousand Pounds Sterling Money of the United Kingdom of Great Britain and Ireland, payable out of the Consolidated Revenue Fund of Canada, and the same shall form the Third Charge thereon.

Salary of Governor General

106 Subject to the several Payments by this Act charged on the Consolidated Revenue Fund of Canada, the same shall be appropriated by the Parliament of Canada for the Public Service.

Appropriation from Time to Time

107 All Stocks, Cash, Banker's Balances, and Securities for Money belonging to each Province at the Time of the Union, except as in this Act mentioned, shall be the Property of Canada, and shall be taken in Reduction of the Amount of the respective Debts of the Provinces at the Union.

Transfer of Stocks, etc.

108 The Public Works and Property of each Province, enumerated in the Third Schedule to this Act, shall be the Property of Canada.

Transfer of Property

Property in Lands, Mines, etc.	109	All Lands, Mines, Minerals and Royalties belonging to the Several Provinces of Canada, Nova Scotia, and New Brunswick at the Union, and all Sums then due or payable for such Lands, Mines, Minerals or Royalties, shall belong to the several Provinces of Ontario, Quebec, Nova Scotia and New Brunswick in which the same are situate or arise, subject to any Trusts existing in respect thereof, and to any Interest other than that of the Province in same.
Assets connected with Provincial Debts	110	All Assets connected with such Portions of the Public Debt of each Province as are assumed by that Province shall belong to that Province.
Canada to be liable for Provincial Debts	111	Canada shall be liable for the Debts and Liabilities of each Province existing at the Union.
Debts of Ontario and Quebec	112	Ontario and Quebec conjointly shall be liable to Canada for the Amount (if any) by which the Debt of the Province of Canada exceeds at the Union Sixty-Two million five hundred thousand Dollars, and shall be charged with Interest at the Rate of Five per Centum per Annum thereon.
Assets of Ontario and Quebec	113	The Assets enumerated in the Fourth Schedule to this Act belonging at the Union to the Province of Canada shall be the property of Ontario and Quebec conjointly.
Debt of Nova Scotia	114	Nova Scotia shall be liable to Canada for the Amount (if any) by which its Public Debt exceeds at the Union Eight million Dollars, and shall be charged with Interest at the Rate of Five per Centum per Annum thereon.
Debt of New Brunswick	115	New Brunswick shall be liable to Canada for the Amount (if any) by which its Public Debt exceeds at the Union Seven million Dollars, and shall be charged with Interest at the Rate of Five per Centum per Annum thereon.
Payment of interest to Nova Scotia and New Brunswick	116	In case the Public Debts of Nova Scotia and New Brunswick do not at the Union amount to Eight million and Seven million Dollars respectively, they shall respectively receive by half-yearly Payments in advance from the Government of Canada Interest at Five per Centum per Annum on the Difference between the actual Amounts of their respective Debts and such stipulated Amounts.

117 The several Provinces shall retain all their respective Public Property not otherwise disposed of in this Act, subject to the Right of Canada to assume any Lands or Public Property required for Fortifications or for the Defence of the Country.

Provincial Public Property

118 Repealed.

[Repealed]

119 New Brunswick shall receive by half-yearly Payments in advance from Canada for the Period of Ten Years from the Union an additional Allowance of Sixty-three thousand Dollars per Annum; but as long as the Public Debt of that Province remains under Seven million Dollars, a Deduction equal to the Interest at Five per Centum per Annum on such Deficiency shall be made from that Allowance of Sixty-three thousand Dollars.

Further Grant to New Brunswick

120 All Payments to be made under this Act, or in discharge of Liabilities created under any Act of the Provinces of Canada, Nova Scotia, and New Brunswick respectively, and assumed by Canada, shall, until the Parliament of Canada otherwise directs, be made in such Form and Manner as may from Time to Time be ordered by the Governor General in Council.

Form of Payments

121 All Articles of the Growth, Produce, or Manufacture of any one of the Provinces shall, from and after the Union, be admitted free into each of the other Provinces.

Canadian Manufactures, etc.

122 The Customs and Excise Laws of each Province shall, subject to the Provisions of this Act, continue in force until altered by the Parliament of Canada.

Continuance of Customs and Excise Laws

123 Where Customs Duties are, at the Union, leviable on any Goods, Wars, or Merchandises in any Two Provinces, those Goods, Wares, and Merchandises may, from and after the Union, be imported from one of those Provinces into the other of them on Proof of Payment of the Customs Duty leviable thereon in the Province of Exportation, and on Payment of such further Amount (if any) of Customs Duty as is leviable thereon in the Province of Importation.

Exportation and Importation as between Two Provinces

124 Nothing in this Act shall affect the Right of New Brunswick to levy the Lumber Dues provided in Chapter Fifteen of Title Three of the Revised Statutes of New Brunswick, or in any Act amending that

Lumber Dues in New Brunswick

Act before or after the Union, and not increasing the Amount of such Dues; but the Lumber of any of the Provinces other than New Brunswick shall not be subject to such Dues.(62)

Exemption of Public Lands, etc.

125 No Lands or Property belonging to Canada or any Province shall be liable to Taxation.

Provincial Consolidated Revenue Fund

126 Such Portions of the Duties and Revenues over which the respective Legislatures of Canada, Nova Scotia, and New Brunswick had before the Union Power of Appropriation as are by this Act reserved to the respective Governments and Legislatures of the Provinces, and all Duties and Revenues raised by them in accordance with the special Powers conferred upon them by this Act, shall in each Province form One Consolidated Revenue Fund to be appropriated for the Public Service of the Province.

IX. Miscellaneous Provisions

General

[Repealed]

127 Repealed.

Oath of Allegiance, etc.

128 Every Member of the Senate or House of Commons of Canada shall before taking his Seat therein take and subscribe before the Governor General or some Person authorized by him, and every Member of a Legislative Council or Legislative Assembly of any Province shall before taking this Seat therein take and subscribe before the Lieutenant Governor of the Province or some Person authorized by him, the Oath of Allegiance contained in the Fifth Schedule to this Act; and every Member of the Senate of Canada and every Member of the Legislative Council of Quebec shall also, before taking his Seat therein, take and subscribe before the Governor General, or some Person authorized by him, the Declaration contained in the same Schedule.

Continuance of existing Laws, Courts, Officers, etc.

129 Except as otherwise provided by this Act, all Laws in force in Canada, Nova Scotia or New Brunswick at the Union, and all Courts of Civil and Criminal Jurisdiction, and all legal Commissions, Powers, and Authorities, and all Officers, Judicial, Administrative, and Ministerial, existing therein at the Union, shall continue in Ontario, Que-

bec, Nova Scotia and New Brunswick respectively, as if the Union had not been made; subject nevertheless (except with respect to such as are enacted by or exist under Acts of the Parliament of Great Britain or of the Parliament of the United Kingdom of Great Britain and Ireland), to be repealed, abolished, or altered by the Parliament of Canada, or by the Legislature of the respective Province, according to the Authority of the Parliament or of that Legislature under this Act.

130 Until the Parliament of Canada otherwise provides, all Officers of the several Provinces having Duties to discharge in relation to Matters other than those coming within the Classes of Subjects by this Act assigned exclusively to the Legislatures of the Provinces shall be Officers of Canada, and shall continue to discharge the Duties of their respective Offices under the same Liabilities, Responsibilities, and Penalties as if the Union had not been made. *Transfer of Officers to Canada*

131 Until the Parliament of Canada otherwise provides, the Governor General in Council may from Time to Time appoint such Officers as the Governor General in Council deems necessary or proper for the effectual Execution of this Act. *Appointment of new Officers*

132 The Parliament and Government of Canada shall have all Powers necessary or proper for performing the Obligations of Canada or of any Province thereof, as Part of the British Empire, towards Foreign Countries, arising under Treaties between the Empire and such Foreign Countries. *Treaty Obligations*

133 Either the English or the French Language may be used by any Person in the Debates of the Houses of the Parliament of Canada and of the Houses of the Legislature of Quebec; and both these Languages shall be used in the respective Records and Journals of those Houses; and either of those Languages may be used by any Person or in any Pleading or Process in or issuing from any Court of Canada established under this Act, and in or from all or any of the Courts of Quebec. *Use of English and French Languages*

The Acts of the Parliament of Canada and of the Legislature of Quebec shall be printed and published in both those Languages.

Appointment of Executive Officers for Ontario and Quebec

134 Until the Legislature of Ontario or of Quebec otherwise provides, the Lieutenant Governors of Ontario and Quebec may each appoint under the Great seal of the Province the following Officers, to hold Office during Pleasure, that is to say,—the Attorney General, the Secretary and Registrar of the Province, the Treasurer of the Province, the Commissioner of Crown Lands, and the Commissioner of Agriculture and Public Works, and in the Case of Quebec the Solicitor General, and may, by Order of the Lieutenant Governor in Council, from Time to Time prescribe the Duties of those Officers, and of the several Departments over which they shall preside or to which they shall belong, and of the Officers and Clerks thereof, and may also appoint other and additional Officers to hold Office during Pleasure, and may from Time to Time prescribe the Duties of those Officers, and of the several Departments over which they shall preside or to which they shall belong, and of the Officers and Clerks thereof.

Powers, Duties, etc., of Executive Officers

135 Until the Legislature of Ontario or Quebec otherwise provides, all Rights, Powers, Duties, Functions, Responsibilities, or Authorities at the passing of this Act vested in or imposed on the Attorney General, Solicitor General, Secretary and Registrar of the Province of Canada, Minister of Finance, Commissioner of Crown Lands, Commissioner of Public Works, and Minister of Agriculture and Receiver General, by any Law, Statute, or Ordinance of Upper Canada, Lower Canada, or Canada, and not repugnant to this Act, shall be vested in or imposed on any Officer to be appointed by the Lieutenant Governor for the Discharge of the same or any of them; and the Commissioner of Agriculture and Public Works shall perform the Duties and Functions of the Office of Minister of Agriculture at the passing of this Act imposed by the Law of the Province of Canada, as well as those of the Commissioner of Public Works.

Great Seals

136 Until altered by the Lieutenant Governor in Council, the Great Seals of Ontario and Quebec respectively shall be the same, or of the same Design, as those used in the Provinces of Upper Canada and Lower Canada respectively before their Union as the Province of Canada.

137 The words "and from thence to the End of the then next ensuing *Construction of* Session of the Legislature," or Words to the same Effect, used in any *temporary Acts* temporary Act of the Province of Canada not expired before the Union, shall be construed to extend and apply to the next Session of the Parliament of Canada if the Subject Matter of the Act is within the Powers of the same as defined by this Act, or to the next Sessions of the Legislatures of Ontario and Quebec respectively if the Subject Matter of the Act is within the Powers of the same as defined by this Act.

138 From and after the Union the Use of the Words "Upper Canada" *As to Errors in* instead of "Ontario," or "Lower Canada" instead of "Quebec," in any *Names* Deed, Writ, Process, Pleading, Document, Matter or Thing shall not invalidate the same.

139 Any Proclamation under the Great Seal of the Province of Canada *As to issue of* issued before the Union to take effect at a Time which is subsequent *Proclamations before* to the Union, whether relating to that Province, or to Upper Canada, *Union, to commence* or to Lower Canada, and the several Matters and Things therein pro- *after Union* claimed, shall be and continue of like Force and Effect as if the Union had not been made.

140 Any Proclamation which is authorized by any Act of the Legislature *As to issue of* of the Province of Canada to be issued under the Great Seal of the *Proclamations after* Province of Canada, whether relating to that Province, or to Upper *Union* Canada, or to Lower Canada, and which is not issued before the Union, may be issued by the Lieutenant Governor of Ontario or of Quebec, as its Subject Matter requires, under the Great Seal thereof; and from and after the Issue of such Proclamation the same and the several Matters and Things therein proclaimed shall be and continue of the like Force and Effect in Ontario or Quebec as if the Union had not been made.

141 The Penitentiary of the Province of Canada shall, until the Parlia- *Penitentiary* ment of Canada otherwise provides, be and continue the Penitentiary of Ontario and of Quebec.

142 The Division and Adjustment of the Debts, Credits, Liabilities, Prop- *Arbitration* erties, and Assets of Upper Canada and Lower Canada shall be *respecting Debts, etc.* referred to the Arbitrament of Three Arbitrators, One chosen by the

Government of Ontario, One by the Government of Quebec, and One by the Government of Canada; and the Selection of the Arbitrators shall not be made until the Parliament of Canada and the Legislatures of Ontario and Quebec have met; and the Arbitrator chosen by the Government of Canada shall not be a Resident either in Ontario or in Quebec.

Division of Records   143   The Governor General in Council may from Time to Time order that such and so many of the Records, Books, and Documents of the Province of Canada as he thinks fit shall be appropriated and delivered either to Ontario or to Quebec, and the same shall thenceforth be the Property of that Province; and any Copy thereof or Extract therefrom, duly certified by the Officer having charge of the Original thereof, shall be admitted as Evidence.

Constitution of   144   The Lieutenant Governor of Quebec may from Time to Time, by
Townships in   Proclamation under the Great Seal of the Province, to take effect
Quebec   from a Day to be appointed therein, constitute Townships in those Parts of the Province of Quebec in which Townships are not then already constituted, and fix the Metes and Bounds thereof.

X. Intercolonial Railway

[Repealed]   145   Repealed.

XI. Admission of Other Colonies

Power to admit   146   It shall be lawful for the Queen, by and with the Advice of Her
Newfoundland, etc.,   Majesty's Most Honourable Privy Council, on Addresses from the
into the Union   Houses of Parliament of Canada, and from the Houses of the respective Legislatures of the Colonies or Provinces of Newfoundland, Prince Edward Island, and British Columbia, to admit those Colonies or Provinces, or any of them, into the Union, and on Address from the Houses of Parliament of Canada to admit Rupert's Land and the North-western Territory, or either of them, into the Union, on such Terms and Conditions in each Case as are in the Addresses expressed and as the Queen thinks fit to approve, subject to the Provisions of this Act; and the Provisions of any Order in Council on that Behalf shall have effect as if they had been enacted by the Parliament of the United Kingdom of Great Britain and Ireland.

147   In case of the Admission of Newfoundland and Prince Edward Island, or either of them, each shall be entitled to a Representation in the Senate of Canada of Four Members, and (notwithstanding anything in this act) in case of the Admission of Newfoundland the normal Number of Senators shall be Seventy-six and their maximum Number shall be Eighty-two; but Prince Edward Island when admitted shall be deemed to be comprised in the third of the Three Divisions into which Canada is, in relation to the Constitution of the Senate, divided by this act, and accordingly, after the Admission of Prince Edward Island, whether Newfoundland is admitted or not, the Representation of Nova Scotia and New Brunswick in the senate shall, as Vacancies occur, be reduced from Twelve to Ten Members respectively, and the Representation of each of those Provinces shall not be increased at any Time beyond Ten, except under the Provisions of this Act for the Appointment of Three or Six additional Senators under the Direction of the Queen.

Constitution Act 1982

Schedule B
Constitution Act 1982

Part I
Canadian Charter of Rights and Freedoms

Whereas Canada is founded upon the principles that recognize the supremacy of God and the rule of law:

Guarantee of Rights and Freedoms

Rights and freedoms in Canada

1 The *Canadian Charter of Rights and Freedoms* guarantees the rights and freedoms set out in it subject only to such reasonable limits prescribed by law as can be demonstrably justified in a free and democratic society.

Fundamental Freedoms

Fundamental freedoms

2 Everyone has the following fundamental freedoms:
(*a*) freedom of conscience and religion;
(*b*) freedom of thought, belief, opinion and expression, including freedom of the press and other means of communication;
(*c*) freedom of peaceful assembly; and
(*d*) freedom of association.

Democratic Rights

Democratic rights of citizens

3 Every citizen of Canada has the right to vote in an election of members of the House of Commons or of a legislative assembly and to be qualified for membership therein.

Maximum duration of legislative bodies

4 (1) No House of Commons and no legislative assembly shall continue for longer than five years from the date fixed for the return of the writs at a general election of its members.

Continuation in special circumstances

(2) In time of real or apprehended war, invasion or insurrection, a House of Commons may be continued by Parliament and a legislative assembly may be continued by the legislature beyond five years

if such continuation is not opposed by the votes of more than one-third of the members of the House of Commons or the legislative assembly, as the case may be.

5 There shall be a sitting of Parliament and of each legislature at least once every twelve months.

Annual sitting of legislative bodies

Mobility Rights

6 (1) Every citizen of Canada has the right to enter, remain in, and leave Canada.

Mobility of citizens

(2) Every citizen of Canada and every person who has the status of a permanent resident of Canada has the right
(*a*) to move to and take up residence in any province; and
(*b*) to pursue the gaining of livelihood in any province.

Rights to move and gain livelihood

(3) The rights specified in subsection (2) are subject to
(*a*) any laws or practices of general application in force in a province other than those that discriminate among persons primarily on the basis of present or previous residence; and
(*b*) any laws providing for reasonable residency requirements as a qualification for the receipt of publicly provided social services.

Limitation

(4) Subsections (2) and (3) do not preclude any law, program or activity that has as its object the amelioration in a province of conditions of individuals in that province who are socially or economically disadvantaged if the rate of employment in that province is below the rate of employment in Canada.

Affirmative action programs

Legal Rights

7 Everyone has the right to life, liberty and security of the person and the right not to be deprived thereof except in accordance with the principles of fundamental justice.

Life, liberty and security of person

8 Everyone has the right to be secure against unreasonable search or seizure.

Search or seizure

Detention or imprisonment	9	Everyone has the right not to be arbitrarily detained or imprisoned.
Arrest or detention	10	Everyone has the right on arrest or detention

10 Everyone has the right on arrest or detention

(*a*) to be informed promptly of the reason therefor;

(*b*) to retain and instruct counsel without delay and to be informed of that right; and

(*c*) to have the validity of the detention determined by way of *habeas corpus* and to be released if the detention is not lawful.

Proceedings in criminal and penal matters

11 Any person charged with an offence has the right

(*a*) to be informed without unreasonable delay of the specific offence;

(*b*) to be tried within a reasonable time;

(*c*) not to be compelled to be a witness in a proceedings against that person in respect of the offence;

(*d*) to be presumed innocent until proven guilty according to law in a fair and public hearing by an independent and impartial tribunal;

(*e*) not to be denied reasonable bail without cause;

(*f*) except in the case of an offence under military law tried before a military tribunal, to the benefit of trial by jury where the maximum punishment for the offence is imprisonment for five years or a more severe punishment;

(*g*) not to be found guilty on account of any act or omission unless, at the time of the act or omission, it constituted an offence under Canadian or International law or was criminal according to the general principles of law recognized by the community of nations;

(*h*) if finally acquitted of the offence, not to be tried for it again and, if finally found guilty and punished for the offence, not to be tried or punished for it again; and

(*i*) if found guilty of the offence and if punishment for the offence has been varied between the time of commission and the time of sentencing, to the benefit of the lesser punishment.

Treatment or punishment

12 Everyone has the right not to be subjected to any cruel or unusual treatment or punishment.

Self-crimination

13 A witness who testifies in any proceedings has the right not to have any incriminating evidence so given used to incriminate that witness in any other proceedings, except in a prosecution for perjury or for the giving of contradictory evidence.

14   A party or witness in any proceedings who does not understand or speak the language in which the proceedings are conducted or who is deaf has the right to the assistance of an interpreter.

Interpreter

Equality Rights

15   (1) Every individual is equal before and under the law and has the right to the equal protection and equal benefit of the law without discrimination, and, in particular, without discrimination based on race, national or ethnic origin, colour, religion, sex, age, or mental or physical disability.

Equality before and under law and equal protection and benefit of law

(2) Subsection (1) does not preclude any law, program or activity that has as its object the amelioration of conditions of disadvantaged individuals or groups including those that are disadvantaged because of race, national or ethnic origin, colour, religion, sex, age, or mental or physical disability.

Affirmative action programs

Official Languages of Canada

16   (1) English and French are the official languages of Canada and have equality of status and equal rights and privileges as to their use in all institutions of the Parliament and government of Canada.

Official languages of Canada

(2) English and French are the official languages of New Brunswick and have equality of status and equal rights and privileges as to the use in all institutions of the legislature and government of New Brunswick.

Official languages of New Brunswick

(3) Nothing in this Charter limits the authority of Parliament or a legislature to advance the equality of status or use of English and French.

Advancement of status and use

16.1   (1) The English linguistic community and the French linguistic community in New Brunswick have equality of status and equal rights and privileges, including the right to distinct educational institutions and such distinct cultural institutions as are necessary for the preservation and promotion of those communities.

English and French linguistic communities in New Brunswick

Role of the legislature and government of New Brunswick	(2) The role of the legislature and government of New Brunswick to preserve and promote the status, rights and privileges referred to in subsection (1) is affirmed.
Proceedings of Parliament	17 (1) Everyone has the right to use English or French in any debates or other proceedings of Parliament.
Proceedings of New Brunswick legislature	(2) Everyone has the right to use English or French in any debates and other proceedings of the legislature of New Brunswick.
Parliamentary statutes and records	18 The Statutes, records and journals of Parliament shall be printed and published in English and French and both language versions are equally authoritative.
New Brunswick statutes and records	(2) The statutes, records and journals of the legislature of New Brunswick shall be printed and published in English and French and both language versions are equally authoritative.
Proceedings in courts established by Parliament	19 (1) Either English or French may be used by any person in, or in any pleading in or process issuing from, any court established by Parliament. (2) Either English or French may be used by any person in, or in any pleading in or process issuing from any court of New Brunswick.
Communications by public with federal institutions	20 (1) Any member of the public in Canada has the right to communicate with, and to receive available services from, any head or central office of an institution of the Parliament or government of Canada in English or French, and has the same right with respect to any other office of any such institution where (*a*) there is significant demand for communications with and services from that office in such language; or (*b*) due to the nature of the office, it is reasonable that communications with and services from that office be available in both English and French.
Communications by public with New Brunswick institutions	(2) Any member of the public in New Brunswick has the right to communicate with, and to receive available services from, any office of an institution of the legislature or government of New Brunswick in English or French.

21 Nothing in sections 16 to 20 abrogates or derogates from any right, privilege or obligation with respect to the English and French languages, or either of them, that exists or is continued by virtue of any other provision of the Constitution of Canada.

Continuation of existing constitutional provisions

22 Nothing in sections 16 to 20 abrogates or derogates from any legal or customary right or privilege acquired or enjoyed either before or after the coming into force of this Charter with respect to any language that is not English or French.

Rights and privileges preserved

Minority Language Educational Rights

23 (1) Citizens of Canada
(*a*) whose first language learned and still understood is that of the English or French linguistic minority population of the province in which they reside, or
(*b*) who have received their primary school instruction in Canada in English or French and reside in a province where the language in which they received that instruction is the language of the English or French linguistic minority population of the province,
have the right to have their children receive primary and secondary school instruction in that language in that province.

Language of instruction

(2) Citizens of Canada of whom any child has received or is receiving primary or secondary school instruction in English or French in Canada, have the right to have all their children receive primary and secondary school instruction in the same language.

Continuity of language instruction

(3) The right of citizens of Canada under subsections (1) and (2) to have their children receive primary and secondary school instruction in the language of the English or French linguistic minority population of a province
(*a*) applies wherever in the province the number of children of citizens who have such a right is sufficient to warrant the provision to them out of public funds of minority language instruction; and
(*b*) includes, where the number of children so warrants, the right to have them receive that instruction in minority language educational facilities provided out of public funds.

Application where numbers warrant

Enforcement

Enforcement of guaranteed rights and freedoms

24 (1) Anyone whose rights or freedoms, as guaranteed by this Charter, have been infringed or denied may apply to a court of competent jurisdiction to obtain such remedy as the court considers appropriate and just in the circumstances.

Exclusion of evidence bringing administration of justice into disrepute

(2) Where, in proceedings under subsection (1), a court concludes that evidence was obtained in a manner that infringed or denied any rights or freedoms guaranteed by this Charter, the evidence shall be excluded if it is established that, having regard to all the circumstances, the admission of it in the proceedings would bring the administration of justice into disrepute.

General

Aboriginal rights and freedoms not affected by Charter

25 The guarantee in this Charter of certain rights and freedoms shall not be construed so as to abrogate or derogate from any aboriginal, treaty or other rights or freedoms that pertain to the aboriginal peoples of Canada including

(*a*) any rights or freedoms that have been recognized by the Royal Proclamation of October 7, 1763; and

(*b*) any rights or freedoms that now exist by way of land claims agreements or may be so acquired.

Other rights and freedoms not affected by Charter

26 The guarantee in this Charter of certain rights and freedoms shall not be construed as denying the existence of any other rights or freedoms that exist in Canada.

Multicultural heritage

27 This Charter shall be interpreted in a manner consistent with the preservation and enhancement of the multicultural heritage of Canadians.

Rights guaranteed equally to both sexes

28 Notwithstanding anything in this Charter, the rights and freedoms referred to in it are guaranteed equally to male and female persons.

29 Nothing in this Charter abrogates or derogates from any rights or privileges guaranteed by or under the Constitution of Canada in respect of denominational, separate or dissentient schools.

Rights respecting certain schools preserved

30 A reference in this Charter to a province or to the legislative assembly or legislature of a province shall be deemed to include a reference to the Yukon Territory and the Northwest Territories, or to the appropriate legislative authority thereof, as the case may be. *Application to territories and territorial authorities*

31 Nothing in this Charter extends the legislative powers of any body or authority. *Legislative powers not extended*

Application of Charter

32 (1) This Charter applies *Application of Charter*
(*a*) to the Parliament and government of Canada in respect of all matters within the authority of Parliament including all matters relating to the Yukon Territory and Northwest Territories; and (*b*) to the legislatures and governments of each province in respect of all matters within the authority of the legislature of each province.

(2) Notwithstanding subsection (1), section 15 shall not have effect until three years after this section comes into force. *Exception*

33 (1) Parliament or the legislature of a province may expressly declare in an Act of Parliament or of the legislature, as the case may be, that the Act or a provision thereof shall operate notwithstanding a provision included in section 2 or section 7 to 15 of this Charter. *Exception where express declaration*

(2) An Act or a provision of an Act in respect of which a declaration made under this section is in effect shall have such operation as it would have but for the provision of this Charter referred to in the declaration. *Operation of exception*

(3) A declaration made under subsection (1) shall cease to have effect five years after it comes into force or on such earlier date as may be specified in the declaration. *Five year limitation*

(4) Parliament or the legislature of a province may re-enact a declaration made under subsection (1). *Re-enactment*

(5) Subsection (3) applies in respect of re-enactment made under subsection (4). *Five year limitation*

Citation

34 This Part may be cited as the *Canadian Charter of Rights and Freedoms.*

Part II
Rights of the Aboriginal Peoples of Canada

Recognition of existing aboriginal and treaty rights

35 (1) The existing aboriginal and treaty rights of the aboriginal peoples of Canada are hereby recognized and affirmed.
Definition of "aboriginal peoples of Canada"

(2) In this Act, "aboriginal peoples of Canada" includes the Indian, Inuit, and Métis peoples of Canada.

Land claims agreements

(3) For greater certainty, in subsection (1) "treaty rights" includes rights that now exist by way of land claims agreements or may be so acquired.

Aboriginal and treaty rights are guaranteed equally to both sexes

(4) Notwithstanding any other provision of this Act, the aboriginal and treaty rights referred to in subsection (1) are guaranteed equally to male and female persons.

Commitment to participation in constitutional conference

35.1 The government of Canada and the provincial governments are committed to the principle that, before any amendment is made to class 24 of section 91 of the "*Constitution Act, 1867,*" to section 25 of this Act or to this Part,

(*a*) a constitutional conference that includes in its agenda an item relating to the proposed amendment, composed of the Prime Minister of Canada and the first ministers of the provinces, will be convened by the Prime Minister of Canada; and

(*b*) the Prime Minister of Canada will invite representatives of the aboriginal peoples of Canada to participate in the discussions on that item.

Part III
Equalization and Regional Disparities

36 (1) Without altering the legislative authority of Parliament or of the provincial legislatures, or the rights of any of them with respect to the exercise of their legislative authority, Parliament and the legislatures, together with the government of Canada and the provincial governments, are committed to
Commitment to promote equal opportunities

(a) promoting equal opportunities for the well-being of Canadians;
(b) furthering the economic development to reduce disparity in opportunities; and
(c) providing essential public services of reasonable quality to all Canadians.

(2) Parliament and the government of Canada are committed to the principle of making equalization payments to ensure that provincial governments have sufficient revenues to provide reasonably comparable levels of public services at reasonably comparable levels of taxation.
Commitment respecting public services

Part IV
Constitutional Conferences

37 (97)

Part IV
Constitutional Conferences

37.1 (98)

Part V
Proceedure for Amending Constitution of Canada

38 (1) An amendment to the Constitution of Canada may be made by proclamation issued by the Governor General under the Great Seal of Canada where so authorized by
General procedure for amending Constitution of Canada

(a) resolutions of the Senate and House of Commons; and
(b) resolutions of the legislative assemblies of at least two-thirds of the provinces that have, in the aggregate, according to the then latest general census, at least fifty per cent of all the population of the provinces.

Majority of members	(2) An amendment made under subsection (1) that derogates from the legislative powers, the proprietary rights or any other rights or privileges of the legislature or government of a province shall require a resolution supported by a majority of the members of each of the Senate, the House of Commons and the legislative assemblies required under subsection (1).

Expression of dissent

(3) An amendment referred to in subsection (2) shall not have effect in a province the legislative assembly of which has expressed its dissent thereto by resolution supported by a majority of its members prior to the issue of the proclamation to which the amendment relates unless that legislative assembly, subsequently, by resolution supported by a majority of its members, revokes its dissent and authorizes the amendment.

Revocation of dissent

(4) A resolution of dissent made for the purposes of subsection (3) may be revoked at any time before or after the issue of the proclamation to which it relates.

Restriction on proclamation

39 (1) A proclamation shall not be issued under subsection 38(1) before the expiration of one year from the adoption of the resolution initiating the amendment procedure thereunder, unless the legislative assembly of each province has previously adopted a resolution of assent or dissent.

Idem

(2) A proclamation shall not be issued under subsection 38(1) after the expiration of three years from the adoption of the resolution initiating the amendment procedure thereunder.

Compensation

40 Where an amendment is made under subsection 38(1) that transfers provincial legislative powers relating to education or other cultural matters from provincial legislatures to Parliament, Canada shall provide reasonable compensation to any province to which the amendment does not apply.

Amendment by unanimous consent

41 An amendment to the Constitution of Canada in relation to the following matters may be made by proclamation issued by the Governor General under the Great Seal of Canada only where authorized by resolutions of the Senate and House of Commons and of the legislative assemblies of each province:

(*a*) the office of the Queen, the Governor General and the Lieutenant Governor of a province;

(*b*) the right of a province to a number of members in the House of Commons not less than the number of Senators by which the province is entitled to be represented at the time this Part comes into force;

(*c*) subject to section 43, the use of the English or the French language;

(*d*) the composition of the Supreme Court of Canada; and

(*e*) an amendment to this Part.

42   (1) An amendment to the Constitution of Canada in relation to the following matters may be made only in accordance with subsection 38(1):   *Amendment by general procedure*

(*a*) the principle of proportionate representation of the provinces in the House of Commons prescribed by the Constitution of Canada;

(*b*) the powers of the Senate and the method of selecting Senators;

(*c*) the number of members by which a province is entitled to be represented in the Senate and the residence qualifications of Senators;

(*d*) subject to paragraph 41(*d*), the Supreme Court of Canada; (*e*) the extension of existing provinces into the territories; and (*f*) notwithstanding any other law or practice, the establishment of new provinces.

(2) Subsections 38(2) to 38(4) do not apply in respect of amendments in relation to matters referred to in subsection (1).   *Exception*

43   An amendment to the Constitution of Canada in relation to any provision that applies to one or more, but not all, provinces, including   *Amendment of provisions relating to some but not all provinces*

(*a*) any alteration to boundaries between provinces, and

(*b*) any amendment to any provisions that relate to the use of the English or the French language within a province,

     may be made by proclamation issued by the Governor General under the Great Seal of Canada only where so authorized by resolutions of the Senate and House of Commons and of the legislative assembly of each province to which the amendment applies.

44   Subject to sections 41 and 42, Parliament may exclusively make laws amending the Constitution of Canada in relation to executive government of Canada or the Senate and House of Commons.   *Amendments by Parliament*

Amendments by *provincial legislatures*	45 Subject to section 41, the legislature of each province may exclusively make laws amending the constitution of the province.
Initiation of *amendment procedures*	46 (1) The procedures for amendment under sections 38, 41, 42, and 43 may be initiated either by the Senate or the House of Commons or by the legislative assembly of a province.
Revocation of *authorization*	(2) A resolution of assent made for the purposes of this Part may be revoked at any time before the issue of a proclamation authorized by it.
Amendments without *Senate resolution*	47 (1) An amendment to the Constitution of Canada made by proclamation under section 38, 41, 42, or 43 may be made without a resolution of the Senate authorizing the issue of the proclamation if, within one hundred and eighty days after the adoption by the House of Commons of a resolution authorizing its issue, the Senate has not adopted such a resolution and if, at any time after the expiration of that period, the House of Commons again adopts the resolution.
Computation of *period*	(2) Any period when Parliament is prorogued or dissolved shall not be counted in computing the one hundred and eighty day period referred to in subsection (1).
Advice to issue *proclamation*	48 The Queen's Privy Council for Canada shall advise the Governor General to issue a proclamation under this Part forthwith on the adoption of the resolution required for an amendment made by proclamation under this part.
Constitutional *conference*	A constitutional conference composed of the Prime Minister of Canada and the first ministers of the provinces shall be convened by the Prime Minister of Canada within fifteen years after this Part comes into force to review the provisions of this Part.

Part VI
Amendment to the Constitution Act, 1867

50 (100)

51 (101)

Part VII
General

52 (1) The Constitution of Canada is the supreme law of Canada, and any law that is inconsistent with the provisions of the Constitution is, to the extent of the inconsistency, of no force or effect.

Primacy of Constitution of Canada

(2) The Constitution of Canada includes
(a) the *Canada Act, 1982,* including this Act;
(b) the Acts and orders referred to in the Schedule; and
(c) any amendment to any Act or order referred to in paragraph (a) or (b).

Constitution of Canada

(3) Amendments to the Constitution of Canada shall be made only in accordance with the authority contained in the Constitution of Canada.

Amendments to Constitution of Canada

53 (1) The enactments referred to in Column I of the schedule are hereby repealed or amended to the extent indicated in Column II thereof, and unless repealed, shall continue as law in Canada under the names set out in Column III thereof.

Repeals and new names

(2) Every enactment, except the *Canada Act, 1982,* that refers to an enactment referred to in the schedule by the name in Column I thereof is hereby amended by substituting for that name the corresponding name in Column III thereof, and any British North America Act not referred to in the schedule may be cited as the *Constitution Act* followed by the year and number, if any, of its enactment.

Consequential amendments

54 Part IV is repealed on the day that is one year after this Part comes into force, and this section may be repealed and this Act renumbered, consequentially upon the repeal of Part IV and this section, by proclamation issued by the Governor General under the Great Seal of Canada.

Repeal and consequential amendments

54.1   *[Repealed]*

55 A French version of the portions of the Constitution of Canada referred to in the schedule shall be prepared by the Minister of Justice of Canada as expeditiously as possible and, when any portion

French version of Constitution of Canada

thereof sufficient to warrant action being taken has been prepared, it shall be put forward for enactment by proclamation issued by the Governor General under the Great Seal of Canada pursuant to the procedure then applicable to an amendment of the same provisions of the Constitution of Canada.

English and French versions of certain constitutional texts 56 Where any portion of the Constitution of Canada has been or is enacted in English and French or where a French version of any portion of the Constitution is enacted pursuant to section 55, the English and French versions of that portion of the Constitution are equally authoritative.

English and French versions of this Act 57 The English and French versions of this Act are equally authoritative.

Commencement 58 Subject to section 59, this Act shall come into force on a day to be fixed by proclamation issued by the Queen or the Governor General under the Great Seal of Canada.

Commencement of paragraph 23(1)a in respect of Quebec 59 (1) Paragraph 23(1)(*a*) shall come into force in respect of Quebec on a day to be fixed by proclamation issued by the Queen or the Governor General under the Great Seal of Canada.

Authorization of Quebec (2) A proclamation under subsection (1) shall be issued only where authorized by the legislative assembly or government of Quebec.

Repeal of this section (3) This section may be repealed on the day paragraph 23(1)(*a*) comes into force in respect of Quebec and this Act amended and renumbered, consequentially upon the repeal of this section, by proclamation issued by the Queen or the Governor General under the Great Seal of Canada.

Short title and citations 60 This Act may be cited as the *Constitution Act, 1982*, and the Constitution Acts 1867 to 1975 (No. 2) and this Act may be cited together as the *Constitution Acts, 1867 to 1982*.

References 61 A reference to the "*Constitution Acts, 1867 to 1982*" shall be deemed to include a reference to the "*Constitution Amendment Proclamation, 1983*."

Questions for Discussion

Chapter 1

1 Developments in technology have made direct democracy more possible. What are the pros and cons of having more direct democracy?

2 Can you think of a recent example where the Canadian government has acted as a tyranny of the majority?

Chapter 2

3 Since Canada is a democracy based on majority rule, why should a minority of provinces be able to block constitutional amendments?

4 If you had to choose between a constitution based on law and a constitution based on convention, which would you prefer?

Chapter 3

5 What are the respective strengths and weaknesses of majority and minority government?

6 Which system of government—responsible government or separation of powers—is more democratic?

Chapter 4

7 Would Canadians be better served by a dominant federal government or by powerful provincial governments?

8 Why should tax dollars from Ontario, British Columbia, and Alberta be transferred to less prosperous provinces under the equalization formula? Shouldn't tax revenues be spent in the part of the country where they are raised?

Chapter 5

9   Was the adoption of the Charter of Rights a good idea?

10   Should the notwithstanding clause be deleted from the Charter?

Chapter 6

11   Given that Canada is a democracy, should the governor general not be elected?

12   Are prime ministers and premiers too powerful?

Chapter 7

13   What do you think could be done to improve the effectiveness of backbenchers?

14   How would making the Senate an elected body improve government? What problems might it cause?

Chapter 8

15   Given that judges have considerable political power, should nominees to the Supreme Court not be examined by Parliament?

16   In your view, what sort of misconduct would justify dismissing a judge?

Chapter 9

17   Is a minority group properly represented in the House of Commons if no MPs are members of that group?

18   What impact would the adoption of an electoral system based on proportional representation have on national unity?

Chapter 10

19   Given that the Bloc Québécois is dedicated to the break-up of Canada as we know it, was it right for that party to be given the role of Her Majesty's Loyal Opposition?

20   If a clear majority of the voters in a riding with a government MP oppose a government bill, how should the MP vote?

Chapter 11

21 If it were practically possible to ban all public opinion polls during election campaigns, would such a measure strengthen our democracy?

22 To what extent do you participate in political life? What prevents you from participating more actively?

Index

Aberhart, William 95
Aboriginal peoples 42-43, 47-48, 258
adjudication
    of private legal disputes 146-47
    of public law cases 147-48
administrative law 148
advertising, electoral 180
Alberta 40, 88, 89, 95
amending formula 40-41, 43-46, 47-48,
    75, 259-62
aristocracy 20, 35
Aristotle 19-21, 22
Auditor-General 133
Australia 27, 74, 86

backbenchers 135-37
bandwagon effect 214
Bennett, R.B. 150
Berger, Justice Thomas 152-53
bicameralism 86-87
Big M Drug Mart v. The Queen 105, 149-
    50, 154
Bill of Rights (Canada) 96-97
Bill of Rights (US) 95-96
bills 132-33
    government 132
    private members' 132, 137-38
    proclamation of 133
    readings of 132-33
Bleus 194
Bloc Québécois (BQ) 62, 176, 193, 195,
    197

British Columbia 40, 88, 89, 131
British North America (BNA) Act 38,
    98(n.1)
brokerage parties 192-93
Brooks, Stephen 153
Bush, George W. 65, 66
by-election 179
Byng, Lord 114

cabinet 57-59, 66-67, 70, 116-18, 120, 122,
    129, 138, 197
    shadow 136, 197
    size of 118-19
cabinet committee system 118-19, 121
cabinet government 58-59
Callbeck, Katherine 206-07
Campbell, Colin 141
Campbell, Kim 60-62, 206
Canada Act, 1982 42
Canada Health and Social Transfer
    (CHST) 83
Canadian Alliance 62, 190(n.1), 193, 196-
    97
Canadian Bill of Rights 96-97
Canadian Broadcasting Corporation
    (CBC) 212
Canadian Constitution 37-49, see also
    Constitution Act, 1867 and *Constitution
    Act, 1982*
    amendments to 40-41, 43-46, 47-48
    basic principles of 53-106
    judicial review of 46-47, 149-50

patriation of 41-42
Canadian Judicial Council 152
Canadian Labour Congress (CLC) 196
Cartier, George Etienne 194
caucus, parliamentary 62, 136
central agencies 123
centralized vs. decentralized federal union 78-79
Charest, Jean 155
Charlottetown Accord 48, 85, 89, 162, 171
Charter of Rights and Freedoms 26, 42, 46, 70, 91-106, 150, 151, 154, 163, 180, 184
  adoption of 94-97
  definition of 91-94
  notwithstanding clause (Section 33) 99-101
  opposition to 97-99
  political impact of 103-06
  Section 1 of 101-03
  text of 250-58
checks and balances 67
Chief Clerk of Privy Council 121
Chief Electoral Officer 179
China 192
Chrétien, Jean 49, 61-62, 65, 118(n.1), 119, 122
Churchill, Winston 33
citizenship
  democratic 214-16
  equality of 24
civil code 147
civil education 214-16
civil service 123-25
civil society 35
Clarity Act 49
Clark, Joe 57, 63, 116, 142(n.1)
Clarkson, Adrienne 112
classical federalism 79-80, 81
classical liberalism 188
Clear Grits 194
Clerk of the House 131, 133
Clinton, Bill 66, 70
closure 135
collective responsibility 56, 117-18
Combines Investigation Act 92-94
common good 20

common law 147
Commonwealth Cooperative Federation (CCF) 193, 195-96
concurring opinion 161
conditional grant 83
Confederation of Regions Party (COR) 195
confidence 56-57, 62-64, 129, 138
conscription crisis 183(n.1)
conservatism 188
Conservative Party, see Progressive Conservative
constituencies, see ridings
Constitution, see Canadian Constitution and US Constitution
Constitution Act, 1867 (CA 1867) 37-41, 53, 77-78, 81-82, 83, 92, 110-11, 112, 116, 119, 123, 127, 139-40, 145-47, 150-51, 154-55, 159, 160, 163, 173, 174, 183
  preamble to 39, 53, 73, 95(n.1), 109-10, 127, 172-73
  Sections 91 and 92, 77-78
  text of 217-49
Constitution Act, 1982 (CA 1982) 38, 40-46, 47, 48, 65, 84, 91, 92, 97, 119, 130, 139(n.2), 152, 169, 179, 183
  amending formulas of 43-46, 75, 259-62
  text of 250-64
constitutional charter of rights, see Charter of Rights and Freedoms
constitutional conventions 32-33, 39, 140-41
constitutional laws 33-37, 38-43
constitutional monarchy 110
constitutional politics, contemporary 47-49
constitutionalism 27, 215
constitutions
  forms of 31-37
  functions of 29-31
conventions 31-33, 37
  constitutional 32-33, 39, 140-41
  of responsible government 56-58
cooperative federalism 80-81
"Court Party" 106
courts, Canadian 156-62

federally created 160
  inferior vs. superior 159-60
  Section 92 v. Section 96, 160
Creditistes 195
Criminal Code of Canada 148
criminal law 148
Crown, the 109-11, 115, 120, 123, 128
  representatives of 111-25
crown attorneys 110

Day, Stockwell 197
decentralization 78-79, 88-90
delegate model 170-71
democracy 20-27, 35
  Charter of Rights and Freedoms and
  98-99
  definition of 20-21
  direct 22
  indirect 23
  liberal 91, 97, 191, 201-02
  parliamentary 22-23
  representative 22-23
democratic citizenship 214-16
Depression 80
deputy minister 125
deputy prime minister 121
Deschenes, Jules 155
Dicey, A.V. 98(n.1)
Dickson, Brian 103
dictatorship 27
Diefenbaker, John 61, 63
Dion, Stephane 56
direct democracy 22
direct taxation 78, 82
disallowance 78
discipline, party 68, 129, 197
dissenting opinion 161
dissolution 114, 130, 179
distinct society 47
division of powers 31, 39, 95
  federal 36-37
dominion 38
Duplessis, Maurice 95
Durham, Lord 55

Earl of Aberdeen 114
elections 57, 129-30, 169-81
  general 179; (1867) 130-31; (1957) 61,
  62; (1963) 63; (1972) 61, 62; (1974) 57;
  (1979) 142(n.1); (1980) 57, 142(n.1),
  176; (1988) 180; (1993) 61, 62, 141,
  175-76, 193, 206; (1997) 65, 130; (2000)
  65, 130, 176, 190, 192
  New Brunswick (1987) 175
  Ontario (1985) 62
  representation and 169-72
  timing of 65-66
electoral system 172-78, 192, 207
emergency federalism 80
entrenchment 35-36, 91-106
enumerators 179
equality 21-24, 215
  before the law 155-56
equalization payments 83-84, 259
estimates 133
executive federalism 81
executive power 29-30, 53-55, 56-57, 59,
  116, 218-20, 228-30
extra-parliamentary wing 191

family compact 55
Fathers of Confederation 22-24, 73, 75,
  77, 78, 84, 87, 145, 160, 171(n.1)
Federal Court of Canada 160
federal parties, Canadian 194-97
federal regime 30, 36-37
federal spending power 82-83
federal union
  centralized vs. decentralized 78-79
  original design of 77-78
  reasons for 75-76
federalism 73-90, 188, 215
  challenge of 84-87
  classical 79-80, 81
  cooperative 80-81
  court system and 157-58
  definition of 73-75
  emergency 80
  executive 81
  fiscal 81-84
  history of 75-81
  quasi- 79
first-past-the-post, see single-member plurality
fiscal federalism 81-84
formation of government 59-62

Forsey, Eugene 64
Founding Fathers 36, 54, 86-87
France 25, 30, 74
Franklin, Benjamin 36
Fraser, John 124
free speech 214-15
Free Trade Agreement 140-41
free votes 138
freedom of the press 214-15
front benches 135-36
fusion of powers 59

"Gang of Eight" 42, 43
general election, definition of 179
Germany 30, 74
Goods and Services Tax (GST) 70, 140-41
government
    definition of 109
    forming a 59-62
government bills 132
governmental power 29-31
    limits of 31
governor general 111-15, 116, 120-21,
    130, 133, 179
    functions of 112-15
governor-in-council 117(n.1), 150
Greece, ancient 20-21, 22
Green Party 192

Hansard 132, 133
harm principle 25
Harper, Elijah 47
head of government 67-68
head of state 67-68
Hnatyshyn, Ramon 61, 112
House of Commons 56-63, 66-67, 68, 70,
    87, 113-15, 122, 123-24, 127, 129-42,
    169-70, 178, 179, 184, 223-27
    business of 132-34
    committees of 136, 137
    distribution of seats in 173-74
    membership and officers of 130-32
    reform of 137-38
    rules of procedure of 134-35
    women in 206
House of Representatives 65, 68, 86

human rights 24-27, 92(n.1), 96-97
Hunter, Lawson 93-94

ideology, parties and 186-88
impartiality 151-54
India 74
indirect taxation 82
individualism 185
inferior courts 159
institutions 109-65
integrated judicial system 158
intensity of opinion 209
Intercolonial Railway 40
interest aggregation 185-86
interest groups 202-05
    women's 207-08
interests, multiplicity of 205
Ireland 74
Israel 27

Japan 27, 74
Japanese-Canadians 98-99
Jefferson, Thomas 36
judges 151-52
"The Judges Affair" 155
judicial commissions of inquiry 148-49
Judicial Committee of the Privy Council
    (JCPC) 38, 160-61
judicial independence 154-55
judicial power 29-30, 53-55
judicial review 46-47, 78, 98(n.1), 100,
    146, 149-50
judicial system, integrated 158
judiciary 92-94, 97, 105, 145-65, 240
    fundamental principles of 150-56
    politicization of 162-64
    role of 145-50

Kennedy, John F. 66
King, Mackenzie 114
kingship 20
Kissinger, Henry 66
Knopff, Rainer 106

language rights 42, 44
Laurier, Wilfrid 79, 114, 195
law, rule of 27, 155-56, 215

laws, constitutional 33-37, 38-43
Lawson Hunter v. Southam 92-94
leadership convention 189-90
Leblanc, Romeo 112
legislative power 29-30, 53-55, 58-59, 116,
    220, 230-34
legislative union 76
Letters Patent 111
Lévesque, René 86(n.1), 100
liberal democracy 91, 97, 191, 201-02
Liberal Party 79, 176, 188, 192, 193, 194-
    95, 196
Liberal-Conservatives 194
liberalism 24-27
    classical 188
Libertarian Party 192
liberty 21, 24-27, 188, 215
lieutenant-governors 111(n.1), 114
line departments 123
lobbying 203-05
local government 74
Locke, John 35-36, 38, 54-55, 69, 146
The Lord's Day Act 149
Lower Canada 54-55
Lyon, Stirling 97-99, 100

M. v. H. 105
Macdonald, John A. 77, 79, 118, 120(n.1),
    194
MacKinnon, Frank 115
Madison, James 36, 205
majority, tyranny of the 21
majority government 62-64
majority opinion 161
mandate 170-71
Mandel, Michael 105-06
Manitoba 40
Manning, Preston 196
Maritime Bank case 80
Martin, Paul 122
Massey, Vincent 112
Mazankowski, Don 121
McNamara, Robert 66
media 210-12
    private vs. public 212
Meech Lake Accord 47-48, 85, 89, 104,
    162, 197

Meighen, Arthur 63, 114
members of Parliament 56-57, 60, 130-33,
    170-71
microcosm theory 171-72
Mill, John Stuart 25
ministerial responsibility 123-25
minority government 63-64, 113
minority rights 26
monarchy 20, 35, 110
    constitutional 110
money votes 227
Montesquieu, Baron de 54-55, 69
Morgentaler, Henry 104
Morton, Ted 106
Mulroney, Brian 47-48, 60, 100, 104, 116,
    118(n.1), 121, 140, 155
multi-party system 191-93
multiplicity of interests 205
Munro, John 155

Narcotic Control Act 102-03
National Action Committee on the Sta-
    tus of Women (NAC) 207
National Energy Policy 130
National Party 192
natural rights 24-27
New Brunswick 40, 42, 139(n.1), 146,
    174, 175, 195, 233
New Democratic Party (NDP) 176, 188,
    193, 195-96
Newfoundland 139(n.1)
Nixon, Richard 66
Northwest Territories 139(n.1)
notwithstanding clause 99-101
Nova Scotia 54, 55, 139(n.1), 146, 233
Nunavut 139(n.1)

Oakes, David Edwin 102-03
Oakes test 103
oligarchy 20
Ontario 42, 44, 79, 131, 139, 146, 230,
    232-33
opinion intensity 209
opinion preference 209
Opposition, official 131, 197
orders-in-council 117(n.1)
organic statutes 33-34, 39, 40

parliament 127-43, 179-80
    dissolution of 114, 130, 179
    role of 128-29
parliamentary calendar 129-30
parliamentary democracy 22-23
parliamentary government 58
parliamentary wing 191
participation, political 169-216
    forms of 201-02
parties, *see* political parties
party discipline 68, 129, 198
party government 197-98
party leadership 189-90, 198
party list system 177-78
party members 170
party politics 197-98
party system 184, 191-93
patriation 41-42, 150
patronage 112
Pearson, Lester 63, 70, 118
plurality 172
political education 215-16
political neutrality 152
political parties 183-99, 203
    federal 194-97
    function of 185-86
    ideology and 186-88
    organization of 189-91
    regional 192-93, 196-97
polity 20
polls, public opinion 212-14
polls, voting 179-80
Powell, Colin 66
powers
    division of 31, 36-37, 39
    fusion of 59
    separation of 54-55, 64-72
pragmatism 187
preamble 39
precedents 147
prime minister 60, 65, 66-67, 113-14, 119-
    23, 130, 179
    deputy 121
Prime Minister's Office (PMO) 121-22
Prince Edward Island 40, 118, 131,
    139(n.2), 174, 207
Principal Secretary of PMO 121
Priorities and Planning Committee 119

private law 146-47
private members' bills 132, 137-38
private sphere 24
    protection of 26
Privy Council 116-17
    Chief Clerk of 121
    Judicial Committee of (JCPC) 38,
    160-61
Privy Council Office (PCO) 121-23
proclamation 133, 227-28
Progressive Conservative Party 176, 180,
    188, 190, 192, 193, 194-95, 196, 215
Progressive Party 192-93, 194, 195
proportional representation (PR) 177-78
prorogation 130
provincial government 74, 77-84, 228-34
Public Accounts Committee 133
public expenditure, scrutiny of 133
public law 147-48
public opinion 208-10
    polls, question of 212-14
Public Service Commission 123
quasi-federal system 78, 79

Quebec 41-42, 44, 47-49, 79, 85-86, 88-
    89, 95, 100, 104, 139, 147, 161, 195,
    197, 230-33
    Bill 101 - 100
    Bill 178 - 100, 104
Quebec v. Ford 104
Queen's Privy Council for Canada, *see*
    Privy Council
Question Period 133-34

R. v. Drybones 96
R. v. Morgentaler 104
R. v. Oakes 101-02, 110
R. v. Sharpe 103
readings of bills 132-33
reference procedure 150
Reform Party 193, 195, 196
Reformers 194, 195
regime principles 19-28
regimes, political 19-21
Reich, Robert 66
report stage 132-33
representation, elections and 169-72
representative democracy 22-23

republicanism 23
reservation of provincial legislation 78
reserve powers 113-15
residual power 31
resolutions 133
responsible government 23, 53-72, 169-72
    as cabinet government 58-59
    conventions of 56-58
    emergence of 53-55
    institutional implications of 64-69
    vs. separation of powers 69-72
Returning Officer 179, 181
ridings 130-31, 173
rights 24-27, 31, 91-106, 215
    human 24-27, 92(n.1), 96-97
    minority 26
    natural 24-27
Roseman, Frank 93
Rouges 194, 195
royal assent 133, 227-28
royal commissions 148-49
rule of law 27, 155-56, 215
"Rupert's Land" 40
Russell, Peter 99, 149, 152
Russia 30

St. Laurent, Louis 61
Saskatchewan 40, 100
Sauvé, Jeanne 112
scrutineers 180-81
scrutiny of public expenditure 133
secession 49
Section 92 courts 160
Section 96 courts 160
self-interest 20
Senate, Canadian 87, 121, 130, 139-42,
    171, 220-23
    reform of 141-42, 196
    size of 139
Senate, US 86, 87, 142
separation of powers 54-55, 64-69
    vs. responsible government 69-72
Sergeant-at-Arms 131
shadow cabinet 136, 197
Singh v. Minister of Employment and Immigration 104-05
single-member plurality (SMP) 173-78,
    192, 193, 214

effects of 174-76
single-party system 192
social contract 35, 38
Social Credit Party 195
social union framework 89
Southam Press 93-94, 105
sovereign authority 74
sovereignty 49, 85, 89
Speaker of the House 131, 135
Speech from the Throne, see Throne
    Speech
spending power, federal 82-83
standing committees 136
Standing Orders 134-35
stare decisis 147
statutes, organic 33-34, 37, 39, 40
superior courts 159
Supreme Court of Canada 39, 42, 49, 92-
    97, 99, 103, 104-05, 150, 154-55, 157,
    160-62, 163-64, 171
Supreme Court of the US 95-96, 158, 161
Sweden 27, 74
Switzerland 74

taxation 78, 81-82
Throne Speech 130
Tocqueville, Alexis de 185, 210, 213
Tories 194
Treasury Board 123
Trudeau, Pierre 26, 42, 57, 61, 96-97, 99,
    116, 118, 119, 121, 130, 142(n.1), 155,
    176
Truman, Harry 71
trustee model 170-71
Tupper, Charles 114
tyranny 20, 54
tyranny of the majority 21

unconditional grant 83
Underhill, Frank 184
Union Government 183(n.1)
Union Nationale 195
unitary regime 30, 73-74, 76
United Kingdom 25, 30, 32-34, 37, 38, 41,
    53-55, 69, 73, 74, 79, 94-95, 109-11,
    127-28, 173
    Bill of Rights (1689) 34
    Parliament Act (1911) 34

Reform Act (1832) 34

United States 23, 25, 30, 34-35, 54-55, 64-72, 98(n.1), 157-58, 164, 205
   Constitution of 36-37, 64
   elections in 65-66
   federalism 73, 75-76, 77, 84-87

United States v. Burns 105

Upper Canada 54-55

utilitarianism 24-26

Valente v. The Queen 154-55

Vanier, Georges 112

veto 44

voting in Canada 179-81

Whigs 194

White, Theodore 204

Wilson, Michael 124

women in politics 206-08

Yukon 139(n.1)